Living Faiths in South Africa

Living Faiths in South Africa

edited by

Martin Prozesky and John de Gruchy

St. Martin's Press   *New York*
Hurst & Company   *London*

Published in the United States of America by
St. Martin's Press, Inc.,
175 Fifth Avenue, New York, NY 10010
and in the United Kingdom by
C. Hurst & Co. (Publishers) Ltd.,
38 King Street, London WC2E 8JT
and in Southern Africa by
David Philip Publishers (Pty) Ltd,
208 Werdmuller Centre, Claremont 7700, South Africa

Printed in South Africa by Clyson Printers,
11th Avenue, Maitland, Cape Town

ISBNs
0-312-12776-6 (St. Martin's)
1-85065-249-X (Hurst)
0-86486-253-9 (David Philip)

Library of Congress Cataloging-in-Publication Data applied for

Contents

Contributors

JOHN W. DE GRUCHY is Professor of Christian Studies in the Department of Religious Studies at the University of Cape Town

ALLEYN DIESEL lectures in Religious Studies at the University of Natal, Pietermaritzburg

JOCELYN HELLIG is Associate Professor in the Department of Religious Studies at the University of the Witwatersrand, Johannesburg

JIM KIERNAN is a Professor in the Department of Social Anthropology at the University of Natal, Durban

PATRICK MAXWELL is Senior Lecturer in the Department of Religious Studies at the University of Natal, Pietermaritzburg

EBRAHIM MOOSA is a Lecturer in the Department of Religious Studies at the University of Cape Town

THILLAY NAIDOO is a Senior Lecturer in the Department of Science of Religion, University of Durban-Westville, Durban

G. C. OOSTHUIZEN is Director of the research unit on New Religious Movements and Independent Churches (NERMIC) in Durban

MARTIN PROZESKY is a Professor in the Department of Religious Studies at the University of Natal, Pietermaritzburg

ARTHUR SONG lectures in the Faculty of Theology, University of Durban–Westville, Durban

LOUIS H. VAN LOON is a part-time lecturer in Buddhist Studies, based in Durban

CHARLES VILLA-VICENCIO is Professor of Church and Society in the Department of Religious Studies, University of Cape Town

1

Introduction

MARTIN PROZESKY

Religion continues to be a significant social force in South Africa. Virtually the entire population professes some kind of faith, and the country has an exceptionally rich diversity of religions. But despite these facts, much of this important phenomenon remains little known and poorly understood, unlike other aspects of South African history and society, such as the political, the economic and even the sporting. Certain parts of it have, of course, received a great deal of attention from scholars, especially where Christianity is concerned, but this does not meet the pressing need for a better grasp of the full range of South Africa's faiths and their histories, and for a more critical interpretation of Christianity in South Africa, written in a way that does not reflect the purposes and interpretations of any single author. The main aim of this book is to help meet this need for a better understanding of the neglected story of religion in South Africa on the part of students, general readers and, indeed, all who are seriously interested in understanding South Africa.

A key point is, therefore, that South Africa does not, or does not yet, have a single religious story; it has many. Moreover, politics and history have so far ensured that there has been and still is no real equality of faiths in this country. Certain kinds of Christians, particularly among whites, have greatly dominated the religious and political stage, as is well known. Other Christians, and especially people from the other religions, have been forced by the politics of the past three centuries into the position of second- and third-class citizens with regard to the legal and constitutional status of their religions, access to public resources and education, and possession of political power. The result is hardly surprising: some parts of the story have enjoyed vastly more attention by scholars and are therefore far more often and more clearly heard than others. A religion with daily or weekly access to publicly funded television or to the nation's classrooms can make its voice heard and its presence felt much more effectively than religions to which these things have always been denied. The religious situation thus shows a resemblance to the inequalities and injustices of the political and economic profile of the country, so that many voices have yet to be adequately heard from the ranks of believers.

This explains why the present book is the work of a team of specialist authors. While all are university scholars and all have written their chapters with the same goal of scholarly fairness and accuracy, they also provide a diversity of outlook, geographical location and background that is intended to help religious voices to be better heard than before. Such a procedure obviously has the drawback of not being able to offer a single, connected interpretation from start to finish. For this we would recommend David Chidester's recent book *Religions of South Africa*. Our own approach is that of telling a rich, often complex and always many-stranded story through the voices of a diversity of writers, each of whom is an expert on the religion he or she discusses, with a long scholarly and sometimes also personal involvement with the South African reality of the religion in question. In this way we hope to contribute something of value to the scholarship of transformation and rehabilitation that South Africa so desperately needs as it both rediscovers and recreates its history and, thereby, also its own identity after apartheid.

Most of the authors of this book were also involved in the writing of its predecessor, *A Southern African Guide to World Religions*. Our concern there was to provide South African readers with reliable information about the religions that have most powerfully influenced human history. The story of these religions in South Africa itself was reserved for the present volume. Where that project was a world map of religions, our present project is a South African map. The period covered is also different. When one discusses the world's main living religions, a time-span of several thousand years is generally sufficient. For religion in South Africa, the time-span is both vastly longer and much shorter. It is longer because religion in this region goes back to now-vanished forms of faith that are immensely ancient, as we shall see later in this Introduction. And it is shorter because the great movements of people, African, European and Asian, that have so radically changed the human fabric of South Africa have taken place within the last two thousand years according to current scholarly estimates, with a dramatic acceleration of the pace of change in the last three or four centuries.

Concerning method

As far as method is concerned, this book shares the basic approach of our earlier volume, namely a policy of accuracy, clarity and fairness, so that each religion is described in a way which reflects as faithfully as possible its historical development in South Africa and its present character. The technical term for this approach is 'the phenomenological method'. What needs to be said here is twofold. Firstly, within this basic approach to the subject, our authors have been free to shape their material as they deem best. For example, while all of them deal with both the history and the religious characteristics of the religions they describe, they differ in how much of each is considered appropriate. Some of our faiths have a largely literate and often affluent membership, which lends itself to the accumulation of written records and thence to detailed histories. Others have been strongly oral and often very poor, with little or no access to scholarly resources. Here the written residue of the past is small or even non-existent, resulting in a diminished ability to produce a detailed recorded history. Some of our religions have established themselves throughout the country. Others are much more localised, for example Hinduism and Judaism, or the faith of the Venda people. Naturally, these variations also lead to variations in the structure and geographical focus of the various chapters.

Secondly, of great importance in the method and structure of this book is the principle of contextuality. Our view as scholars is that human existence is affected, sometimes very profoundly, by the context in which it develops, and that this is also to be observed in the religious life – a principle which is not in itself in conflict with the conviction on the part of many believers that their faith has its ultimate source in divine revelation. An example of contextuality from Christianity is the way ancient European culture affected it, for example the word 'Easter'. According to the early English historian Bede, this came from the name of the pre-Christian goddess of spring, Oestre, a deity absorbed into and transformed by the church as it took root in Europe after its Near Eastern beginnings. Members of the earliest church in and near Jerusalem would not have understood the term, yet it has come to stand for one of the most sacred occasions in the Christian calendar. Similarly, some of our indigenous Southern African religions have a pronounced interest in rain-making, which obviously makes sense in a drought-prone region. Ancient Egypt, while virtually rainless, had plenty of water from the Nile and showed no such pronounced interest in rain-making. Instead, there is a wealth of religious symbolism linked with the sun. Here too, the influence of the context is clear.

The South African context

The story of religion in South Africa cannot therefore be understood apart from its geographical, political, cultural and historical context, though which of these is most relevant varies from faith to faith. For example, the religion of the San people owed a great deal to its geographical setting, as we can see from the use of natural features like caves and rock overhangs for their religiously significant rock art, and in the spiritual symbolism of the praying mantis or the eland in their culture. By contrast, the socio-political factors that greatly affected Christianity in South Africa, such as the rise of merchant capitalism, appear to have played no part in shaping San religion, except of course for the dreadful fact of its extinction within the boundaries of the present-day Republic of South Africa – an instance of religious and cultural violence which must be seen against the background of the history of white settlement and of violent conflict between the settlers and the San. Islam, on the other hand, came to South Africa directly as a result of political and economic factors, and its history in South Africa has not been much shaped by the geography of the subcontinent.

While it is not the function of a book like this to present the details of the

South African context so far as religion is concerned, a brief indication of the main points is necessary. With regard to geography, an important factor is the division of the region into areas where rainfall is sufficient to sustain settled patterns of existence, chiefly in the eastern half of the country and in the southwest, and regions which are generally arid. The distribution of the San, Khoikhoi and black African peoples, and certain differences of lifestyle and religion between sections of the black African people, reflect this factor. Another instance of geographical factors affecting the development of religion is the mineral wealth, employment opportunities and consequent rapid urbanisation of the Witwatersrand, which partly accounts for the concentration of certain religious communities in that area, such as our largest Chinese and Jewish communities, as well as sizeable Hindu and Islamic communities.

Of greater contextual importance, however, is the political and economic history of South Africa, and here the single outstanding factor is the three great migrations of people that have dramatically changed the human texture of the region, together with the drama of conflict, conquest, resistance and liberation associated with the second of them. Before about 2 000 years ago, according to archaeological evidence, the people of the area south of the Limpopo River were the San and the Khoikhoi, whose presence, possibly going back to a single ancestral Khoisan culture, is thought to date back at least 30 000 years, with a human and proto-human presence in the region going back an immensely long time before that.

It is in that very distant past that we find what may well be the oldest sign of religious activity anywhere on earth, and certainly the oldest in South Africa. In a cave known as the Border Cave near the Phongolo River in the far north of Natal, the remains of a child's body have been found, bearing traces of red ochre. Scholars date the remains to about 100 000 years ago. If religion can be taken to mean the belief that our present existence is not the only reality, and that reality as a whole includes a dimension which is not bounded by bodily death, then the act of applying red clay to a body before burial may well be a symbolic ritual act expressing that conviction. In that case, Border Cave near the Phongolo River would be the oldest known site of religious significance in South Africa and, indeed, in the world. The religions of the Khoikhoi and San are thus much more recent, but are nonetheless the oldest faiths in South Africa of which we have detailed information. They are discussed in the first of Jim Kiernan's chapters, in which he deals with the indigenous religions of the area.

From about 2 000 years ago onwards, this longstanding situation of a subcontinent evidently peopled by just the San and Khoikhoi slowly began to undergo momentous change through the arrival from adjacent parts of the subcontinent of black African people with metal-working and farming skills. Though their descendants exhibit some important linguistic differences, scholars nonetheless classify their languages, along with certain other African languages, as a discrete group, usually designating those in question as Sintu-speaking or Bantu-speaking people; the latter being a technical term that must be clearly differentiated from the way the word 'Bantu' came to be misused in the idiom of apartheid. In time, the forebears of these people would come to populate virtually all of the arable portion of the country, with the important exception of the southwestern corner of the Cape. While little is known of the details of the following millennium and a half, there are linguistic, cultural and archaeological indications that point to sustained coexistence and contact between the newcomers and the older, Khoisan population. For example, it is thought by some linguists that the click sounds of the Nguni languages may have been acquired through long contact with the Khoisan peoples, whose languages are especially rich in these sounds. The religions of these black African people, especially before the process of white settlement and conquest began to affect them, form the subject of the rest of Jim Kiernan's chapter on South Africa's indigenous religions.

No less momentous, but spelling the end of what may plausibly be seen as a long chapter of coexistence by South Africa's peoples from around 2 000 to about 350 years ago, was the second great movement of people: the arrival of steady increments of Europeans, starting with the Dutch in 1652 and followed from 1795 and especially 1806 onwards by the British in sizeable numbers, as well as by much smaller numbers of other Europeans. It is a process that has continued to the present. In recent years an influx of people of European extraction from formerly white-ruled areas of Southern and East Africa has added its quota to this process. The third movement, roughly coterminous with the one from Europe, brought people from Asia to South Africa. We shall return to it later in this Introduction.

In the judgement of the present author, the phenomenon of a significant, though always minoritarian and incomplete, Europeanisation of the southern end of Africa constitutes the decisive context for the story of our religions after 1488, when the first known Christian contact took place,[1] but especially from 1652 onwards when Dutch coastal trading practices with no interest in settling in South Africa led to a much more potent form of European interest in the area: that of the permanent settler who retained few or no geographical ties with Europe. It is essential to be quite clear about the priorities of the first Dutch settlers and their successors. These related to the basic needs of independent subsistence as farmers no longer in the pay of the Dutch East India Company, and thus involved as a first consideration access to arable land. This in turn could not fail to mean conflict with the Khoi, who had long been the established, though nomadic, people of the southwestern Cape. As pastoralists, their existence depended absolutely on continued access to grazing and water for their flocks. If we add to this the mutual strangeness of the two cultures and significant differences in matters such as the concept of individual land ownership, then the recipe for conflict was even stronger. And if we add the fatal further ingredient of the possession of firearms and horses by the Europeans, then it is equally clear that what began as conflict would become a process of conquering and subduing the indigenous communities, heroic resistance notwithstanding.

Further increments of white settlers and the potent imperial interests of the British in the nineteenth century intensified and extended this basic reality to the entire subcontinent. This led in due course to the vanishing of the San as a distinct people and of the Khoikhoi as a distinct culture, as well as to the destruction of all the once independent black African polities, their resistance once again notwithstanding. These themes continue in the dramatic changes which have taken place recently in South Africa. For this reason we have, in creating a structure for the present volume, selected the theme of conquest, resistance and liberation as the basic contextual reality in relation to which we can periodise the story of South Africa's religions.

So far, this factor of settlement and conquest has been introduced by identifying the primary, material interests of the settlers as human beings with natural needs, wants and limitations. This must not blind us to the wider historical context that drove that more personal and individual process. For this we must shift our attention from the Cape in the mid-seventeenth century to Europe. Of the various important forces then reshaping society or beginning to do so, such as the rise of nation states, science and modern philosophy in the aftermath of Renaissance humanism, or the Reformation, the one that is most relevant is capitalism. By the time Jan van Riebeeck's ships sailed for the Cape, European life was already being transformed by a movement away from a feudal and largely rural culture to one characterised by trade, the rise of towns and cities linked with trade, the hunger for new markets and sources of goods, the creation of banking and of a middle class based upon skill and education rather than landed wealth or labour, and by the incentive to innovate.[2] This is the world of merchant capitalism, and it is the matrix underlying European interest and settlement in South Africa.

The apartheid state, with its self-justifying notions of a civilising and Christianising mission underlying white domination, and with its control over education and the media, did much to prevent a clear awareness forming of the overriding self-interest at work in the tide of settlement and conquest that flowed to South Africa from Europe. That this was a fundamental force is, however, quite clear, for the logic of a trade-driven social transformation fits the facts of European settlement in South Africa all too well: traders need goods to sell and markets to sell them in. Competition among the traders drives them to find new goods and new markets, making for a natural, expansionist dynamic. This in turn means that seafaring countries or cities will be important for their ability to extend the network of trade beyond the seas. Just as clearly, the commercial ventures to which this trend gave rise would prioritise profitability rather than philanthropy, so that service for the company would tend to be arduous and foster in its bolder spirits a search for something more satisfying, like independence. The fit between this dynamic and the process of settlement at the Cape and elsewhere is obvious. (Interestingly, it may be that an important factor behind the prominence of maritime Western European nations in this process was itself at least partly subject to religious forces, in the form of the spread of Islam and the ability of Muslims to block or impede overland trade routes to India and other Eastern regions. The capture of Constantinople by Islam in 1453 would well exemplify this possibility.)

Later developments such as imperialism and colonialism can then be seen as extensions of the economic trend discussed above, which means that the story of religion in South Africa unfolds against a background not just of relentless white settlement and conquest and the resistance provided by the black populations, but also of powerful international economic and political forces aimed primarily at enriching Europe and its white surrogates over the seas, and not at bringing benefits to the people of Africa. This in turn generates a much more critical context in which to reconsider the place of religion, especially Christianity (including black Christianity), in South African history, for example by asking to what extent our religions have been the abetters rather than the critics of the kinds of consciousness and social structures that accompany and exemplify these great economic and political forces.

Religious aspects of the context

The judgement that economic and political forces were paramount does not mean losing sight of the religious aspect of European settlement in South Africa, which is the subject of the first of John de Gruchy's two chapters, but it does enable us to see it in perspective. Unlike the Puritans in North America, our own earliest European settlement did not happen for primarily religious reasons, despite other possible similarities. It happened as a commercial enterprise, the Dutch East India Company; moreover, the first Europeans to settle here were farmers and not missionaries. The religious element was much more of a priority for the French Huguenots who joined them in 1688 as Calvinist religious refugees,[3] but they were fewer in number and were deliberately assimilated into the older Dutch-speaking population, so that in the long run their contribution to the attempted Europeanisation of South Africa has, ironically for people of a somewhat austere lifestyle, been judged to have much more to do with their wine-making skills than with their faith. British and other European settlers were in much the same position as the Dutch, except of course for the very small number who came to South Africa as missionaries dedicated to converting the African people to some or other form of Christianity. Even they, of course, have been interpreted as, wittingly or otherwise, serving the political and economic interests of European imperialism.[4]

We may thus conclude that the European impact on South Africa was neither in its origins nor in its subsequent main line of development primarily motivated by religious conviction, and especially not by any great missionary concern for the soul of Africa. Its interests, all too humanly, were much more a matter of obtaining, by force when necessary, the conditions for a better life that would be African in location but European in culture. Christian faith would, of course, be an important component in the identity of the people involved, products as they were of a religious age in which modern secularity was quite unknown, but it would not on the whole be the mainspring of their lives. This may tell us why the Christianity of white South Africa has managed to coexist with and, indeed, even foster the politics of racist domination in such a striking departure from the evident ethical intentions of its founder and its Scriptures.[5]

Having related the religious character of the European settlers to more basic and potent social forces, we can now note the main features of that religious character. Here the key contextual issue is again to be found in Europe in the form of the Reformation. As a result of this sixteenth-century upheaval in the religious life of Catholic Europe, the Netherlands and Britain were both Protestant by the time the first settlers arrived at the Cape, the former Calvinist and the latter a mixture of denominations. This is, of course, a main reason for the numerical preponderance of Protestants over Catholics in South Africa today. Another reason is the religious intolerance of the day. The Reformation had been followed by serious conflict in Europe. As early as 1555 at the Peace of Augsburg, a guiding principle in the search for a solution was that territories should follow the religious affiliation of their rulers (*cuius regio eius religio*). Modern notions of freedom of belief and worship were unknown at that time, and things were not much changed a century later. The restrictions on non-Calvinists at the Cape were thus severe. Lutherans – fellow Protestants of the Dutch Calvinists – were only permitted to build their own churches over a century after the coming of the Dutch. Catholicism was severely curtailed until after the second British occupation of the Cape in 1806. And although Muslims were present at the Cape from very early in the Dutch period because of slavery and the exile of Islamic leaders from the East Indies, the practice of Islam was severely restricted. The regulations governing the situation were the Statutes of India, which stipulated that Muslims were forbidden to hold private or public meetings under penalty of the so-called priest being put in chains.[6] Thus the religious hostilities and intolerance of seventeenth-century Europe were exported to South Africa and ensured that from the beginning the Christian faith would be a factor in separating its peoples and strengthening the politics of domination rather than equality, even in the ranks of Christians.

A further religious influence concerns the Bible. Protestantism in general treats the Christian Scriptures as its central authority. Modern secular influences have obscured for many of us the extent to which it was once consulted, not just on matters of faith and morals, but also as an historical and scientific guidebook, moreover in a manner that would strike most readers today as highly uncritical and misguided. The fact that Christianity took root in South Africa in seventeenth-century Protestant form meant that from the start there would be a much stronger (and generally uncritical) reliance on biblical guidance than was the case in areas of Catholic or even Anglican domination. We can see the effects of this at the highest levels of power. The statue of Paul Kruger in Pretoria's Church Square carries several inscriptions on its base, one of them to the effect that Kruger made Scripture his guide, not just in religious matters, but also in the affairs of state. A similar appeal to the Bible has been made even in very recent times. It is not a long step from this belief to the further belief that one's policies therefore have divine backing.[7] Thus the religious context underlying the implanting of Christianity in South Africa goes a long way towards clarifying the exceedingly close alliance between white political domination and strong Christian conviction of the kind just indicated, above all (but not only) among members of the Dutch Reformed churches.

When the control of the Cape passed from Dutch to British hands in 1806, the way opened for a steady inflow of English-speaking Christians with their own division into denominations – Anglican, Methodist, Presbyterian, Congregational, Catholic, Baptist and the like – thereby increasing rather than easing the divided state of their religion and, in due course, contributing to a further fracturing of the ranks of black South Africans. There had, of course, been no single culture or political entity embracing all the black people of South Africa, which was itself a factor favouring the Europeans and their African-born descendants in the process of conquest. The subsequent conversion of blacks on a very great scale (such that today some three-quarters of all black South Africans report a Christian affiliation) added the significant further dimension of religious disunity to the existing geographical, linguistic and political fragmentations. What was good for the soul of black South Africa, from a Christian point of view, appears therefore to have been a political disaster, though this judgement must be carefully balanced against the important positive, liberating resources black Christians have said they find in their faith.

In any event, missionary Christianity in South Africa is clearly as important as it is controversial, so that we have varied the general structure of this book by including a case study of it, concentrating on the region where its unfolding has perhaps been most revealing, namely the Eastern Cape. This case study, where greater detail is possible than in other aspects of our coverage of Christianity, will be found in the chapter by Charles Villa-Vicencio. The missionary movement, itself a consequence of the rise of evangelical interests in Europe's Protestant churches in the eighteenth and nineteenth centuries, rather than a product of any great local zeal for missions by the settler Christians (at least initially), has clearly been a potent factor behind the extensive shift to Christianity by the black people of South Africa. Even so, conversion appears only to have begun to be significant after armed conquest or other kinds of violent dislocation, such as that which befell the Mfengu people.[8] These military and missionary forces thus made major inroads into the identity of the African peoples of the region, as well as fostering important creative responses. The initial phase of this complex and important matter is dealt with in the second of Jim Kiernan's three chapters.

Developments in Europe just before the second British occupation of the Cape had a further important influence on the story of South Africa's religions: this was the turn towards greater religious tolerance early in the nineteenth century. For this we must thank the Enlightenment, one of the fruits of which was the rise of a strong sense of human rights (though other factors also contributed, including religious ones). Thus by the late eighteenth century this new way of thinking had issued in declarations of human rights in France and America, with religious liberty among them. The Netherlands in the period of the Batavian Republic was strongly influenced by this development and extended it to areas like the Cape, which fell under the rule of the Batavian Republic from 1803 to 1806. In 1804 its Commissioner, J. A. de Mist, issued a proclamation of religious tolerance. Thus he ensured that a century and a half of Dutch influence at the Cape would end on a very different note, so far as the position of non-Calvinists and non-Christians was concerned, from the one that was sounded at the beginning. The door was also now open for the adding of a further strand to the tapestry of faiths then being woven for South Africa, in the form of the arrival from Europe at various times throughout the nineteenth century and thereafter of a small but significant Jewish community, which is the subject of chapter nine in this book, by Jocelyn Hellig.

People from Asia

We are now in a position to begin to appreciate just how deep and far-reaching the impact of European trends has been on religion in South Africa, firstly through the movement of large numbers of Europeans to this country and, secondly, through the circumstances that prevailed in Europe at that time, especially in the fields of politics, economics and religion. With these matters in mind we can now return to the three great movements of people that have so massively changed the human face of South Africa in the past two millennia. Two of these – African and European – have been discussed. Now it is time to turn to the third one, which concerns Asia.

Its beginnings in South Africa have already been noted, involving the forcible settlement, from very early in the period of Dutch presence and control, of Islamic people from what is now Malaysia and elsewhere at the Cape. The chapter on Islam in South Africa by Ebrahim Moosa deals with this and, of course, subsequent developments. What concerns us now is the continuation of this movement of people from Asia to the southern end of Africa. The numbers involved were much smaller than those from Europe but the religious and cultural diversity was perhaps greater. From 1860 onwards, people from India arrived at Natal, firstly as workers for the sugar-cane plantations, and secondly as independent migrants, many of whom were merchants. While most of the former were Hindus from South India, the second category also involved Muslims and came in the main from parts of north India. The Muslims who settled in Natal were thus culturally distinct from the older Islamic population of the Western Cape. Together with the newly forming Natal Hindu community (which is the subject of the chapter by Patrick Maxwell, Alleyn Diesel and Thillay Naidoo), this Natal Muslim community added a significant further dimension to the growing religious diversity of South Africa, especially of Natal. The Natal Indian community also involved small numbers of Buddhists. Their activities, and more recent developments in the small South African Buddhist community, form the subject of the chapter by Louis van Loon. Also with roots in India are the very small Jain and Parsee communities, described in the chapter by G. C. Oosthuizen.

South Africa's Chinese community was formed initially through the arrival of merchants and also mine-workers in the Witwatersrand towards the end of the nineteenth century. Other Chinese immigrants followed. In this way something of the diverse religious experience of the Chinese has been added to South Africa, though the numbers have never been large, as will be seen from Arthur Song's chapter in this book. And as with the Natal Indian communities, here too it is clear that economic factors were significantly present in creating the conditions that produced these new South Africans from Asia. Clearly, then, migrations from parts of Asia to South Africa have notably diversified its religious character, especially in Natal, though the religions involved today represent a very small percentage of the total population.[9]

Periodisation

An important consideration in a book which contains historical material by a team of authors is to work according to agreed historical periods. Our policy has been as follows. Each of the religions covered in this book has its own, internal history and thus its own significant periods and events. Naturally, none of these apply to the rest. So we cannot turn to any of the religions themselves for our periodisation. What we have done, instead, is to work from our basic methodological principle of presenting the religions against the background of the broader context of South African history, interpreting it by means of the central theme of conquest, resistance and liberation associated with the arrival of settlers from Europe. This provides a basic periodisation of the history, into a time before European settlement, followed by the process of conquest which reached a military climax in the British defeat of the Boer Republics in 1902 and a political climax in 1910 when the Union of South Africa was created as a state based on white political and economic control, followed in turn by the twentieth-century history of the rise of the apartheid state and its recent demise through the ultimate success of the liberation struggle. In this way we have attempted to give an adequate account of the earlier history of our religions until the beginning of the present century, while also giving some prominence to twentieth-century developments. This is especially evident in John de Gruchy's second chapter, in which he deals with these developments in connection with Christianity, and in Jim Kiernan's third chapter dealing with the African Independent Churches, the enormous proliferation of which has been such a striking feature of the history of religion in South Africa this century.

As will be seen from the chapters that follow, our periodisation corresponds more directly to the stories of black African religions and Christianity than to most of the others. This is revealing in several ways. For a start, between them these two complex religious formations include the vast majority of the total population, so that their interaction has inevitably been profoundly and directly affected by the political history of the subcontinent. The other faiths are in a somewhat different position. Their smaller numbers have made them particularly vulnerable to the tide of white, Christian-orientated conquest and domination. Christian perceptions of them have almost always been negative. For many of their members, poverty has made this vulnerability even greater. The result, all too understandably, has often been that community survival depended on directing all available resources inward at sustaining a religious identity. This has sometimes been misperceived as a lack of religious engagement in the resistance struggle, but a more empathetic reading of the same realities would see them as resistance in perhaps its most basic mode, that of the maintenance of a religious identity judged alien and inferior by the conqueror. Thus, even in South African religions where our general periodisation does not correlate directly with significant internal developments, its relevance remains undiminished.

By way of conclusion, it may help readers if some of the key themes that emerge from a comprehensive study of the religions of South Africa are noted. First of all, it is clear that in South Africa religion is a dynamic force with a very extensive following, unlike the heavily secularised societies of Western Europe and some other parts of the world. Thus, while it certainly is true that the faiths in question in South Africa have been greatly affected by political and economic factors, it is also true that these factors have been influenced by religion. Education policies are a case in point.

A second important feature is the hegemonic relationship that has existed between the various religions since European settlement began, with Christianity having a position of constitutional (as well as numerical) dominance until recently.

Thirdly, there is the remarkable religious transformation of black South Africans which is still proceeding, involving a wealth of creativity in highly adverse circumstances. While there clearly has been a major Christianising of black South Africa, so too has there been a major Africanising of Christianity by black people in this country, to the extent that it probably no longer makes much demographic sense to talk about the European-derived Christian denominations as the 'mainstream' churches, as though the African Independent Churches were a social side-issue. That is very far from being the case.

A fourth and related theme is what has happened to African traditional religions, prompting the question whether conversion to Christianity has in fact meant the eroding and abandoning of traditional religion or its adaptation to new conditions and its adoption of new forms. The evidence is that traditional ways have proved extremely resilient and capable of adaptation to new circumstances.

Another important theme that emerges in and from a consideration of the chapters that follow is the place of the various religions in the processes of conflict, conquest, resistance and liberation. What has it meant to be a Muslim, a Jew, a Hindu or a traditionalist Xhosa in the face of white, Christian-orientated conquest? Has this experience created distinct South African forms of these religions? How deeply has support for apartheid injured Christianity in South Africa? These are some of the questions to which the material presented in this book gives rise and for which answers can be found in the following pages, though some of them doubtless also need further investigation as research into the subject continues. In this connection it is a great benefit that the country possesses important academic resources to foster such research. These take the form of long-established disciplines like history and anthropology as well as the newer discipline of religious studies.

Lastly, what of the future? Religious affiliation is likely to remain high and may grow; and religious diversity is sure to remain pronounced. What do these two realities mean for a country in search of a new, national identity?

Will they foster or impede it by ensuring that we enter that future with the fractured religious consciousness that we have inherited from the past? Or will the remarkable moral convergence of these religions prove to be a significant source and inspiration for the task of humanising what apartheid, political as well as religious, has ravaged? The following chapters shed much valuable light on these and many other important matters.

NOTES

I wish to acknowledge with thanks the valuable suggestions of Professor John Wright of the Department of Historical Studies at the University of Natal, Pietermaritzburg, concerning various parts of this Introduction.

1. Martin Prozesky (ed.), *Christianity in South Africa*. Johannesburg: Southern Book Publishers, 1990. First published under the title *Christianity amidst Apartheid: Selected Perspectives on the Church in South Africa*. London: Macmillan, 1990.

2. Leo Huberman, *Man's Worldly Goods: The Story of the Wealth of Nations*. New York: Monthly Review Press, 1936 and 1963.

3. Randolph Vigne, 'The Rev. Pierre Simond: "lost leader" of the Huguenots at the Cape', *Journal of Theology for Southern Africa*, 65, (December 1988).

4. Nosipho Majeke, *The Role of the Missionaries in Conquest*. Johannesburg: Society of Young Africa, 1952; James Cochrane, *Servants of Power: The Role of English-speaking Churches in South Africa: 1903–1930*. Johannesburg: Ravan Press, 1987.

5. J. A. Loubser, *The Apartheid Bible: A Critical Review of Racial Theology in South Africa*. Cape Town: Maskew Miller Longman, 1987; Martin Prozesky (ed.), *Christianity in South Africa*. Johannesburg: Southern Book Publishers, 1990. First published under the title *Christianity amidst Apartheid: Selected Perspectives on the Church in South Africa*. London: Macmillan, 1990, pp. 122ff.

6. A. Davids, 'Early Muslims at the Cape', *'Iqra Research Journal*, 1, 1 (July 1978), p. 10.

7. Michael Cassidy, *The Passing Summer: A South African Pilgrimage in the Politics of Love*. London: Hodder & Stoughton, 1989, pp. 299, 352.

8. T. R. H. Davenport, *South Africa: A Modern History*. Johannesburg: Macmillan, 1987, pp. 179ff.

9. J. J. Kritzinger, *Statistiese Beskrywing van die Godsdienstige Verspreiding van die Bevolking van Suid-Afrika*. Pretoria: ISWEN, 1985.

SELECT BIBLIOGRAPHY

Cassidy, Michael, *The Passing Summer: A South African Pilgrimage in the Politics of Love*. London: Hodder & Stoughton, 1989

Chidester, David, *Religions of South Africa*. London and New York: Routledge, 1992

Cochrane, James, *Servants of Power: The Role of English-speaking Churches in South Africa: 1903–1930*. Johannesburg: Ravan Press, 1987

Davenport, T. R. H., *South Africa: A Modern History*. Johannesburg: Macmillan, 1987

Huberman, Leo, *Man's Worldly Goods: The Story of the Wealth of Nations*. New York: Monthly Review Press, 1936 and 1963

Kritzinger, J. J., *Statistiese Beskrywing van die Godsdienstige Verspreiding van die Bevolking van Suid-Afrika*. Pretoria: ISWEN, 1985

Loubser, J. A., *The Apartheid Bible: A Critical Review of Racial Theology in South Africa*. Cape Town: Maskew Miller Longman, 1987

Majeke, Nosipho, *The Role of the Missionaries in Conquest*. Johannesburg: Society of Young Africa, 1952

Prozesky, Martin (ed.), *Christianity in South Africa*. Johannesburg: Southern Book Publishers, 1990. First published under the title *Christianity amidst Apartheid: Selected Perspectives on the Church in South Africa*. London: Macmillan, 1990

Prozesky, M. and J. W. de Gruchy (eds.), *A Southern African Guide to World Religions*. Cape Town: David Philip, 1991

2

African Traditional Religions in South Africa

JIM KIERNAN

The titles of this and other chapters use the term 'African traditional religions' to refer to all the indigenous religions of the area. This is more inclusive than the use of the term as a label solely for the faiths of the various black African, Bantu-speaking peoples, because it refers also to the religions of the San and the Khoikhoi. In the present chapter South Africa's traditional, indigenous religions in this wider sense will be described in terms of their characteristics independently of the influence of white settlement. In chapter five, after we have surveyed the planting of Christianity in South Africa, our attention will move to the initial consequences of that development for the indigenous religions of the region.

A religious system exhibits a number of basic features. First of all, religion is a mode of transcending everyday experience; a way of rising above the routine, the mundane; a way of communicating with an order of being(s) at a remove from the limitations of space and time. Secondly, by transcending experience, religion gives to it a dimension of meaning it would otherwise lack, by explaining anomalies and dilemmas arising out of experience which are impervious to rational and empirical resolution. Thus it provides a problem-solving mechanism or technique.

Thirdly, as a special mode of explanation, religion provides the basis for a charter of action. It spells out the limitations and possibilities of a relationship with the transcendent by mapping out a moral terrain of avoidances, prohibitions and injunctions, and by constructing a system of ritual observances for approaching the transcendent and wresting advantage from it. Religion thus hedges the transcendent with notions of right and wrong, reward and punishment, to produce a code of conduct which regulates an ordered existence.

Fourthly, as a transcendental explanatory and moral system, religion does not exist in a vacuum but in a definite social context of organised human relations and interactions. There will be some degree of correspondence and of mutual influence between the social and religious spheres – religion is shaped by society, and society benefits from religion. The one bolsters the other, and a change in one will have repercussions for the other.

Fifthly, religion also has its roots in nature, in so far as it draws on symbols for ritual renewal and replenishment. For the most part religious symbols are natural things, whether inanimate, animal or human, which are impressed with social and mystical meanings. These meanings are then released in collective rituals to achieve effects on the religious level, often of a therapeutic nature.

Sixthly, while religions may differ as to degree of symbolic investment, such symbolic expression and other collective sentiments can engage and release powerful human emotions to produce a heightened experience. Religion appeals not merely to the intellect but also to the emotions, and thus holds out to its devotees the possibility of their emulating and drawing closer to sacred and quasi-sacred beings by temporarily overstepping the limits of space and time. The inducement of trance or possession states is a good example of this.

Finally, there is a tendency for religious systems to be operated by a core of specialists who, by training, induction or experience, or merely by virtue of the place they occupy in society, can lay claim to unusual powers and expertise. This augmented capacity enables them to fulfil a vital role in initiating and facilitating exchanges between the natural, social and mystical spheres.

Khoisan religion

We would expect any religion to display most, if not all, of these features in a greater or lesser measure, and we can certainly find them clearly expressed in the indigenous religions of Southern Africa at the time of white infiltration; indeed, they are still manifest even today. When whites first began to settle in South Africa, this territory was largely occupied by two distinct cultural traditions impinging on one another: the Khoisan people in the southwest and the steadily encroaching Bantu-speakers, well established on either side of the Drakensberg.

The Khoisan had evolved into two distinct cultural strains of the same genetic stock. The San, or Bushmen, maintained a hunter-gatherer way of life, relying on the uncultivated supply of fruit and vegetable yielded by the land and supplementing this with wild game. Essential to this way of life was their dependence on the movement of game, antelope in particular, and the supply of fresh water, ultimately in the form of rainfall. Both features of their environment brought a degree of unpredictability to bear on their lives, which they contrived, especially by religious means, to control. To exploit their environment by social means, the San were organised into small roving bands, internally stressing the values of egalitarianism and sharing. These groups were not isolated from one another but rather intermingled, interacted and intermarried.

The Khoi, or Hottentots (sometimes referred to as Khoikhoi), had for centuries departed significantly from this way of life by developing an existence that embraced the herding of domesticated animals and the smelting of iron to provide implements and weapons. They were largely confined to scattered settlements along the western and southern coast, although their presence extended over the whole of the western half of the country. More sedentary than the San, with large fixed central settlements, the Khoi were nevertheless nomadic pastoralists, moving in smaller groups with their animals within their tribal territory as pasture and water became less accessible. The meat supply was derived mainly from hunting and fishing. Organised into clans and clan segments, the Khoi had hereditary chiefs and headmen, whose authority was light and circumscribed by consultative elders, to regulate communal undertakings. As their pastoral interests steadily encroached on the game preserves of the San, the San's resistance was overcome by superior weaponry and the ability to mobilise loose-knit but larger formations. The San were even less of a match for the Bantu-speakers on the east and had been driven to refuge in the Drakensberg. Although the outcome of contact with Bantu-speakers and with Khoikhoi was ultimately damaging to the San, it tends to blur the extent of peaceful exchange which took place between these cultures, resulting in much mutual influence.

Contact with whites gave rise to the erroneous notion that Khoisan worshipped the moon and that the San also worshipped the Mantis. Of course, moonlight (or firelight) was an essential setting for energetic rituals sensibly performed after sunset, but it was a means rather than an end. Possibly the waxing and waning of the moon represented the possibility of life after death, though neither San nor Khoikhoi had any clear idea of what such an afterlife might be. The influence of the dead was mischievous, often being the cause of illness, but there was no organised cult of the dead remotely approaching ancestor worship.

The San recognised a supernatural creative being called !Kaggen, 'the master of all things' who, because he resided in what he had created, could assume a variety of forms, including the Mantis. He was thus regarded as a trickster, the master of disguise. Under certain circumstances, the Mantis could therefore be considered an auspicious omen; at other times, observation of its actions could be interpreted as oracular in predicting or divining the outcome of uncertain ventures such as hunting. Indeed, !Kaggen himself was an expression of an essentially unpredictable nature. Hence he was identified with the thunderstorm, the most unpredictable of events, at once benign, rain-bearing, and dangerous. While he was protective of man and assisted him in the hunt, he also tried to save the eland and the hartebeest, his favourites, by laying down conditions or moral bounds to be observed in hunting them. Such capricious intervention in the hunt may be seen as a way of evening the contest and of maintaining a balance between man and nature, between scarcity and plenty.

Reflective of !Kaggen's omnipresence, there was a supernatural energy possessed by diverse things, and within people themselves, called *n/um*. It could be tapped by religious specialists, now referred to as medicine men or medicine owners, for therapeutic and other purposes. This was achieved in the trance (fostered by communal dancing), which is the central religious experience of the San, linking society with the supernatural. In the dance, the specialists contrived to bring their *n/um* to the boil, at which point it over-flowed in sweat and nasal bleeding; the odour of these emanations was said to repel evil things. But evil was also extracted from sufferers by the sniffing of specialists, who then sneezed it away. Other rituals were conducted to control rainfall and to regulate the transition from adolescence to adulthood.

The explanatory principle of the Khoikhoi departed from the San notion of a single ambivalent 'god' in asserting the existence of a duality of spirit: Tsui//Goab, the giver of rain and plenty, who was propitiated with animal sac-rifice performed by the chief; and another male figure, //Guanab, who was unambiguously associated with evil. In practice, however, this did not remove uncertainty about the source of misfortune. Scarcely satisfied with the two annual rain-making and first fruits rites, the beneficent spirit was capable of spiteful retaliation, in effect trespassing on the preserve of his counterpart. However difficult it was to reconcile the perceived opposition between the two with the confusion resulting from their converging interventions, this dualism was confined to the dispensing of good and bad fortune on a communal scale. The fate of the individual was governed by a being of a quite different order. Heitsi Eibab (sometimes also called Heitsi Eibib) was a dead heroic figure, essentially human, corresponding to a national original ancestor of the Khoi-khoi in general. Exceptional magical powers were attributed to him, and because he was believed to have risen from the dead many times before defini-tively dying, his 'graves' are plentifully distributed. Here he is approached and invoked for success, for example in hunting, and here offerings of various kinds are deposited.

The material and social welfare of individuals could also be manipulated by sorcerers, who could employ medicines derived from the local environment to harm their fellows. But those knowledgeable about medicines could be approached to provide an antidote to rid one of an affliction and, in this capacity, they functioned as socially supportive medicine men, restoring health and well-being to the victims of sorcery.

It can readily be seen that Khoikhoi religion made separate provision for the individual and his or her circumstances and for the communal interests of a large-scale tribal unit; whereas in San religion, the individual is catered for only as an integral part of a small-scale sharing and caring group. This closely corresponds to their differing forms of social organisation: in the one case small and intimate hunting bands wherein each member contributed to the changing fortunes of everyone else; and in the other, a larger pastoral associa-tion, which underwent a repetitive fusion and fission of its constituent parts and within which the individual was but loosely aggregated. Although more could be said about Khoisan religion, the written record not only is thin on matters of detail, but gives rise to conflicting viewpoints. However, such diver-gence of opinion on finer points may simply reflect a real variation in the detail of religious belief and observance between like communities separated by great distance. Discrepancies of this kind almost certainly existed between the San of the southern Cape and those situated further to the north. Further-more, we must continually remind ourselves that what we now know of the indigenous religions of Southern Africa before white penetration is derived almost entirely from the accounts of early white observers and interlocutors, whose Christian bias all too often produced misunderstandings that are now very difficult to correct.

The religions of Bantu-speaking African people

The Bantu-speaking people of South Africa introduced farming to Southern Africa, including cattle-herding, and they brought with them the skill of fashioning iron to productive and aggressive purposes. Although herding required a certain limited amount of movement, their cultivation of the soil imposed on them an essentially sedentary way of life. Maritime records attest to the widespread presence of their long-established settlements in the interior of the east coast as early as the sixteenth century, and in all likelihood they had by then settled the central region beyond the Drakensberg quite extensively. Existing archaeological evidence from sites throughout the eastern half of the country shows that they were already there well into the first millennium CE. This southeastern Bantu-speaking group included the Zulu–Xhosa–Swazi, the Sotho–Tswana, the Venda, the Shona and others.

These people developed distinctive lifestyles, depending on whether they settled in the eastern grasslands or on the inland plateaux roughly to the west of the Drakensberg. Both sets of people were endowed with similar knowledge and techniques and exploited the environment within well-organised chiefdoms. But they deployed their assets and labour to adapt to the differences of altitude, climate, soil and plant cover obtaining in the east and in the west. The chiefs controlled internal boundaries and regulated the pattern of work and use of resources best suited to the environment of each area; and the mode of regulation itself differed, from greater centralisation of control in the west, to greater delegation in the east.

There were good reasons for the concentration or distribution of organising authority in each case. In the east, an economic unit or settlement could be small because, in these well-watered and productive lands, a sufficient variety of resources was available in its immediate surroundings to supply all the needs of a mixed economy. Typically, a settlement occupied a ridge, with valley fields for cultivation and grazing along the slopes. Within a district, any settlement could be within hailing distance of its neighbours but had no need to canvass this wider range of relationships to wrest a living from the environment. It was economically self-sufficient and could comfortably regulate its own access to vital resources without encroaching on those of others. Transgressions that would require the intervention of higher authority (the chief) might only arise with an increase of population density coupled with a limit to territorial expansion. But the basic pattern was one of numerous dispersed, but independent, economic and political units dotting the countryside.

This concentrated exploitation of the environment was not possible in the west. Large expanses of uniform country and an inconstant water supply meant that people had to cover large areas in order to find the variety they needed for subsistence. Regulation of access to such dispersed resources and of their utilisation had to be of corresponding wide span, hence the emergence of centralised authorities and the concentration of the population in centrally located large settlements, from which people could attend to their scattered investments. (Some fields could be as far as 40 kilometres apart, and sparse pasturage increased the distance cattle had to travel.) Returns on such thinly spread investments were so uncertain that any individual had to have a broad range of social relationships through which to negotiate alternative arrangements should things go wrong. For these reasons, the social and political units in the west were of relatively large span (thousands of people), of concentrated residence with centralised control, and at great distances from one another.

The ancestors

We would expect religious beliefs and practices to reflect the human concerns that gave rise to these distinctively different social patterns, but to draw on much the same spiritual repertoire in doing so. The common element of religious approach lies in a pragmatic emphasis on contemporaneous reward and its roots in social structure, membership of a cult group being determined by descent, and cult spirits being contained within existing social boundaries. These spiritual agents are of human origin, an element of the living ensemble surviving death to inhabit an afterlife where its major function is to supervise the lives of living descendants. There is little consensus over where dead ancestors reside – underground, in the skies, on the western horizon and so on – but a persistent feature is their constant attachment to the living space of their progeny. Whereas the afterlife, vaguely depicted, is for all, ancestral status is not automatically accorded to everybody, and it can vary in the value placed upon it. This is because it is really conferred by the living and ultimately depends on their continued willingness to honour it.

In the first instance, it is granted only to those who during their lifetime represented some span of authority and responsibility towards subordinates, for example heads of families, lineage or clan heads, and royalty. Ancestral influence is thus an extension of a secular role, and the relevance of the ancestors is a function of their social position while alive. This eliminates minors and childless people and it means that women less frequently become ancestors than men. Secondly, ancestors are recollected and honoured to the extent that they serve the dominant interests of the living, in spelling out the separate identity of one group vis-à-vis another, asserting the linkages between two or more groups, or preserving the internal unity of a corporate descent group. Should there be a shift in any of these arrangements, the relevance of an ancestor as a structural pivot would diminish, he would recede from the centre of living preoccupations, and be pushed into the relative anonymity of the collective body of ancestors. In the course of time, ancestors become distanced from human affairs. Sometimes the term 'shades' is employed to distinguish ancestors of recent provenance who are most active in human concerns from those more removed from the theatre of human action.

There are limits, therefore, to the perceived usefulness of ancestors, whose recall as singular active spiritual agents is thus affected. Aside from royal figures who constitute a special case, the hierarchy of identifiable ancestors varies in depth from at most three generations, in the case of local descent groups, to five and more generations for ancestors whose function it is to articulate the connectedness of numerous local groups. Thus, as ancestors become more distant, their span of influence expands and becomes more diffuse, but the intensity of their involvement in issues of immediate living concern diminishes. Royal ancestors, the progenitors of chiefs and monarchs, are remembered longest, over ten or more generations, but neither the span nor intensity of their influence is much affected by genealogical regression, because a single line of succession is being preserved rather than a whole web of genealogical connections.

However, entitlement in terms of lifetime responsibility and structural position does not automatically confer ancestral status. A transition of status has to be negotiated and legitimised, through a ritual process organised by the living. In other words, the social qualifications of an ancestor must receive a religious impress in order to endow him with mystical powers which are socially supportive. This ritual transition takes the form of mortuary rites which, like any other rite of passage, are conducted over a variable period of time, from three months in one place to two years or more in another, thus permitting the ancestor to gradually relinquish living responsibilities and to assume and settle into the new role of ancestor. Typically, a burial rite is followed by a customary period of mourning. This is terminated by a second ritual, sometimes referred to as the 'second funeral', at which the first sacrifice is made for the new ancestor, thus confirming his new ancestral status. The sacrifice should be performed by the male heir, so that it is the heir who ultimately confers ancestorhood on the parent. To die without male issue would condemn the person concerned to limbo, but steps could be taken, even retroactively, to circumvent this awful possibility. Should the person die before marriage and reproduction, a kind of 'ghost marriage' can be arranged on his behalf; his wife thus acquired by bridewealth[1] could produce an heir in cooperation with a kinsman and so end the mourning period. If a deceased person is bereft of male issue only, a daughter could similarly supply him with male progeny by contracting a 'woman marriage' (both partners being women) in which she would assume the male role, except of course in reproduction. Nevertheless, despite the availability of these adjustive mechanisms, it was still conceivable that a man could die far from home without the knowledge of those who had the power to establish him ritually as an ancestor, in which case death would translate him into a rogue spirit, capricious and indiscriminately harmful. The mystical powers of such a person would not be socially anchored but would be essentially anti-social.

It can be seen, then, that the religious remembrance of ancestors is a way of extending authoritative roles beyond the grave in such a way as to support a social order which rests simultaneously on the distinctiveness of small groups and on their combination to form broader social and political units. The dead who cannot be pressed into the service of this scheme either are forgotten or become troublesome and anti-social, a threat to the established order. There is, therefore, a marked correspondence between the religious system and the social order, and variations in the social order will yield differences in religious observance. Thus, where most of a person's activities and relationships are encompassed by the small independent unit, as in the east, he will attend more to ancestors whose influence is focused on the distinctiveness and internal cohesion of that group and less to those serving broader but more fragile bonds. If, on the contrary, he lives the bulk of his life within a single large settlement under the close supervision of a chief, as in the west, he is likely to devote more attention to the royal ancestors, while other ancestors may be *selected* for their position in the network of relationships he has built to afford him access to dispersed opportunities. In fact, a pattern based on this difference of emphasis does emerge when we compare east and west. The cult of the royal ancestors was noticeably more marked in the west than in the east, reaching its most developed expression among Venda and Shona, a point to which we shall return shortly; later developments in the east were to redress this difference somewhat. On the other hand, ancestors of an order of descent in the male line *only* were not exclusively cultivated in the west, as they were in the east, and were accommodated within a wider spread of recognised ancestors, all specified in their particularity; thus included would be a man's father and grandfather besides ancestors on the mother's side, the mother's brother being especially important.

Ancestors inhabit a world of spirit in which they are endowed with the capacity to influence mystically the orderly life of the group or the individuals for whom they assume structural or instrumental significance. In religious terms, their function is to be supportive and protective of the living, to ensure an ordered and fruitful existence for them. As long as ancestors fully discharge their assigned role, their descendants should enjoy a life of peace and prosperity, and neither would have reason to reproach the other or, indeed, take more than occasional notice of the other. But life is never that perfect, and the course of practical religion does not run quite that smoothly. In fact, relations between the living and the dead are fraught with uncertainty. Ancestors are capable of reneging on their responsibilities and of turning against descendants, appearing to be capricious and unreliable guardians and meriting the reproach of the living. Similarly, the living can be remiss in fulfilling their obligations to the dead, who justifiably take offence and respond angrily. On this contentious ground, the religious explanation of misfortune is partly worked out.

Communicating with the ancestors

The living communicate with the dead by regular ritual sacrifice and invocation, the priest or officiant at which is the family head, or the senior group representative where ancestors of larger groups are being addressed. Through the medium of sacrifice, the living not only honour the dead, but thank them for benefits received and plead for future favour. Moreover, their enduring membership of the social or interest group is reconfirmed, and they are sustained by being offered a share in the sacrificial substance, which is consumed commensally. Choice of sacrificial victim varies according to economic circumstances, but it is usually a beast, cattle being the ideal, and may be accompanied by a beer or grain offering where an animal is not considered sufficient. In any case, the ancestors should not go hungry, and stinginess on the part of the living invites their angry retaliation, typically registered as an impairment of health or a reduction of resources.

Such retaliation is of course one of the ways in which ancestors communicate with the living. But besides, ancestors may manifest themselves as animals; the appearance of a harmless snake is commonly interpreted as a propitious symbol of good fortune. And they can be identified in dreams, often by way of premonition against an intended course of action which could prove harmful. While punitive intervention is only one of a number of chan- · nels of communication, it is the most telling, and demands a response from the living to repair the damage and re-engage ancestral benevolence. Ancestors may also strike out at any challenge to the social order which they uphold, such as a serious breach of customary behaviour, particularly when it adversely affects the harmony and cooperation that should mark relations between kinsmen. The religious response is a specific sacrifice to repair the relationship with the ancestors, while other steps are taken to heal the social rift.

Witches and sorcerers

Yet even when ancestors are at their most punitive, their intervention is admonitory rather than vindictive. It is taken for granted that they always act in a socially supportive role. The same cannot be said of another kind of fully human mystical agency, witches and sorcerers, who also are given prominence in the explanation of misfortune. Although those who believe in this source of malevolence do not clearly distinguish between witch and sorcerer, the distinction is not without its usefulness. There are witches who, with or without animal accomplices, unleash their inherent potency without conscious effort, and those who can switch it on and off at will. Sorcerers, on the other hand, generate this power externally for specific purposes, by collecting and mixing substances ('medicines') which they arm with incantation. Most witches are women, as if their position in society alone disposes them towards witchcraft, whereas everyone has more or less equal access to harmful medicines. It appears too that in the west the accent was on the harm that men could do, while in the east there was a much greater fear of the mystical powers of women.

The explanation of misfortune rests on the conjunction of anti-social and pro-social forces, the combination of living evil-doers and deceased ancestors. In their protective capacity, ancestors shield their descendants from the depredations of nature and from the designs upon them of witches and sorcerers. When ancestors punish transgression, they do not directly inflict harm. Rather, they temporarily relinquish their role as guardians, leaving their wards defenceless against attack from witch or sorcerer.

Diviners and herbalists

In general terms, this religious system of ideas provides a theory of causation regarding deprivation, illness and distress. But the problem for individuals is that of extracting from this system, and from the alternatives it sets out, the precise cause of their particular malady, so that they can take appropriate measures to remedy it. Once again, the ancestors come to their aid by supplying them with a special channel of communication, enlightenment and clarification. This is the diviner, commonly a woman, who knows how to operate the levers of the religious system so that it 'works'. She is singled out for this specialisation, 'called' to it by her ancestors, who stake their claim to her by marking her with a specific sickness in which the signs of possession, pain, bodily convulsion and mental dissociation are discernible. This close communion with her ancestors empowers her to act as their medium, but her powers have to be channelled and socialised by her subjection to a one- or two-year period of training during which she is removed from the community and apprenticed to an experienced diviner. The techniques imparted permit the development of a number of specialisations within the divining profession. One definite pattern that emerges is the prevalence of the 'sniffing-out' technique in the east and the use of bone- or dice-throwing in the west.

Being in direct communication with the ancestors, the diviner has a clearer vision of what ancestors require of the living. She is equipped to clarify the meaning of dreams by means of which ancestors imperfectly communicate with the living; she can diagnose the cause of misfortune, determine in what measure it has its origin in the ancestral relationship or in disturbed living relationships expressed as sorcery or witchcraft, and in each case indicate the particular relationship concerned. She can prescribe the action to be taken to remedy the situation – the performance of sacrifice, the application of healing medicines, recourse to mystical counter-attack, or the resolution of social conflict. She may even have the capacity to recover lost or misplaced property.

The diviner is, therefore, a specialist who orchestrates a religious response to crisis and adversity which is conducive to the restoration of normality. Yet not all of these measures are entirely within the competence of the diviner. The resort to curative and retaliatory medicines is a male specialisation based on an acquired knowledge of herbal and vegetable potencies. Medicines provided by the herbalist are put to a range of uses: to promote harmony, fertility and prosperity in the community; to protect property of all kinds; to settle interpersonal conflict; to stimulate sexual attraction; and to restore health and well-being. They can be ingested or otherwise consumed, applied externally or worn simply as charms against the whims of nature. Clearly, the activities of diviner and herbalist are mutually dependent, but there was a tendency in the west to combine them within a single profession, that of the doctor (*ngaka*), who was usually a man, whereas they were practised separately in the east.

Some functions of religion in Bantu-speaking societies

For Bantu-speaking societies religion upholds and conserves the moral order. More precisely, upright living is guaranteed to yield the good life, moral deviance precipitates disaster, and religion articulates, mediates and services this connection. The ancestors, with the collaboration of diviners and the support of herbalists, are the guardians and defenders of the moral order. Their primary concern is that their descendants should behave in a manner which promotes harmony, solidarity and mutual support among themselves. But they are also concerned with how descendants conduct themselves towards others outside their ranks – their neighbours. Any serious departure from the code of right conduct will result in a withdrawal of benefits and a suspension of protection, so that offenders will register the pain of physical and social disorder. Similarly, a breach of good neighbourliness, such as an assertion of selfishness, a failure of hospitality, or inordinate success, can excite the envy or hostility of others sufficiently for it to assume the form of an attack of witchcraft or sorcery; alternatively, one's anti-social behaviour runs the risk of being stigmatised as harming others by mystical means. In all of these ways, religion sanctions time-honoured social arrangements and disciplines deviance from them. And ultimately, it is the ancestors, through the offices of the diviner with the assistance of the herbalist, that provide the means of renewing the moral order once it has been upset.

On the evidence presented so far, there can be little doubt that this religion is an expression of humanism, in the sense of emphasising human or this-worldly concerns. All its active features – ancestors, diviners, herbalists, sorcerers and witches – are essentially human agents without any pretensions to divinity. Secondly, it is unashamedly devoted to the realisation of purely human interests, and this can be seen in two ways. It is overtly preoccupied with the temporal promotion of physical health, economic well-being and human development. It is a system of ideas and practices aimed at the delivery of human welfare and human therapy. But, it is equally concerned with the regulation and management of human social relations, and with the easing of social conflict. Thus, there is no suggestion in it that religion transcends the level of purely human engagement or that it is subsumed within a design conceived by a deity, or negotiated between several deities, out of time and out of this world.

The question of belief in a supreme being

How then are we to account for the commonly made assertion that the Bantu-speaking people recognised the existence of a variously named Supreme Being, a Creator God? In fact most portrayals of African religion begin right here, with a mandatory reference to a Creative Spirit, if only to dispose of him as being too peripheral to human affairs to merit much attention from anybody. Having set things in motion, he no longer evinces much concern with his own creation.

The evidence for this belief comes from a body of sketchy 'creation myths' which have been preserved, but since only the Zulu–Swazi versions describe anything that might correspond to an act of creation, they might be better described as 'myths of origin'. A myth of origin, being an explanation of antecedents, would logically posit a first being, which in terms of human procreation could be said to propagate or cause others. A first cause in this sense would not necessarily mean a First Cause, that is a supernatural creator. Even the Zulu and Swazi myths are quite consistent with an emphasis on human origin rather than on divine creation. The first being of these myths (known as uNkulunkulu or Modimo) conforms to the notion of the 'first of our kind to settle in these parts and to initiate [cause] our way of life here', hence an original progenitor and first settler. Many of the myths make it clear that they are dealing with ancestral origins, but even here there is the further implication that the myths deal with royal ancestry, because the idea of 'first settler' had to be conceived as 'a leader of the first settlement'. The Shona regional cults have long been described as addressing a High God, but closer analysis reveals that here too we are dealing with claims to territory through the invocation of autochthonous or original royal settlers, who legitimate these claims through their control of rainfall and of fertility.

Nor is there much need to go beyond the basic humanism of African religion to explain the belief in the indwelling spirits of nature and of natural things, which for the most part seem to be manifestations or associations of forgotten ancestors who have slipped the harness of structural usefulness. The Zulu goddess of spring, Nomkhubulwana, seems to be a genuine exception, but the Zulu 'Sky God', who controls lightning and storm, is not. The more correct rendering is 'Chief of the Sky', by which the Zulu apparently meant that the mystical counterpart of the living chief controlled the sky, and this leads back to the influence of royal ancestors.

Despite some confusion, the conclusion is inescapable that at the heart of Bantu-speakers' religion lies the cultivation of the ancestors, of the human spirit released from the constraints of time and place. Because initially our knowledge of these religions came to us through the early missionaries and other Christian observers, distortions understandably crept in. One of these put a gloss of divinity on one aspect of ancestral religion. The 'discovery' of elements of Judaeo-Christian religion in Africa was hard to resist, for it seemed to hold out hope of easing the work of conversion. Nevertheless, it was an imposition foreign to the humanism of the ancestor cult. Of course, the missionaries would have their way in the end, but that is another story.

NOTE

1. A 'dowry' paid by the prospective husband to the family of the bride.

SELECT BIBLIOGRAPHY

The primary source on Bushmen beliefs is the Bleek collection, supplemented by Orpen, both based on early oral evidence. Fresh and compelling insights are to be gained from modern studies of the rock art record, notably those of Lewis-Williams and Vinnicombe. The most reliable source on the Khoikhoi (Hottentots) is Schapera, who also provides the basis of comparison with the San (Bushmen). Schapera has also edited a useful collection on the Bantu-speaking people of South Africa, and his Select Bibliography is a helpful guide to early work on various aspects, inclusive of religion, of not only Bantu-speaking culture but that of the San and the Khoikhoi as well. Most anthropological studies and compilations on Bantu-speaking societies, such as Junod and Krige, have a section devoted to religion. Of particular interest with reference to Zulu religion are Berglund and Callaway. Kiernan is a more specialised treatment of the religious explanation of misfortune.

Berglund, Axel-Ivar, *Zulu Thought Patterns and Symbolism.* Cape Town: David Philip, 1976

Bleek, D. F., 'Beliefs and Customs of the /Xam Bushmen', parts v and vi. *Bantu Studies,* 7, 2 (1933)

Bleek, D. F., 'Beliefs and Customs of the /Xam Bushmen', part vii. *Bantu Studies,* 9 (1935)

Bleek, D. F., 'Beliefs and Customs of the /Xam Bushmen', part viii. *Bantu Studies,* 10 (1936)

Callaway, H., *The Religious System of the Amazulu.* Cape Town: Struik, reprint 1970

Junod, H. A., *The Life of a South African Tribe,* part II. New York: University Books, reprint 1962

Kiernan, J. P., 'The Problem of Evil in the Context of Ancestral Intervention'. *Man,* NS 18 (1982)

Krige, E. J., *The Social System of the Zulu.* Pietermaritzburg: Shuter and Shooter, reprint 1962

Lewis-Williams, J. D., *Believing and Seeing: Symbolic Meanings in Southern San Rock Art.* London: Academic Press, 1981

Orpen, J. M., 'A Glimpse into the Mythology of the Maluti Bushmen'. *Cape Monthly Magazine,* NS 9, 49 (1874)

Schapera, I., *Select Bibliography of South African Native Life and Problems.* London: Oxford University Press, 1941

Schapera, I. (ed.), *The Bantu-speaking Tribes of South Africa.* Cape Town: Maskew Miller, 1966

Vinnicombe, P., *People of the Eland.* Pietermaritzburg: Natal University Press, 1976

3

Settler Christianity

JOHN W. DE GRUCHY

Christianity developed in South Africa along two distinct paths. In the first instance, it was the established religion of the European powers, both Dutch and later British, who colonised the Cape from the mid-seventeenth century onwards. A consequence of this process of colonisation was the influx of settlers who were Christian by tradition. This led to the planting of European churches, the established Nederlandse Gereformeerde Kerk (Dutch Reformed) and German Lutheran to begin with, followed later in the nineteenth century by the full range of denominations then existing in Great Britain, as well as the Roman Catholic Church. As other European settlers came to the shores of Southern Africa, so their respective churches usually followed, or else they were absorbed into other denominations.

The second strand in the development of Christianity came as a result of missions to the indigenous peoples or to those who had been brought to the Cape as slaves from the East. A full account of all these missions and their endeavours is beyond the scope of this volume, but a significant part of that story from its beginnings to the end of the nineteenth century is told and assessed elsewhere in this volume.[1] It is a story which is both complex and full of ambiguity. Complex, because of the many different missionary societies which began work in Southern Africa after the British occupation of the Cape; ambiguous, because of the way in which the missionaries were often co-opted, wittingly or not, into serving colonial interests.

Our specific focus in this chapter is on the transplanting of European Christianity and its various church denominations to the soil of South Africa. While we shall refer in passing to some missionary endeavour, our main concern is to outline the way in which settler Christianity developed on the subcontinent alongside of, but without any meaningful relation to, mission Christianity. If the missionaries often found themselves the servants of colonialism, the settlers were the colonists, and the 'settler churches' a significant element within the process of colonisation.[2]

The settler churches existed to serve their constituencies in a new geographical environment. This meant, in effect, helping settlers cope with and adapt to their new and rather alien location by providing the necessary pastoral care, as well as a community of familiar symbols, rituals and values. In this way the churches became a cultural link with the 'old country'. Such a task was very different from that undertaken by the missionaries, whose main concern was the evangelisation of the 'heathen', and in the process turning them into 'civilised persons' who would meet the cultural norms of the 'old country'. On the other hand, the settler churches and their leaders assumed that Europeans were Christian by definition (unless they happened to be Jewish) even though they might need to be rebuked and reproved for failing to live accordingly.

As the word 'transplanting' suggests, the development of settler Christianity and churches in South Africa took place along lines which mirrored the ecclesiastical situation in Europe. The same confessional and theological differences which divided the churches there into Protestant and Catholic, Reformed and Lutheran, Anglican and Nonconformist, took root. These differences were reflected, as in Europe, in everything from church architecture and liturgy to the way in which church members related to society and politics. It is not possible to give an exhaustive account of this process of 'transplanting' in what follows. Our aim is, first of all, to provide a brief introduction to the main church denominations which were established at the Cape in the nineteenth century and which subsequently took root elsewhere in emergent South Africa, especially after the Great Trek and the discovery of diamonds and gold. Secondly, we shall consider the relationship between the Dutch Reformed and the English-speaking churches in the final decades of the century, and especially during the events which culminated in the Anglo-Boer War.

The origins and ethos of the churches

The first settlers at the Cape, whether Dutch, German or French, were Protestants. From the beginning, Jan van Riebeeck, the first commander, regarded the establishment and promotion of the Reformed religion as part of his mandate.[3] Reformed Christianity, which derived from the Swiss Reformation led by John Calvin in the first half of the sixteenth century, had already become the established religion in Holland by 1579, after that country had won its independence from Catholic Spain. Not surprisingly, the Dutch East India Company expressly forbade the practice of Roman Catholicism in its colonies. Thus the Nederlandse Gereformeerde Kerk, or Dutch Reformed Church (DRC), became the established church at the Cape of Good Hope under the supervision of the church authorities (*classis*) in Amsterdam.[4]

The first Dutch Reformed congregation was established in Cape Town in 1665, and a growing number were founded during the second half of the seventeenth century and the first half of the eighteenth, as the settlers spread into the hinterland. Soon after the French Huguenots arrived in 1688 they were absorbed into the Dutch church, having been prevented from organising their own congregations by the authorities. German Lutherans who settled at the Cape, on the other hand, managed to retain their own identity and eventually, though only in 1779, obtained permission to erect their own church buildings.

In what follows we shall not refer again to the Lutheran Church, not because it lacked significance, but because it tended to remain self-contained within the German-speaking community. There were both social and theological reasons for this. Socially, while the Lutherans were much closer to the Dutch-speaking community than to the English, they had to struggle to ensure that their Lutheran identity was not forfeited. Lutheran congregations were established wherever there were German settlements, and they retained strong links with their respective church communities in Germany. Likewise, the various German missionary societies (notably the Berlin, Rhenish and Hermannsburg Missionary Societies) which came to South Africa during the nineteenth century tended to keep to themselves. The same was generally true of the Scandinavian Lutheran settler congregations and missions. Synodical development of the Lutheran Church in South Africa was much later in coming than for the other European settler churches, and in many ways more complex.[5]

The Dutch Reformed Church in the nineteenth century

During the Batavian rule of the Cape (1803–1806), which followed the first brief British occupation (1795–1803), Commissioner De Mist introduced a new church law (1804) which separated church and state, but also ensured that the church was still subordinate to the state. Under this arrangement, many Dutch Reformed congregations and clergy continued to receive state funding, a situation which was to be maintained even under British rule until 1875. Indeed, when the second British occupation began in 1806, the new colonial authorities continued to recognise the pre-eminent position of the DRC, even though the Church of England was now the established church of those in power.

As a result of the new political dispensation the DRC had great difficulty in obtaining ministers from Holland. Lacking its own theological training facilities at the Cape, it had to depend upon the services of Scottish Presbyterian ministers whom the British authorities brought to the Cape for this purpose. This *verengelsing* was to play an important role in the shaping of the DRC during the years ahead, both politically and theologically. The Scottish *dominees* were British in their loyalties, a factor which influenced the attitude of the DRC towards the Great Trek. And they were strongly evangelical in their theology and piety, typified pre-eminently by Andrew Murray, jun., in contrast to the hyper-Calvinism, or else more liberal theology, of most Dutch-trained *predikante*.[6]

In 1824 the local DRC gained its autonomy from the church in Holland and held its first synod. This signified the establishment of the first South African-controlled church denomination, though Political Commissioners still retained a position of authority at the synods and all resolutions had to be approved by the Governor. In 1842, the passing of Ordinance 7 finally established the independence of the church from the state, but limited the work of the DRC to the Cape Colony. This limitation had far-reaching repercussions because it meant that the DRC in the Cape had no authority to minister to those who, as a result of the Great Trek of the mid-1830s, had now established communities beyond the colony. Indeed, the Trekkers had had to rely on the services of missionaries from the LMS and Wesleyan Methodists and of, most notably, Daniel Lindley of the American Board. However, in 1853 a Dutch minister, Dirk van der Hoff, arrived in the Transvaal from Holland, and became the first *predikant* of the newly constituted Nederduitsch Hervormde Kerk. The Hervormde Kerk became the state church of the South African Republic (Transvaal) in 1860.

The church situation in the Transvaal was made more complex with the arrival of Dirk Postma from Holland in 1858. Postma, a minister of the Christelike Afgeskeie Gemeentes, which had recently broken away from the state church in the Netherlands, helped establish the Gereformeerde Kerk in the Transvaal in 1859. The Gereformeerde Kerk (or Doppers) rejected the 'evangelical songs' of the DRC, and also stood for a more strictly Calvinistic theology based on the articles of faith of the Synod of Dort (1618–19). DRC congregations were, however, also established in the Transvaal, as well as in the Orange Free State and Natal. Eventually, in January 1885, a union was achieved in the Transvaal between the Hervormde Kerk and the Dutch Reformed Church (now referred to as the Nederduitse Gereformeerde Kerk – NGK) with the formation of the Nederduitse Hervormde of Gereformeerde Kerk. Some Hervormde congregations remained outside of the union, thus perpetuating a division which has continued until now.[7] These developments meant that by early in the second half of the nineteenth century, three separate and distinct Dutch Reformed churches existed in what was eventually to become South Africa.

A further development within the NGK, and one of far-reaching significance, was the decision of the Cape Synod in 1857 to allow the racial segregation of congregations. This decision was the result of a long and heated debate which stretched back almost to the beginning of the Dutch settlement at the Cape. It related, in the first instance, to the question of the evangelisation and baptism of slaves and indigenous people.[8] But then, where these had been baptised, it concerned membership within local congregations, and all that this implied at a social level. The focal point became the question of sharing together in the Lord's Supper. Segregation at Holy Communion was practised in many rural congregations, and there was considerable pressure upon the Cape church to provide the necessary sanction. The issue was debated at several successive synods, with segregation rejected on theological grounds. But eventually permission was granted by the Synod of 1857.[9] The resolution reveals something of the unease of the Synod in taking such a step:

> The Synod considers it desirable and according to the Holy Scripture that our heathen members be accepted and initiated into our congregations wherever it is possible; but where this measure, as a

result of the weakness of some, would stand in the way of promoting the work of Christ among the heathen people, then congregations set up among the heathen, or still to be set up, should enjoy their Christian privileges in a separate building or institution.[10]

While the motivation given was that the decision would help in the evangelisation of 'the heathen', it was clearly a concession to settler racial prejudice. The next logical step was the creation of a separate church denomination for 'coloured' (or mixed race) people. This occurred in 1881 when the Nederduitse Gereformeerde Sendingkerk was established. Eventually this also led to the creation of separate Dutch Reformed churches for Africans (NG Kerk in Afrika in 1910) and for Indians (Reformed Church in Africa in 1951).

The situation in the Afrikaner Republics to the north was even more racially rigid than in the Cape. If we keep in mind the fact that these Republics were the result of a trek away from a more liberal British dispensation in the south, symbolised by the ending of slavery, it is not surprising that Africans were excluded from both membership in the church and any kind of political representation. Indeed, in article three of its constitution the Hervormde Kerk expressly excluded blacks from membership in the church. While this was never part of the constitution of either the NGK or the Gereformeerde Kerk, in practice segregation became the norm. Moreover, it was eventually regarded not as a concession to 'the weakness of some' but as a divine mandate derived from Holy Scripture. Thus in due course the NGK and its sister Reformed churches provided the theological legitimation for the policy of apartheid, a development which would eventually be declared a heresy by other churches.[11]

The formation of the Church of the Province

The Anglican Church came to the Cape Colony as the established Church of England, and therefore the church of the British colonial authorities.[12] Initially it was comprised of civil servants and soldiers, and to begin with there were no parishes but only a few congregations meeting in an assortment of buildings, including, for a while, the vestry of the DRC Groote Kerk in Cape Town. These congregations were served by military and colonial chaplains, and received episcopal ministrations from the Bishop of Calcutta as he passed through Cape Town en route to or from India.

The arrival of the 1820 Settlers in the Eastern Cape, followed by successive groups of British immigrants to the Cape and Natal, led to the establishment of a growing number of parishes. The first Anglican missionary society, the Society for the Propagation of the Gospel, began work in the Western Cape in 1821, concentrating on evangelising the Muslim population. On the whole, the chaplains who served the settlers were not marked by diligence or competence, and there was a lack of direction and oversight within the church. Moreover, the Governor had full administrative and juridical authority over its affairs.

The situation changed under the leadership of Robert Gray, who became the first Bishop of Cape Town in 1848. Gray's diocese was enormous, stretching from the Cape to Natal, and included the Island of St Helena. Within a few years Gray embarked on a series of visitations to each part of his diocese, establishing new parishes and strengthening those already created. In 1853 new dioceses were established in Grahamstown and Natal, and soon the Church of England developed into a well-organised, predominantly settler church in South Africa.

Gray and most of the other bishops who were elected to the new sees were influenced by the Anglo-Catholic Tractarian movement within the Church of England, though Gray himself was not a Tractarian. This meant that from early on the character of the Anglican Church in South Africa tended to be Anglo-Catholic in orientation, though there were some more evangelical clergy and parishes. This Anglo-Catholic tendency was strengthened by the arrival of religious orders, such as the Society of the Sacred Mission (1867), the Society of St John the Evangelist (1883) and the Community of the Resurrection (1903), which pioneered much of the missionary work of the Anglican Church in Southern Africa.[13] The fact that the bishops, as well as these religious orders, were also influenced by a growing social conscience within the church in England, had an impact on the development of the Anglican Church in South Africa.

Gray was convinced that the church could not really grow and develop within the South African context if it remained under the authority of the British crown. In this respect his views coincided with those who were seeking to bring to an end the last vestiges of church–state establishment at the Cape. For while there was no official state church, a large number of NGK congregations continued to receive grants-in-aid, as did Church of England, Wesleyan Methodist, Presbyterian and Catholic settler parishes and congregations. On principle, the Baptists and Congregationalists, who strongly maintained the need for the separation of church and state, refused any state assistance.

Already in 1854 a debate was introduced into the Cape Parliament on the Voluntary Principle, which meant in effect the end to state funding of churches. Its main proponent was Saul Solomon, a distinguished Jewish liberal politician who had converted to Christianity and joined the Congregational Church. While Solomon's goal was not finally achieved for another twenty years, the public debate on the issues had far-reaching ramifications. In a celebrated letter of 15 November 1856 to the clergy and laity of his diocese, Bishop Gray had intimated that the public debate about such matters as the Voluntary Principle, and more especially the pastoral and leadership needs of the church, required the establishment of a Synod which, while adhering to the faith and practice of the Church of England, would have legislative powers in determining its own affairs.[14]

The disestablishment of the Church of England in South Africa as well as all other churches, while occurring within this context, was inadvertently furthered by one of the staunchest defenders of Erastianism, Bishop John William Colenso of Natal. Colenso was a remarkable person.[15] A highly erudite biblical scholar, internationally known for his research on the Old Testament, he was also very advanced in his thinking about the relation between Christianity and indigenous culture. He had, in fact, demonstrated the significance of his views by establishing a strong missionary work amongst the Zulu, whose rights he also staunchly defended against British imperialism. Unfortunately his views on the Bible and on other points of Christian doctrine smacked of heresy to some of his clergy. As a result he was cited by Bishop Gray to appear before a court of bishops in 1863. In responding to Gray's charge, Colenso refused to accept the jurisdiction of the courts of the church in South Africa and appealed to the Privy Council in England.

Ironically the Privy Council, which upheld Colenso's appeal against the authority of Gray, also indicated that the Anglican Church in South Africa fell under the legal jurisdiction of the South African courts, and therefore not under the authority of the crown. Colenso was eventually found guilty of heresy and excommunicated by Gray in 1866. Colenso then established his own diocese in Natal, comprised of a handful of parishes which stood by him. This laid the foundation for the much later establishment of the Church of England in South Africa in 1934, though the immediate cause of that event concerned developments in Cape Town. Meanwhile Gray and the rest of the bishops, dioceses and parishes proceeded with the inauguration of the Church of the Province of South Africa (CPSA), the first Synod of which was held in Cape Town in 1870. The Province was acknowledged by the Archbishop of Canterbury and the world-wide Anglican communion. Gray's vision had, in many respects, been fulfilled, and by the time he died a few years later, there were well-organised dioceses throughout South Africa.

English Nonconformists and Scottish Presbyterians

The Congregational, Presbyterian and Baptist churches originated in the Protestant Reformation in the sixteenth century. While the Presbyterians could trace a direct line, like the Dutch Reformed Church, from the work of John Calvin in Geneva, both the Congregationalists and Baptists, though Reformed in many respects, were also influenced by ideas on the 'left wing' of the Reformation, notably those regarding the freedom of the church from the state. As a result, Congregationalists and Baptists and, later, Methodists – collectively referred to as the Nonconformists – were in the forefront of the struggle for the separation of church and state in England. This was also true of the sizeable contingent of Baptists who came to South Africa from Germany. While some Presbyterians came to South Africa from England, most were members of either the Church of Scotland or the Free Church of Scotland, the latter being strongly evangelical in character. In some respects the Presbyterians were closer in ethos to the Cape NGK, not least because of the influence of Scottish ministers within that church, and though they were English-speaking and closely related to the English-speaking Nonconformists, their links with Scotland gave them a strong sense of Scottish national identity.

The Congregational and Presbyterian settler churches trace their origins in

South Africa to the British soldiers who served at the Cape, some of whom formed the 'Calvinist Society' in 1807. As their numbers increased with the arrival of British settlers, a congregation serving both Congregationalists and Presbyterians was established in 1820 in Cape Town. The congregation split in 1824 into two separate churches, Union Congregational and St Andrew's Presbyterian. By the middle of the nineteenth century, many Congregational (or Independent) congregations were established in various parts of the country, and regional structures had been formed both in the Cape and in Natal. The Congregationalists established the Evangelical Voluntary Union in 1860, made up of settler congregations and former London Missionary Society congregations established amongst the 'coloured' community. This became the Congregational Union in 1877, a forerunner of the United Congregational Church of Southern Africa (UCCSA) formed a century later in 1967.[16] Another branch of Congregationalism, which eventually helped create the UCCSA, was the American Board Mission, the first missionary society to begin work in Natal amongst the Zulu, in 1836.

Presbyterian congregations developed along with the growth of English-speaking settler communities in the Western and Eastern Cape and in Natal, where the first presbytery was established in 1844. The presbytery of the Transvaal was established in 1890 shortly after the discovery of gold, but it was not until 1893 that the first presbytery was established in Cape Town. The Presbyterian Church of Southern Africa (PCSA) was only constituted in 1900. Meanwhile, the Glasgow Missionary Society had begun missionary work in the Eastern Cape at Lovedale in the 1820s, laying the foundations for what eventually became the University of Fort Hare. The Disruption of the Church of Scotland in 1843, which led to the formation of the Free Church of Scotland and then, in 1847, to the formation of the United Presbyterian Church, complicated developments on the eastern frontier. The Free Church and then, after reunion, the Church of Scotland became responsible for the work at Lovedale, and eventually the establishment of the Bantu Presbyterian Church (1923), now renamed the Reformed Presbyterian Church. The missions of the United Presbyterian Church then became part of the Presbyterian Church of South Africa. Attempts to unite all Presbyterian churches in South Africa during the twentieth century have thus far been unsuccessful.

Methodism was the product of the Evangelical Revival led by John Wesley in England in the early eighteenth century. Wesley had not intended to create a new church, and to the end of his life regarded himself as a Church of England clergyman. But Methodism did become a separate institution, and soon divided into several groups, notably the Wesleyan Methodists and the Primitive Methodists. Strongly evangelical in orientation, the Methodists influenced the other English Nonconformist churches, contributing also to their interest in and commitment to missionary endeavour. Indeed, without the Evangelical Revival there would have been no London Missionary Society or, for that matter, any other.

Like the Congregationalists and Presbyterians, there were a significant number of Wesleyan Methodists amongst the soldiers who came to the Cape in 1806. There was also a particularly strong group of Wesleyans amongst the 1820 Settlers, which soon led to the formation of a number of Methodist societies in the Albany and Algoa regions. Meanwhile Wesleyan, Methodist missionaries penetrated into the Northern Cape as early as 1816, and others developed a chain of stations in the Eastern Cape after the arrival of the 1820 Settlers.[17] Later, in 1870, the Primitive Methodists began missionary work in the northeastern Cape, and the British Wesleyans in the Transvaal. The Wesleyan Methodist Church was constituted in 1882, and its first Conference was held the following year. These three branches of Methodism united in 1931 to form the Methodist Church of South Africa.[18]

The first Baptist congregation was founded in Grahamstown, in 1823, also as a result of the arrival of the 1820 Settlers. They were strengthened by the arrival of German Baptists in the 1860s in British Kaffraria.[19] Although the German Baptists did not join the Baptist Union when it was formed in 1877, most did so the following year. There were also a growing number of Dutch-speaking Baptists within the Union, leading in 1886 to the formation of the Afrikaanse Baptiste Kerk. Thus while the Baptist Union has its origins within the broad context of the English-speaking churches, its settler constituency was more varied than the others, and its theology tended to be more conservative.

Throughout the country, as English-speaking communities spread, particularly in the larger towns and cities, the parochial life of England was reproduced. Anglican parish churches co-existed with Baptist, Congregational, Methodist and Presbyterian congregations, as did their denominational structures at a national level. Church architecture, hymnody and liturgy reminded the church members of 'home'. And as the English-speaking community was the more affluent, there was a close connection with the growing and expanding mercantile class. This wealth made possible the development of such typically English institutions as private church schools, which have played a significant cultural role in South Africa, particularly within the more elite English communities.

The Roman Catholic Church

While there was a small Roman Catholic presence at the Cape from the very earliest colonial times, the Catholic Church virtually disappeared from South African history between 1686 and 1804.[20] A government ordinance of 1804, which decreed that 'all religious societies' should enjoy equal protection by the state, paved the way for the arrival at the Cape of several priests who sought to gather together the remnants of a somewhat scattered flock and minister to Catholic soldiers. This fundamental change in policy was welcomed by neither the NGK nor the British authorities who took over control of the Cape in 1806 and who ordered the priests to leave the colony soon after. While a fear of Roman Catholicism in terms of both religion and politics would continue well beyond the nineteenth century, toleration of the Roman Catholic Church was, however, gradually accepted. Indeed, it is recorded that in 1832, along with Dutch Reformed, Anglican and other church ministers, at least one priest's salary was paid by the state in accordance with policy originally established by De Mist.

In 1818 Pope Pius VII erected the Vicariate Apostolic of the Cape of Good Hope and adjacent territories, and appointed Bishop Bede Slater as the first Vicar Apostolic. The position of the church was further strengthened in 1837 when the Pope made the Cape of Good Hope a separate vicariate, and appointed Bishop Patrick Griffith as its Vicar Apostolic. This meant that for the first time a Roman Catholic bishop was permanently resident in Cape Town. Ten years later, Bishop Devereux was appointed to Grahamstown.

As was the case with the other churches at the Cape, the initial concern of the hierarchy was to provide for the needs of the Catholic community. But gradually the church began to grow as a result of evangelisation amongst the indigenous population. Meanwhile, various religious orders began to work in other parts of Southern Africa, notably the Oblates of Mary Immaculate in Natal, so that in 1885 the Vicariate of Natal was established embracing Natal, Zululand, the Orange Free State, Transvaal, Kaffraria and Basutoland, as well as parts of Mozambique. A year later, after the discovery of gold on the Witwatersrand, the Prefecture Apostolic of the Transvaal was formed. It was not until 1951, however, that Pope Pius XII established the Ecclesiastical Hierarchy in South Africa, thus giving to the Catholic Church in the country its full status. But even then, the Roman Catholic Church remained ever conscious of the widespread antagonism to Catholicism within the dominant Afrikaner society, a consciousness which tended to make the church reticent and hesitant to participate fully in the public and political arenas.

The Dutch Reformed and the English churches in the late 1800s[21]

Strange as it may now seem, one of the major resolutions passed at the first Synod of the Church of the Province in 1870 concerned the possibility of church union with the NGK. On the instruction of the Synod, Bishop Gray wrote to the Moderator of the 'Dutch Church' in the Cape, Dr P. Faure, to explore the possibility of such a union. This was then taken up by the Cape NGK at its own Synod in November that same year, and led to the following resolution being adopted:

> That this Synod, even though the numerous difficulties in the way of an outward and visible re-union of the Churches under a common Government are of such a nature that it cannot flatter itself with the expectation that the desire after Union can be realised in the immediate future, is nevertheless prepared to take into serious and friendly consideration proposals having its object in view, and emanating from any Protestant sister Church.[22]

The theological gap between Anglicans and Dutch Reformed was, however, far too great to bridge. In particular, fundamental differences on the issue of episcopacy brought a speedy end to any expectations that such a union might come about. Nonetheless, this very early expression of ecumenism remains significant, though it was very short-lived.

Despite their rejection of Erastianism, Anglicans in South Africa had a strong sense of being the established church which served the needs of the colonial nation as a whole. Within the South African context, however, it was impossible to be a national church without the NGK, which, after all, had by far the largest membership, especially within the settler community. What was at stake in seeking church union was, therefore, not simply the unity of the church but the need for a united nation in which English and Dutch settlers shared together and were served by a common church. Thus in Gray's initial letter to Faure he wrote that 'this land ... with its various races and languages, appears eminently to need Unity of action through one Church, to overcome antipathies and soften asperities, and mould its population into one nationality and one Christian people'.[23] It is tempting to consider the impact such a union might have had on the future social history of South Africa. But that was not to be; on the contrary, events would result in a growing alienation between these churches and their constituencies.

While the CPSA Synod had resolved to approach other Christian communions as well as the NGK about unity, nothing came of this decision either; indeed, it is not clear whether the CPSA even followed up the issue. There was, in fact, a much greater desire to be in ecumenical relationship with the NGK than with the other churches, even though the former was so strongly Dutch Calvinist and the latter were English-speaking. Indeed, there was considerable antipathy between Anglicans and the heirs of British Nonconformity in South Africa, and little awareness of a common identity as 'the English-speaking churches'. Only much later, in the middle of the twentieth century, would Anglicans and other 'English-speaking churches' discover common interests and goals, and seek ways to express their Christian unity.

The Voluntary Act finally became law in the Cape in 1875. This meant that while the NGK and the CPSA remained the dominant settler churches, all denominations and, by extension, all religious faiths were rendered equal. Much later, the Voluntary Principle was enshrined in the constitution of the Union of South Africa, though the pre-eminence of Christianity was upheld by succeeding governments and constitutions, and assumed by most of the churches. Indeed, the Christendom notion that the state has a responsibility to ensure that Christian values and truth are upheld in the public arena, even if it does not contribute financially to the maintenance of the churches, determined government policy for virtually the whole of the twentieth century.

Meanwhile, diamonds had been discovered in the Northern Cape in 1867. This event, followed soon after by the discovery of gold on the Witwatersrand, signalled the beginning of the process which brought modern South Africa into existence. It also had far-reaching consequences for the numerous mission stations which dotted the landscape of the Northern Cape, the Orange Free State and the Transvaal, and for the growth of the settler churches. Missionaries, especially those of the London Missionary Society, had long found themselves trapped in the middle between the interests of their African followers and those of the Boers and settlers. Generally they had sought to take the side of the Africans, even to the extent of being accused by the Boers of acting as gun-runners for the Africans. But now, with the discovery of diamonds in their own backyard, the missionaries found themselves embroiled in a far larger and bitter dispute, and their position and role became more ambiguous. At stake were no longer the interests of Tswana and Boer alone, but the more powerful interests of the British colonial government as well as the European diggers, entrepreneurs and traders who flooded into the interior. Inevitably the distinction between missionaries and other whites became blurred in the minds of many Africans in the ensuing struggles, and there was a growing awareness of the discrepancy between what the missionaries preached and what European settlers in general practised.[24]

The discovery of diamonds provided a powerful economic base for the English-speaking community, and therefore for the further expansion of British interest. By 1889 the De Beers Mining Company, controlled by Cecil John Rhodes, had already achieved a monopoly in diamond mining. Even more significant in the long term than the discovery of diamonds, however, was the discovery of gold on the Witwatersrand. This led to a massive influx of foreigners or *uitlanders*. Most of them were skilled or semi-skilled artisans who had been forced by economic factors to leave Britain. Their primary political loyalty, especially when it served their self-interests, was to the Empire. In so far as they were church-goers, they either were Anglicans or belonged to one of the British Nonconformist denominations, predominantly the Wesleyan Methodists. Thus within a few months of the founding of Johannesburg, churches serving the needs of the new settlers were established. But the gold miners were not well known for their commitment to religious values. Johannesburg, like many another city built on a 'gold rush', was, as one church newspaper editorial of the day described it, 'the quintessence of 19th century life, with all the pinchbeck glare and glitter of its follies and fashionable vices, all its business, push and hurry and bustle, and all its arrogance of success'.[25]

The Transvaal Republic was ruled by an oligarchy in Pretoria headed by President Paul Kruger. Ever since its establishment as a result of the Great Trek, the Republic had excluded indigenous blacks from participation in its political structures. 'There is no equality', declared the *Volkswet*, 'in church or state.' Indeed, no person who was not a male member of one of the Dutch Reformed churches had the vote. Moreover, as early as 1860 the Volksraad (legislature) had decreed that no Roman Catholic or Protestant churches and missionaries other than those authorised by the state could work in the Transvaal.[26] This was changed in 1870 when all churches, including Roman Catholics, were granted freedom to worship. But despite this opening up on the religious front, matters were far more problematic in the struggle for political power.

Cecil Rhodes, a key player in the unfolding political drama that was shaping the future South Africa, was the acknowledged hero of the settler community in the Cape Colony. An editorial in the Anglican periodical, *The Southern Cross*, describes an 'enthusiastic reception' which Rhodes received 'by all classes of our fellow-colonists' as 'a tribute to the man who has added a territory of 2,000 by 1,000 miles to the Empire, and who has opened that territory to Christian civilisation by his dauntless energy, keen forethought, and indomitable pluck.'[27] It is not surprising that Rhodes became Prime Minister of the Cape in 1890. A few years later, in 1895, he was the brains behind the abortive Jameson Raid, which tried to wrest power from the Boers in the Transvaal with the support of the *uitlanders*. While this destroyed the relationship which Rhodes had forged with the Afrikaner Bond and led to his fall from office, there was no doubt in the minds of English-speaking church leaders that, however foolish the Jameson Raid was as a strategy, and however much sympathy should be shown towards the 'misguided' Boer rank and file, it was of vital importance to get rid of the anachronistic Kruger regime in Pretoria. In fact, according to the editor of *The Southern Cross*, Dr Jameson's enterprise 'will live in the pages of history as having exposed the Hollander–German plot to turn the Transvaal and Free State into States of the German Empire'.

It was all very well writing positively about Rhodes, and even the Jameson Raid, from Cape Town. It was another matter trying to be a clergyman of an English-speaking church, especially the Anglican, at this time in the Transvaal. According to the Rev. Edwin Farmer of Pretoria,

> Jameson's raid and the strained diplomatic relations have caused an extreme bitterness in the Boer mind against the English, including the clergy, and the wild talk that has been going on unsettles the natives. Several times I have heard that they have been warned against having anything to do with the English missionaries, and the natives have told me that I should not be well treated if I went amongst them.[28]

Yet Farmer was adamant that he was not going to kowtow to the Boer authorities, and he spoke about the work at St Cuthbert's College, Pretoria, which he hoped would lead to 'the beginning of a native ministry'.[29]

In 1897 Sir Alfred Milner was appointed British Governor of the Cape and High Commissioner for Southern Africa. Milner was determined to sort out the South African situation as swiftly as possible, and within two years of his arrival Britain and the two Boer Republics were at war. Understandably, there was enormous pressure placed on English-speaking churches in the Republics and other Boer-controlled areas, and many clergy had to leave.

After initial setbacks, Bloemfontein, Johannesburg and Pretoria were occupied by the British army in 1900, the Transvaal became a British colony, and Paul Kruger went into exile in Switzerland. However, the war was to drag on for a further two years of bitter conflict as the Boers waged an intense guerrilla campaign. The British, in a determined effort to wipe out resistance, began a scorched earth policy of destroying Boer farms, and then interned thousands of Boer women and children as well as many black people in concentration camps. In anguish, the Nederduitsch Hervormde Kerk in the Transvaal wrote an open letter to the Christian churches in Great Britain and Ireland, pleading for an end to the senseless killing.[30] Likewise, ministers of the NGK in the Cape expressed their support for the just cause of the Boer Republics, condemning the war and the methods employed in carrying it on. They appealed to God 'to move the British nation to retrace its steps, and at once to stop the war'. In so doing it will extinguish the bitter race feeling by which the two dominant European races in South Africa are now estranged from one another, it will efface the injurious and dangerous impressions which this war between two white races is creating in the heathen native mind, and it will open the way for establishing lasting peace and prosperity in all South Africa.[31]

There were, on the other hand, isolated voices within the NGK who pleaded with their fellow ministers to stop supporting the ongoing Boer guerrilla war. H. A. du Plessis, minister at Lindley in the OFS, pleaded to his colleagues in the Cape NGK to recognise that further guerrilla resistance was futile and to ensure that the NGK use 'her influence to bring our people to subjection to the British Empire' rather than 'spurring them on to resist her rule'. Indeed, it was his opinion that the war was God's punishment for unrighteousness in the Transvaal.[32]

Sir Alfred Milner's war policy received strong support from the Nonconformist,[33] Anglican[34] and Roman Catholic church leaders.[35] They were convinced that a peaceful and stable future was only possible through a British victory and the establishment of a united nation under the British crown. This, they believed, would not only lead to mutual acceptance amongst the Afrikaner and English-speaking whites, but it would also be in the long-term best interests of the indigenous people.[36] Implicit in this was the assumption that the English-speaking churches, particularly the Anglican and Methodist (by far the largest), would play a leading role. Nonconformist leaders personally visited Milner and told him:

> We very distinctly hold the belief that the well-being of the whole of South Africa is dependent upon the indisputable establishment of British supremacy and sovereignty, and we do not hesitate to affirm that when the end is accomplished and the neighbouring territories are placed under a pure and wise government, in accordance with the policy that prevails in other provinces of the British Empire, disaffection will cease, and the whole population without distinction of race or language will be welded into a peaceful and loyal community.[37]

The English-speaking churches, and especially their missionaries, regarded the war a result of Boer aggression and unjust policies towards *uitlanders* and natives.[38] Typical of statements made by other denominations was that issued by the Baptist Union: 'the interests of the Kingdom of Christ, especially in relation to the Native races of this Continent, are intimately associated with the success of British arms …'[39] This connection between a British victory and the future well-being of Africans was a constantly reiterated theme in the pronouncements of English-speaking church and political leaders and was used to legitimate the claim that the Boer Republics must be taken over and placed under British rule. The Rev. J. S. Moffat, one of the leading Nonconformist churchmen of the day, and son of the famous missionary Robert Moffat, argued that the real issue at stake – as in the case of the Civil War in the United States – was the status of the native. In support of his case, Moffat, using material from the Rev. Charles Phillips, who had recently been forced to flee the Transvaal, compared the lot of blacks in the Transvaal with that of blacks in the Cape. Indeed, for Moffat as for many others it was 'no exaggeration in speaking of the native question as one of the principal causes which have led to the present war ...'[40]

While the distinction between the way in which the Boer and British authorities treated the Africans might hold in some respects, it is not one which can be maintained without qualification. Moreover, and in anticipation of what is yet to come, we must note that this rhetoric, however well meant, was in striking contrast to what happened after the war when everything was done by the British to conciliate the Boers and no heed was taken of the black voices of protest. Indeed, there was 'virtually no protest from either Anglican clergy or those of other denominations to Article Eight of the Peace of Vereeniging, which deferred decision on an African franchise until after the granting of self-government to the annexed Boer states'.[41]

> Wartime propaganda had led many [Africans] to expect some form of recognition at least of the political rights of Africans living in the conquered Boer republics, in line with what was already enjoyed in the Cape Colony, and the claims made in the British press and elsewhere that the war was being fought in the interests of true Christianity and an imperial order based on equality before the law and 'equal rights for all civilised men'.[42]

But Milner and the imperial government 'were in no doubt that the question of extending political rights to Africans should not be allowed to stand in the way of reconciling Boers and English-speaking South Africans to the new imperial order that was being created for southern Africa. The contribution of black South Africans to the war effort, in other words, was to be without tangible political reward.'[43] Colonial clergy, as distinct from many missionaries, and settler churches, as distinct from mission-educated Africans, saw the future in terms of white unity rather than black rights. This became the post-war agenda of the English settler churches as they sought to foster reconciliation with their former enemies and promote the cause of the Union of South Africa in line with British foreign policy.

NOTES

1. See chapter 4.

2. For a more detailed account of the relationship between mission and settler Christianity see John W. de Gruchy, *The Church Struggle in South Africa.* Grand Rapids: Eerdmans, and Cape Town: David Philip, second edition, 1986, pp. 1ff.

3. For a more detailed account, see chapter 4.

4. A. Moorrees, *Die Nederduitse Gereformeerde Kerk in Suid-Afrika, 1652–1873.* Cape Town: Bible Society, 1937.

5. Hans W. Florin, *Lutherans in South Africa.* Durban: Lutheran Publishing Co., 1967.

6. De Gruchy, *Church Struggle,* pp. 18f.

7. G. B. A. Gerdener, *Boustowwe vir die Geskiedenis van die Nederduitse Gereformeerde Kerk in die Transgariep.* Kaapstad: Nasionale Pers, 1930.

8. Jonathan N. Gerstner, *The Thousand Generation Covenant: Dutch Reformed Covenant Theology and Group Identity in Colonial South Africa, 1652–1814.* Leiden: E.J. Brill, 1991.

9. See Chris Loff, 'The History of a Heresy', in John W. de Gruchy and Charles Villa-Vicencio (eds.), *Apartheid is a Heresy.* Grand Rapids: Eerdmans, and Cape Town: David Philip, 1983.

10. Quoted in *ibid.,* p. 19.

11. See De Gruchy and Villa-Vicencio, *Apartheid is a Heresy.*

12. Peter Hinchliff, *The Anglican Church in South Africa.* London: Darton, Longmann & Todd, 1963.

13. *Ibid.,* pp. 225f.

14. See Cecil Lewis and C.E. Edwards (eds.), *Historical Records of the Church of the Province of South Africa.* London: SPCK, 1934, pp. 147f.

15. Jeff Guy, *The Heretic: A Study of the Life of John William Colenso, 1814–1883.* Johannesburg: Ravan, 1983.

16. D. Roy Briggs and Joseph Wing, *The Harvest and the Hope: The Story of Congregationalism in Southern Africa.* Johannesburg: UCCSA, 1970.

17. See chapter 4.

18. Leslie A. Hewson, *An Introduction to South African Methodism.* Cape Town: Methodist Publishing House, 1951.

19. Sydney Hudson-Reed (ed.), *By Taking Heed: The History of the Baptists in Southern Africa: 1820–1977.* Roodepoort: Baptist Publishing House, 1983.

20. J. E. Brady, OMI, 'History of the Church in South Africa', in *The Catholic Church and South Africa.* Cape Town: The Catholic Archdiocese of Cape Town, 1951, p. 115.

21. For a more detailed account see John W. de Gruchy and Charles Villa-Vicencio, *The Social History of the Church in South Africa,* vol. 2, forthcoming.

22. *The Unity of Christendom: A Correspondence Relative to Proposals for Union between the English and Dutch Reformed Churches in South Africa.* Cape Town, 1871, p. 9.

23. *Ibid.,* p. 7.

24. Jean and John Comaroff, *Of Revelation and Revolution: Christianity, Colonialism, and Consciousness in South Africa,* vol. 1. Chicago: Chicago University Press, 1971, p. 188ff.

25. *The Southern Cross,* 15 March 1896, p. 27. *The Southern Cross,* now the name of a Roman Catholic newspaper, was then the title of the newspaper published by the Church of the Province (Anglican).

26. Gerdener, *Boustowwe,* p. 765.

27. *The Southern Cross,* editorial, 15 January 1887.

28. Article in *The Mission Field* (Anglican), 2 August 1897, p. 302.

29. *Ibid.,* p. 305.

30. 'Beroep op Kristelike Kerk in Anglo-Boer-Oorlog', in Gerdener, *Boustowwe,* pp. 771–2.

31. The statement is contained in a letter to Governor Sir Alfred Milner, December 7, 1900, to inform him about the matter. See *British Command Papers* (Cd. 903), April 1901, no. 22.

32. H. A. du Plessis, 'Open Letter to the Clergy of the D.R. Church in the Cape Colony', published in the *Cape Times*, 12 February 1901.

33. See G. C. Cuthbertson, 'The Nonconformist Conscience and the South African War, 1899–1902'. Doctoral dissertation, University of South Africa, 1986.

34. Margaret Blunden, 'The Anglican Church during the War', in P. Warwick (ed.), *The South African War: The Anglo-Boer War 1899–1902*. London: Longman, 1980.

35. See *The Voice of the Churches in Support of the Imperial Policy*, published by the South African Vigilance Committee, Cape Town, 1900.

36. See, for example, Allan B. Webb, *Some Questions on the Settlement in South Africa*. London: Skeffington & Son, 1900. Dr Webb had been Anglican bishop of Bloemfontein and then Grahamstown.

37. Statement addressed to Milner by Nonconformist church leaders in Cape Town, 18 June, 1900. From M. J. Farrelly, *The Settlement after the War in South Africa*. London: Macmillan, 1900, Appendix III, p. 276.

38. Blunden, 'Anglican Church', pp. 282, 284.

39. *The Voice of the Churches in Support of the Imperial Policy*.

40. Rev. J. S. Moffat, a member of the South African Vigilance Committee, which published his pamphlet on *The Black Man and the War*, Vigilance Papers, no. 8 (1900).

41. Blunden, 'Anglican Church', p. 290.

42. Willan, *The South African War*, p. 104.

43. *Ibid.*, p. 104.

SELECT BIBLIOGRAPHY

Briggs, D. Roy and Joseph Wing, *The Harvest and the Hope: The Story of Congregationalism in Southern Africa*. Johannesburg: UCCSA, 1970

Brown, W. E., *The Catholic Church in South Africa, from its Origins to the Present Day*. London: Burns & Oates, 1960

Chidester, David, *Religions of South Africa*. London and New York: Routledge, 1992

De Gruchy, John W., *The Church Struggle in South Africa*. Grand Rapids: Eerdmans, and Cape Town: David Philip, second edition, 1986

De Gruchy, John W., and Charles Villa-Vicencio, *The Social History of the Church in South Africa*, vol. 2, forthcoming

Florin, Hans W., *Lutherans in South Africa*. Durban: Lutheran Publishing Co., 1967

Hewson, Leslie A., *An Introduction to South African Methodism*. Cape Town: Methodist Publishing House, 1951

Hinchliff, Peter, *The Anglican Church in South Africa*. London: Darton, Longman & Todd, 1963

Hinchliff, Peter, *The Church in South Africa*. London: SPCK, 1968

Hofmeyr, J. W., J. A. Millard and C. J. J. Froneman, *History of the Church in South Africa: A Document and Source Book*. Pretoria: Unisa, 1991

Hudson-Reed, Sydney (ed.), *By Taking Heed: The History of the Baptists in Southern Africa: 1820–1977*. Roodepoort: Baptist Publishing House, 1983

Moorrees, A., *Die Nederduitse Gereformeerde Kerk in Suid Afrika, 1652–1873*. Cape Town: Bible Society, 1937

4

Mission Christianity

CHARLES VILLA-VICENCIO

Long before the first whites set foot on the southern tip of the African continent, Bantu-speaking Africans had already settled the area that is today known as South Africa; and the Khoikhoi had already been in the southern parts of the country from before the beginning of the Common Era.[1] In this context the first European mariners landed at the Cape in the fifteenth century, in search of a sea-route to the East.

In what follows, comment is offered on the religious implications of the early Dutch settlement at the Cape and thereafter on the expansion of missionary activity that coincided with the British occupation of the Cape in 1795 and again (permanently this time) in 1806. Although the focus of attention is on the activity of English missionary societies on the Eastern Cape border (as an example of the broader missionary work in other parts of the subcontinent) reference is also made to other missionary activity, across the Orange River, in Natal and elsewhere.[2]

The Dutch settlement 1652–1795

The first significant colonial development at the Cape occurred with the establishment of a Dutch East India Company (DEIC) settlement in 1652. As was the case with the Portuguese endeavours, the original intention behind the settlement was limited. The purpose was to provide no more than a service to passing ships. This is partly seen in the decision to send Van Riebeeck, a merchant under censure for having violated Company regulations governing free trade in the East, to oversee the project. He was instructed to maintain peaceful relations with both indigenous people and foreign traders who might call at the Cape. The Company was at the same time bound by a stipulation of the Second Charter of the Netherlands government of 1622 which required it to promote and protect 'public religion' (in other words, Reformed orthodoxy). This religious policy would shape the character of social structures at the Cape, and determine the nature of the slave trade in the region until its abolition in 1834.

Religious conflict

Reformed orthodoxy at the Cape was further strengthened with the arrival in 1689 of the French Huguenots – Calvinist victims of religious persecution. As they were refused access to a French minister, cultural differences in time disappeared, and the Huguenots were absorbed into the Dutch settler community.[3] Roman Catholics were, in turn, prevented from engaging in public worship. German Lutherans who arrived in the Cape during the period of Dutch settlement were also not permitted to engage in public worship until 1778.

The exclusivism of the Reformed faith, however, gave way in time to religious tolerance at the Cape, as a result of a new European spirit emanating from the French Revolution. This had made its presence felt in the Netherlands when the Batavian Republic replaced the Dutch monarchy. At the Cape, Commissioner De Mist issued in 1804 a Church Order, which permitted the practice of other religious beliefs.[4] The result was that the Dutch Reformed Church (DRC) was no longer the state church, although it would continue to be the dominant church, enjoying certain privileges over other churches and religions, a situation which prevailed even after the British occupied the Cape. Despite a general liberalising policy, the tiny Jewish community at the Cape did not build a synagogue until 1841, and Islam continued to be confined to the slave community. Three Roman Catholic priests, however, arrived in Cape Town soon after the Church Order had been promulgated, initiating the ministry of the Roman Catholic Church in South Africa. De Mist, at the same time, never deviated from the essential social ideology which shaped the Dutch colonisers' attitude to religion, which was to assist the state in the maintenance of social order. The only difference was that it now became the task of all religious groupings to exercise this role.

Before De Mist's policy of liberalisation was enacted, Christian missionary work had already begun, primarily among the Khoikhoi. The response of the DRC and Company officials to the arrival of the first missionary in 1738, the Moravian George Schmidt, clearly indicated the kind of ideological control which religion was expected to exercise in the colony. Although he was armed with a letter of authority from the Company's directors in the Netherlands, and commenced work at Baviaanskloof (later to be renamed Genadendal), his work soon aroused the suspicions of DRC ministers in the Cape who saw Schmidt's evangelical piety and proclamation of universal salvation as a violation of Reformed orthodoxy. Company officials, in turn, feared that independent congregations of Khoikhoi could undermine their jurisdiction. Rather than submit to the kind of control which the authorities tried to impose on him, Schmidt insisted on his right to preach the gospel without submitting to any particular confession, and left the colony in 1744. The result was the virtual disappearance of mission work from the Cape for almost fifty years. The London Missionary Society (LMS) did not enter the territory until 1799, to be followed by other missionary developments. Before these initiatives are considered, it is necessary, however, to give attention to another important development in this period, namely religion in the slave community.

Slavery

In accordance with Company policy of not enslaving the indigenous people in the place of settlement, Van Riebeeck had to wait for the importation of slaves from elsewhere. They came from countries as diverse as West Africa, Mozambique, Madagascar, present-day Java, Bali, Timor, the Malayan peninsula, China and various parts of India.

Within the slave community the work of Shaykh Yusuf, Abd Allah ibn Qadi Abd al-Salam (later known as Tuang Guru) and other Muslim leaders was important in promoting the Islamic faith. The Christian church showed little interest in working with slaves, although later, British missionaries and authorities alike would lament the failure of slaves to adopt the Christian faith.

The Islamisation of slaves can be attributed to a number of factors. Many of the slaves, originating as they did from the East, were at least nominally Muslim at the time of their arrival in South Africa. Robert Shell suggests that their assimilation into the Muslim faith was motivated by a variety of additional factors – the adoption by Muslims of neglected and abandoned children, the provision of marriage ceremonies for slaves (often denied them by the church), the availability of burial services (again neglected by Christians) and the teaching of the Quran in schools under the control of the Islamic community. Not least, slaves were attracted to Islam by the promise of freedom: the emerging Muslim culture in the Malay (or 'coloured') community promoted the well-being and liberation of slaves.[5] Although required neither by the Quran nor the Sha'ria (Islamic law), such humanitarian actions were seen as works of great piety, Muslim slaves frequently being freed by Muslim slave-owners. There is also evidence of slaves having been bought by Muslim people of means, specifically in order to free them.

In addition to the positive appeal of Islam, it was also the negative attitude of the church to slaves, enshrined in the Charter of the Company, which contributed to the growth of Islam at the Cape. This was the consequence of an article of Reformed doctrine laid down by the Synod of Dort in 1618 which determined that the children of heathens were not to be baptised even if they were taken into Christian households. It was, however (ironically perhaps), another requirement of the Synod of Dort which was decisive in shaping the attitude of slave-owners to slaves. This stated that Christian slaves were to be set free – a belief eventually incorporated into law in 1770. A direct consequence was the growing opposition of slave-owners to Christian mission work among slaves. Within a few years of the passing of this legislation, the benches reserved for slaves in the Groote Kerk in Cape Town were no longer needed.[6]

Class distinction between slave-owners and slaves was entrenched in the settler community, and neither the rulings of Company officials nor the theology of Dort was sufficient to erode this. Further, there is evidence that some slave-owners encouraged their slaves to become Muslims because the Islamic prohibition on the drinking of alcohol and other social vices made Muslim slaves reliable workers and better servants.[7]

Early British colonialism: 1795 and 1806 onwards

The South African Missionary Society was established in 1799, with the fifth article of its constitution reaffirming the relationship between church and state: 'The attention of the Directors of this Society is most earnestly directed to the general duty of every Christian, to render all submission and reverence to temporal Power, for the Lord's sake, and carefully to refrain from anything which may be repugnant to the rules that have been promulgated in things civil and ecclesiastical.'[8] It was a policy in line with earlier Company policy, one which the British were happy to inherit. The year 1799 also saw the arrival of Dr Johannes van der Kemp of the LMS, marking the beginning of a new and different missionary era.

Shortly before, in 1792, the Moravians had returned to Baviaanskloof.[9] Although the reaction of the Dutch settlers was negative, DRC mission work among the Khoikhoi was beginning to develop. M. C. Vos, working within this church, was partly responsible for establishing the South African Missionary Society.[10] The major missionary impulse was, however, to come from the LMS, a non-denominational initiative which emerged from the Evangelical Revival in Europe. Anglicans, Methodists and others soon chose to work independently. The LMS in South Africa gave birth to the Congregational Church in the country. Its work was initially personified in the ministry of Van der Kemp, which was to have far-reaching social and economic implications in the region.

Van der Kemp and the Khoikhoi

Proceeding into the Zuurveld in the Eastern Cape, Van der Kemp first made missionary contact with the Xhosa people under Ngqika. The social and political infrastructure of Xhosa society was, however, still intact and the response to his overtures was limited. The disintegration of the social order among the Khoikhoi was, on the other hand, already well advanced by the time Van der Kemp turned his attention to this community, ensuring a more positive response.[11]

In brief, a consideration of missionary history suggests that it was only after traditional structures had given way under the impact of imperialism that the indigenous population looked to missionaries to satisfy their basic needs. The church played an ambiguous social and political role in the colonial process. Ministering to the basic needs of the people, it also contributed to the collapse of the very infrastructure that was required for Africans to resist the imperial onslaught. Eager to engage in evangelism, missionaries attracted their prospective converts to mission stations where they were taught European ways and customs – these were regarded as an inherent part of the Christian life.

Van der Kemp's work among the Khoikhoi started in Graaff-Reinet in 1801; here he was assisted by James Read, who had arrived in the country the previous year. Van der Kemp earned the wrath of the Boer settlers for refusing to allow segregated worship.[12] Deeply engaged in the conflicts between Khoikhoi and Boer, the LMS missionaries were virtually driven out of the area. In

1803 they were allowed to establish a mission station at Bethelsdorp, near Algoa Bay. Again controversy emerged around their ministry.

Despite their confrontation with the colonists and government alike, the LMS missionaries were also not unwilling to cooperate with colonial officials when it was in their interest to do so. The problem was that this invariably led to certain compromises with the government. One such instance occurred prior to Van der Kemp's departure for Bethelsdorp. The Graaff-Reinet land-drost, H. C. D. Maynier, offered Van der Kemp land on the Sundays River for a mission station. This he willingly accepted and in return felt obliged to support the recruitment of Khoikhoi into the Hottentot Corps. And later, when the British Governor, Sir Francis Dundas, asked Van der Kemp to intervene in a conflict between the settlers and Khoikhoi, Van der Kemp persuaded Klaas Stuurman (a local Khoikhoi leader) to accept a settlement in return for certain privileges. A direct outcome was the loss of support for Stuurman among the Khoikhoi and a further undermining of Khoikhoi unity.

The words of Van der Kemp's biographer are sufficient to tell the other side of this story: 'Like a tigress defending her cubs, Van der Kemp tirelessly defended the rights and well-being of his people. Once again he acted as their spokesman, conveying their complaints to the government ...'[13] Eventually he was summoned to Cape Town to make their complaints known to the Governor. A circuit court was appointed to hear the charges which were brought against the Boers. By this time Van der Kemp was exhausted; he eventually died in December 1811 at the age of 64. Read continued the work, and although he has earned the criticism of many historians for being ineffectual and unable to provide the kind of mission leadership that was required, Christopher Saunders's reassessment of Read suggests that a great deal of this criticism is unjustified. Stubbornly seeking to defend the cause of the Khoikhoi and Xhosa-speaking peoples, he has been viewed with suspicion by colonisers and historians alike.[14] H. A. Reyburn's careful study of evidence before the circuit courts, in turn, shows that despite the rejection of many of the charges brought against the settlers by Read as the chief complainant, he 'came out of the ordeal with reasonable credit'.[15] The Khoikhoi, on the other hand, found the decisions of the courts in favour of the farmers outrageous. This deepened the suspicions of the Khoikhoi towards the colonial authorities.

Notwithstanding the importance of mission work among the Khoikhoi, it was the Xhosa-speaking peoples who in the early nineteenth century were fast becoming the focus of both colonial and missionary expansionism. Although reluctant at first to support missionary activity in the area, as they regarded missionaries as subversive of colonial interests, the authorities slowly began to see the value of missionary endeavour for colonialism. Thus when the Rev. John Campbell, a representative of the directors of the LMS, visited the Cape in 1813–14, the Governor, Sir John Cradock, granted permission for additional land to be made available for mission work. In the wake of these developments, John Philip was appointed superintendent of the LMS in South Africa in 1819.

Xhosa-speaking people

To understand missionary work among the Xhosa, it is necessary to recall early developments in this regard. Tradition suggests that Van der Kemp, during his short sojourn among Ngqika's people, made contact with Ntsikana, a diviner who helped shape an emerging African manifestation of the gospel.[16]

Significant missionary contact with the Xhosa-speaking peoples had nevertheless to wait until Lord Charles Somerset (who replaced Cradock as Governor in 1814) decided he needed to exercise influence on Ngqika, the dominant Xhosa chief in the area. Read travelled twice to the area between the Tyume and Kat rivers, arranging with Ngqika for the appointment of Joseph Williams as resident missionary. Williams, however, soon realised what the government expected of him. He was required to act in a dual capacity, as both missionary and government agent. His unwillingness to cooperate at this level made him unpopular with the colonial administration. He was ultimately accused of adultery by the Rev. George Thom, who became a severe critic of those missionaries opposed to government policy. When Williams died in 1818, Colonial Secretary Bird contacted the Rev. John Brownlee to express his concern about Williams's tendency to 'waver and hesitate' in his relations with the Colonial Office. He encouraged Brownlee to take up the post of resident missionary, and assured him of the necessary financial and administrative support of the Governor. Tensions between Ngqika and his rival, Ndlambe, were intensifying at that stage, and mission activity in the region had to wait until later.

Perhaps more significant than direct missionary activity for the emerging church in the area were developments concerning Ntsikana and Nxele, Ndlambe's counsellor and diviner. They responded differently to the influence of missionaries on their people, prefiguring two alternative types of religious resistance which would mark the history of the black struggle in South Africa. These alternative responses can, to a large degree, be attributed to their different contexts. As diviner in Ngqika's homestead, Ntsikana gained prominence during the period when Ngqika was obliged to cooperate most closely with the colonial government, whose support he needed to ward off the challenge to his authority from the hostile and more independent Ndlambe. Nxele was, in turn, diviner to Ndlambe, whose forces on two separate occasions defeated Ngqika. Ngqika managed to survive as chief only because of British support.

When Nxele's visions predicted the military victory of Ndlambe's forces over the British garrison in Grahamstown, Ndlambe decided to attack the settler town. Promising Ndlambe that the bullets of the British would turn to water, Nxele taught his followers to sing, as they went to war, of the day when whites would be driven into the sea:

> To chase the white men from the earth,
> And drive them to the sea.
> The sea that cast them up at first,
> For Ama Xhosa's curse and bane,

Howls for the progeny she nursed
To swallow them again.[17]

Ndlambe's attack on Grahamstown on 22 April 1819 failed. Nxele was sentenced to life imprisonment on Robben Island, and later drowned while trying to escape. The millenarian religious resistance personified by Nxele would nevertheless become a recurring feature in the black struggle against white domination in South Africa.

Ntsikana's response was equally important. Having initially had his divining powers rejected by the more independent Ndlambe, he turned to Ngqika. His attitude to missionary religion was clearly shaped by Ngqika's forced accommodationist response to colonialism, just as Nxele's attitude was shaped by the more independent response of Ndlambe. Ntsikana's contribution to the development of an Africanised Christianity is recorded in his 'Great Hymn'.[18] The continuing struggle by African Christians in the mainline churches and the African indigenous churches to give expression to a contextual African Christianity bears witness to the importance of Ntsikana's response to the missionaries.

At another level both his and Nxele's responses characterise the central dilemma that faced the Xhosa arising from the presence of the missionaries. 'Nxele was a wardoctor and his cosmology was one of battle between good and evil,' writes Peires. 'Ntsikana was a man of peace and submission, and his cosmology was one of peace and submission.'[19] This observation reaches to the heart of the challenge that colonialism and the Christian religion presented to the indigenous peoples: rejection or accommodation.

The response of the colonial authorities to Ndlambe and Ngqika was ultimately very similar. When the need arose for the British to settle the Mfengu people, who were fleeing the effects of the Mfecane, Ngqika was compelled to surrender three thousand square miles for the settlement. The Methodist missionary John Ayliff actively promoted the plan. Ngqika's observation says it all: 'Though protected, I am rather oppressed by my protectors.'[20] The ambiguous missionary involvement in the colonial subjugation of the Xhosa-speaking peoples had, in fact, only just begun. The religious culture which emerged from the kinds of responses offered by both Ntsikana and Nxele would, in turn, live on among the Xhosa of the Eastern Cape – each response in its own way contributing to the African Independent church movement.

The arrival of the 1820 Settlers

It was essentially the arrival of the 1820 British settlers that set the scene for what was to come. The established churches of the Cape Colony remained the DRC and the Anglican Church, both of which drew their membership largely from the white settler community. The situation of the dominant missionary societies – essentially, the LMS and the Wesleyan Missionary Society – was different. They emerged largely from a Nonconformist background, and the focus of their activity was essentially the indigenous population. Their ministry had at the same time ambiguous consequences, often aggravated by the many different (at times competing) missionary societies operating in the Cape, each fuelled with evangelistic zeal for the souls of the heathen. In the words of Dr John Philip:

> It is the incalculable worth of the human soul which gives to missionary labours their greatest importance ... it is to this principle that we are to trace the philanthropy, the energy, and wisdom, which have given rise to Bible and Missionary Societies ... and were this spirit extinguished, ignorance and barbarism would speedily resume their wonted empire.[21]

Differences among missionaries and clashes between some missionaries and the colonial settlers came about essentially as a result of conflicting perceptions of how converts could best be won and the extent to which the church should become directly involved in political conflicts. Some missionaries were more concerned with social issues than others, while the emancipation debates of the 1820s often exacerbated the differences between them.

Slavery

Before we pursue the impact of these developments on the mission work among the Xhosa-speaking people, passing comment on missionary attitudes towards slavery in the period preceding emancipation is appropriate. Noting the social advantages for slaves who converted to Islam (referred to earlier), the LMS missionaries, William Elliott and John Philip among them, began to work for reforms in state and church, to ensure a more favourable attitude towards the Christian faith.[22] While Barnabas Shaw of the Wesleyan Missionary Society was not himself directly involved in the anti-slavery campaigns, he writes of the morning when slaves were freed (1 December 1834): 'I awoke at about two o'clock with the words, "Africa is free" powerfully impressed upon my mind, and felt a longing desire that all her sons might be free indeed.'[23]

This interest in the cause of the slaves stands in contrast to the lack of obvious missionary concern for the emancipation of slaves in the earlier period, suggesting that the apparent shift in missionary attitudes was essentially a reflection of a general changing attitude towards slavery in the Empire. While the reasons for emancipation cannot be addressed here, it is important to note the economic climate which probably contributed to the freeing of the slaves.[24] In brief, slavery belonged more to the feudal age than a capitalist economy. Free labour was significantly cheaper than slave labour, not least because it required no capital outlay. In a free market, labour could be hired and dismissed at will. Without this economic reality the moral appeal of abolitionists would probably not have met with the success it ultimately enjoyed. Abolitionists used this changing social milieu, and the cause of emancipation thus gained ground. This having been said, the direct involvement of the churches in the fight against slavery in South Africa was limited, although individual missionaries, notably Van der Kemp and Philip, did involve themselves in the call for an end to slavery.

The Northern Cape

Missionary involvement on the northern border of the Cape in the 1820s came about as a result of the Mfecane. A band of marauding Sotho refugees swept westwards across the plains of what is today known as the Orange Free State, playing a crucial, if unintended, role in the establishment of a Christian presence amongst both the Bechuana and the Ndebele of Mzilikazi.

The local people, the BaTlaping among them (although hitherto fairly indifferent to the LMS mission in Kuruman), now had no option but to look to the missionaries, taking refuge on mission stations and ultimately availing themselves of the influence of missionaries to gain colonial protection. This recurring development is seen most vividly during the time of the ministry of Robert Moffat and Mary Smith at Kuruman; they were able to call on Andries Waterboer at Griquatown for assistance when the Sotho threatened to over-run the BaTlaping. On 23 June 1823, the Griqua chief led a group of mount-ed men armed with rifles against the invaders, driving them off. The outcome was increased influence for the missionaries among the BaTlaping. Moffat recorded that a general spiritual awakening occurred at Kuruman. A church building was completed and the first six converts were baptised. Political instability and religious awakening indeed went hand in hand.

Mzilikazi's response to Moffat further reflects the growing social impact of the missionaries. Having heard of the missionary influence among the BaTla-ping, Mzilikazi invited Moffat to visit him. A lifelong friendship developed which opened the way for the Paris Missionary Society to work among the Sotho.

The impact of the migrating Sotho on missionary work was also felt else-where. In November 1822, Thomas Hodgson and Samuel Broadbent crossed the Vaal River to work among the Baralong chiefdom of the Bechuana. Here they were attacked by the advancing Sotho. Eventually they were succeeded by James Archbell, who was able to persuade Moshoeshoe to agree to allow the Baralong to settle at Thaba Nchu, which would become a centre for extensive missionary work in the area.[25]

In brief, the missionaries offered a way out of the crisis of insecurity faced by weaker chiefdoms unable to withstand the Mfecane. The mission stations became places of refuge and aid for the weak and the helpless. Philip reports that many women also saw the mission stations as a vehicle for escaping the imposition of menial work and exploitation by men – which was especially prevalent at this time of social collapse in African traditional society.[26]

A further missionary development in the interior occurred among the Namaquas. Lilyfontein was established as the centre of Wesleyan mission work in the area. Barnabas Shaw, William Threlfall and Jacob Links (the first African to be ordained to the Methodist ministry in South Africa) pioneered the work, with the assistance of a young convert, Johannes Jager. In 1825 Threlfall, Links and Jager travelled north of Warm Bath, and became the first Christian martyrs in the area.[27]

The eastern frontier

In 1819 the British government settled upon emigration as a solution to the problems of unemployment in Britain; the Cape Governor, Lord Charles Somerset, saw settlers as a solution to the border conflict, a first line of defence against the African chiefdoms in the area.

Of working-class origin, most settler families were Nonconformists and Wesleyans, with only two of the settler parties choosing a minister from the Church of England. The dominant Sephton settler group brought with them a Wesleyan minister, the Rev. William Shaw. He articulated a vision of mission work beyond the confines of the settler community, dreaming of a chain of mission stations from the western colonial border to Delagoa Bay, and applied to the Governor for permission to cross the Fish River. This was granted, and in November 1823, supported by Ann Shaw and colleague William Shepstone, William Shaw's work began.

It was not long before Shaw demonstrated his usefulness to the colonial authorities by arranging a meeting between their representatives and the Xhosa chief Pato, which secured the chief's cooperation. As a result the Mount Coke station was established among the people of Dushane, the son of Ndlambe. Stephen Kay, assisted by Richard Tainton, was entrusted with this mission station and the task of influencing local people who had thus far resisted colonial advances. Missionary cooperation with the government was also evident when in 1827 William Shrewbury sought the aid of the land-drost of Albany to persuade the Gcaleka chiefdom under Hintsa to allow the establishment of Butterworth, the third mission in the chain.[28] Other mission stations followed: in May 1829 William Shepstone established Morley at the capital of the Bomvana chief, Mdepa. Clarkbury, the fifth in the series, was established by Richard Haddy in April 1830, among the Tembu people led by Vusani; and the sixth, Buntingville, was founded by William Boyce 120 kilometres north of the Umtata River among the Mpondo, led by Faku.

Within seven years a chain of mission stations stretching 300 kilometres to the north was established, with government permission. The activities of previously unknown African people now aroused the interest of colonial officials. The colonial expectations for these missions will be discussed later – as well as the extent to which many of the missionaries lived up to them. Dr Philip, when reflecting on the role of the missionaries during this period, conceded that it had not been the intention of missionaries to bring the chiefdoms 'into a state of subjection to the colony'. He recognised, however, that (intentions apart) 'our missionaries have conciliated the chiefdoms on the borders of the colony to the colonial government, and have been the instruments in preserving them in peace with the colony'.[29] The extent of direct missionary cooperation with colonial officials in the subjugation of the indigenous people soon became the cause of bitter friction between Shaw and Philip. Writing in defence of the stance of Wesleyan missionaries, Shaw insisted that the watchword for Wesleyan missionaries was 'justice to the kaffirs – security to the colony'.[30] Their work exposed what Shaw saw to be the dilemma facing missionaries who desired to be both 'loyal British subjects and yet friends of the Kaffer nation'.

Philip saw things differently. Although on his arrival he was influenced by settler views, he soon became embroiled in the struggle for the rights of the Khoikhoi. He objected to the effects of the pass system, conscription into the armed forces, compulsory labour, and taxation on the Khoikhoi – engaging the wrath not only of the Governor, but of the British settlers, the Boers and often other missionaries. Undeterred, he won the support of William Wilberforce, who persuaded the British parliament to appoint a commission of inquiry into the general conditions of the slave and Khoikhoi population. The outcome was that on 15 July 1828 the British government decreed that instructions be given 'as shall most effectively secure to all the natives of South Africa the same freedom and protection as are enjoyed by other free people of the colony, whether English or Dutch'.[31] Two days later, the Acting Governor of the Cape, General Bourke, promulgated Ordinance 50, which provided the equality called for by Britain.[32] In reality, the Ordinance did not change much. James Read observed that the Khoikhoi 'have not been much elated by hearing of the liberty; in fact, it will not so much affect them, except in the pass system'.[33] Ordinance 50 left the Khoikhoi economically helpless, forcing many to remain landless serfs at the mercy of white landowners. In an attempt to ameliorate this situation, the government established the Kat River Settlement, designed to provide farming land for the Khoikhoi and a buffer between the Xhosa and the settlers. Because of its location, the size of plots and a range of social problems, however, the settlement failed to meet the expectations of the Khoikhoi. The white farmers, in turn, saw the settlement as attracting labour away from their farms.

The labour situation was further aggravated by the emancipation of slaves in 1834, and by pressure for the introduction of vagrancy laws to ensure a regular supply of labour for settler farms. The LMS missionaries, led by Read, supported the Kat River residents in their opposition to the legislation, and the laws were not passed. Settlers and colonial officials often succeeded all the same in making demands on the Khoikhoi and other residents of the settlement which exceeded what the existing legislation allowed.

The broader missionary reaction was mixed. The Wesleyan superintendent, William Shaw, and others were critical of the resistance of the indigenous people, while John Philip criticised the Wesleyans for being 'eulogists' of the colonial authorities.[34] The already acrimonious relationship between the LMS and Wesleyan missionaries intensified. Shaw saw fit to respond to the charges of Philip in a pamphlet entitled *A Defence of the Wesleyan Missionaries in Southern Africa*. Signed jointly by the missionaries working in the area, the pamphlet stated that the colonial government's war against the Xhosa-speaking chiefdoms (whose land they were occupying) was an act of 'self-defence and of absolute necessity ... carried out in the strict accordance with the principles of justice and mercy'.[35] Other missionaries tended to support the view of the Wesleyans.[36] Colonel Harry Smith, responsible for the colonial attacks on the local black population, wrote to his sister:

Although that Satan Dr Philip has been the great author of the savages' delinquency and atrocities ... all view the fanaticism of his conduct in its true light and abhor the practices by which he has endeavoured to attain ascendency in what he calls the Christian world. Your brother Harry has destroyed the enemy, while every Missionary says 'Colonel Smith, God Bless you'.[37]

This was also the time when Boer trekkers sought to escape the impact of what they saw as unsatisfactory labour relations. They left the Cape Colony, in the words of Piet Retief's Manifesto on trekker grievances, to 'preserve proper relations between master and servants'.[38]

Another major development in this period was the arrival of further missionary societies and groupings. The Paris Evangelical Missionary Society established its work with the Sotho in 1833 and the American Board of Commissioners for Foreign Mission began work in Natal. In 1835 the Anglican missionary Allen Gardiner also commenced mission activity in Natal, and Francis Owen of the Church Missionary Society arrived two years later. Mission work in this area was initially received by Dingane with hesitation. Wanting to avail himself and his people of the educational opportunities the missionaries offered, Dingane, the king of the Zulus, nevertheless anticipated the danger that the presence of whites signalled. A minor chief, Jacob Simbate, warned that 'one white man after another would come into the country, and want to build a house, and live in the country, till at last an army would come and take the country from them'.[39] Eventually the Boer trekkers arrived in 1838, and Piet Retief, together with a party of his followers, was killed when Dingane's suspicion intensified. The missionaries withdrew in anticipation of an ensuing war between Zulu and Boer. Dingane was succeeded by Mpande, whose survival as Zulu king was dependent on the Boer Volksraad. The Boers were never able to conquer Zululand, and had to be content with the area south of the Tugela River. The British were initially faced with the same reality when they occupied Natal in 1843. Defeated at Isandlwana in 1879, the British won a decisive battle at Ulundi later the same year, and Zululand was occupied by the settler community for the first time. 'The House of Shaka', it was reported, 'shall never rise again.'

Among the missionaries who best understood the Zulu cause was John Colenso. An ardent supporter of Zulu independence and of a gospel with roots in Zulu culture, he observed in 1879:

Was it a political success, or any more than a bloody but barren victory?... The burning of Ulundi and other kraals means nothing in Zulu eyes, as I hear from natives. And there is no clear evidence as yet that the loss of so many warriors ... has broken the spirit of the natives.[40]

It was, nevertheless, the tried and tested policy of British rule to pit the indigenous rulers against each other. Cetshwayo, the Zulu king, who had been forced to spend four year in exile, was eventually allowed to return – but faced with the rival chief Zibhebhu, he was obliged to rely on British support. Dinuzulu, who succeeded him, defeated Zibhebhu, but soon had his territory annexed by the British. He, in turn, was arrested and banished to St Helena. When he returned ten years later, Zululand was a formal part of Natal. His presence was at the same time enough to rekindle Zulu loyalties, and the Bambatha Rebellion broke out in 1906.

This comment on Natal takes us beyond the confines of the historical period of this chapter. It is also outside of the declared focus on the Eastern Cape, to which we return.

The War of the Axe

Tensions had intensified between the Xhosa and the settlers since the fateful attack on Grahamstown by Ndlambe. The alliance that followed between Ngqika and the British was eventually shattered when Governor Somerset confiscated the land between the Fish and Keiskamma rivers to create a new buffer zone, arguing that the Xhosa chief was unable to exercise adequate control over his own people. Then in 1829 in the midst of severe drought, Maqoma, the brother of Sandile (Ngqika's successor), was expelled from the Kat River valley to make way for the Kat River Settlement. When war eventually came in 1834, it united the Xhosa, and gave occasion for the ruthless Colonel Harry Smith to unleash his army against them. When peace was declared the following year, the tension continued, essentially because there was no support from either the Xhosa or the settlers for the imposed treaties designed to limit further conflict. The final spark which led to the next war came when Tsili, a member of Sandile's people, was imprisoned for the theft of an axe from a Fort Beaufort shopkeeper. He was freed by a group of Xhosa, who cut off the hand of the Khoikhoi prisoner to whom he was handcuffed; this resulted in the so-called War of the Axe (the seventh frontier war, 1846–7). The Xhosa lost, and were required to acknowledge the sovereignty of the British crown.

The eighth frontier war in 1850–1 (which came about because of the failure of the 'peace treaty' subsequent to the seventh war) was the longest and most costly in which the Cape Colony was ever engaged. It marked the end of Xhosa independence. Their political structures were fragmented, their culture was destroyed by missionary endeavour, and their land and cattle depleted. Only a miracle could save them. A young woman prophet, Nongqawuse, told of a vision which required the killing of cattle and refusal to cultivate the lands, in response to which the ancestors would replenish the Xhosa people's riches and drive the whites from the region.[41] Almost half a million cattle are thought to have been killed, and thousands of Xhosa died of starvation. Devastated and reduced to starvation, thirty thousand Xhosa surrendered to the colonists, offering their labour in return for sustenance.

It is often suggested that desperation and religious fervour had given rise to this act of national suicide. More plausibly, it needs to be seen as an act of national sacrifice in reaction to the hunger, oppression and alienation of a proud people, devastated by colonial exploitation and expropriation.[42] Whatever the cause, the incident contributed significantly to fulfilling the colonists' need for wage labour, and to Sir George Grey's 'civilisation policy', which was designed to make the Xhosa economically and politically dependent on the Cape Colony.

In brief, the religious consequences of the collapse of Xhosa independence were twofold: accommodation and resistance. Broadly speaking, they were the kinds of responses earlier offered by Ntsikana and Nxele. This time, however, accommodation and resistance were reflected in cooperation with missionaries on the one hand, and the emergence of the African Independent church movement on the other. The responses showed themselves in attitudes such as those displayed by the black Presbyterian church leader, Tiyo Soga. 'Be proud of what you are,' he told black Christians. He remained, however, within the institutional church structure and some saw him as an accommodationist. For others, he offered an important challenge to white missionary domination.[43]

But religious resistance also came in the form of a more aggressive response to the missionaries. In 1884 the Rev. Nehemiah Tile broke away from the Methodist Church, in response to accusations that he was 'taking part in political matters [and] stirring up a feeling of hostility against the magistrates'.[44] A pioneer of the African Indigenous church movement (or Ethiopianism as it was called), he founded the first mass-based African movement of a truly national kind. The Rev. Moses Mangena Mokone and Rev. J. M. Dwane also broke with the Methodist Church, and Dwane later established the Order of Ethiopia, which became affiliated to the Anglican Church. In 1896 a manifesto released by the Ethiopian leadership declared their intent:

> To unite together Christians of the African race and of various denominations in the name of Jesus Christ to solemnly work towards and pray for the day when the African people shall become an African Christian nation ... To place on record ... the great wrongs inflicted upon the African by the people of Europe and America and to urge upon Christians who wish to be clear of African blood on the day of God's judgement, to make restitution ... Finally to pursue steadily and unswervingly the policy of AFRICA FOR THE AFRICANS and look for and hasten by prayer and united effort the forming of the AFRICAN CHRISTIAN NATION by God's power and in his own time and way.[45]

White missionary activity also reflected the changed political climate. While seeking to provide for the needs of the indigenous people, missionary policy would soon be drawn closer to colonial ideals.

Later missionary praxis

We need to comment on three aspects of the consequences of the later missionary period which began with the arrival of the 1820 Settlers.

The gospel of work

It is sufficient to note that the missionaries, no less than other members of their society, were not isolated from their communities, and that the churches they represented were an integral part of the socio-economic and political structures of the time. This suggests that despite the fact that individual missionaries championed the cause of the African people, they simultaneously helped undermine the African social fabric and therefore the base from which resistance could be launched against colonisation. Selope Thema observed, for example, that despite certain important differences, the attitudes of Boer and Brit as well as of missionary and colonial officials towards indigenous people were essentially the same: African traditional society, says Thema, 'was condemned by both missionaries and colonists as a life of laziness and indolence. They both agreed that the African should be taught the dignity of labour.'[46]

Early missionaries, especially Van der Kemp and Read, at times opposed colonial attempts to force the indigenous people to work on settler farms. They also insisted that the laziness of the Khoikhoi had to be overcome. Reporting to the LMS in London, Van der Kemp and Read wrote: 'Laziness is the most prevalent evil among our people which exposes them to the greatest distresses.'[47]

By contrast, James Stewart of Lovedale was representative of a mission policy that was less critical of colonialism. He understood the gospel to be the basis of social renewal; the New Testament message needed to be linked to what he defined as the 'gospel of work'. This gospel, he argued, 'does not save souls, but it saves people ... Lazy races die or decay. Races that work prosper on earth. The British race, in all its greatest branches, is noted for its restless activity. Its life motto is Work! Work!'[48] John Philip was, in turn, more committed to the well-being of the indigenous people than many other missionaries. Yet he too found himself trapped in the ideology of imperialism. He unabashedly argued that the missionaries were 'by the most exceptional means, extending British interests, British influence and the British empire'. Among the tasks of the missionary, he contended, was to 'teach them [Africans] industrious habits, and create a demand for British manufactures'. And the mission stations were in his view 'the cheapest and best military posts that a wise government can employ to defend its frontiers against the predatory incursions of savage chiefdoms'.[49]

Although they were fervently convinced that the most important gift they could impart was the gospel, the heart of the missionaries' gospel could scarcely be distinguished from the values of the Empire. 'Conversion', writes Greg Cuthbertson, 'was ... the initial phase in the subversion of African societies by Europeans, the psychological basis for a politics of colonialism'.[50] The *Christian Express,* mouthpiece of the missionaries at Lovedale, was remarkably explicit, in an editorial written in 1878, in defining the social goal of the Christianising process:

We want to see the natives become workers ... And ... we believe Christianity will be a chief cause of their becoming a working people ... How this ... comes to be is twofold. Christianity creates needs. Generally speaking, every man will work just as much as he is required to do and not more. There will be a constant relation between the time a man works and his necessities ... If you want men to work, then, you must get them to need. Create need and you supply stimulus to work; you enlist the worker's own will on the side of labour. Few men anywhere, and certainly no heathen men, ever work for the mere pleasure of working. Now, the speediest way of creating needs among these people is to Christianise them. As they become Christianised, they will want more clothing, better houses, furniture, books, education for the children, and a hundred other things which they do not have now and never have had. And all these things they can get by working, and only by working. But Christianity also teaches the duty of working, and denounces idleness as a sin. So to Christianise a Kaffir is the shortest way, and the surest, to make him put his hand steadily and willingly to the work that is waiting to be done. This will make it both his interest and his duty to work, will enlist, besides his bodily appetites, his home affections, his mental powers, and his conscience, on the side of industrious habits.[51]

However, the central dilemma facing the early missionaries was how to minister to the needs and well-being of both the white settlers and the indigenous population at the same time. Clearly, the missionaries sought on many occasions to work on the conscience of the settlers by speaking out on behalf of the indigenous people in the struggle for land, human rights and social justice. Yet because of their shared pastoral concern for the well-being of the settlers, commitment to the indigenous population was not unequivocal, and the missionaries were often accused by discerning black opinion of capitulation to settler demands. With this sense of dual responsibility to both black and white, to both oppressor and oppressed, the die was cast for internal conflict and compromise, which still characterise the English-speaking churches today.

Land and taxes

Land meant survival to all the indigenous people, in that it meant cattle and cattle meant wealth, but it also formed an inherent part of their social structure. Land meant agriculture, hunting and political power. With the loss of land went the loss of political identity and social cohesion. On the other side, the demand for more land by frontier farmers dovetailed not only with the official colonial desire to dominate the Xhosa-speaking people but also with the concern of missionaries to liberate indigenous people from what they saw as the reactionary power of chief and chiefdom, while exposing blacks to the 'benefits' of Western values and skills. Historians writing from other perspectives tell the story differently. De Kiewiet, although generally favourable toward the missionaries, describes the syndrome as the 'unintentional collusion' between the humanitarian desire of missionaries and the selfish, exploitative motives of others.[52] However altruistically conceived by liberal historians, the outcome was the same: black people were squeezed out of their traditional pattern of living and made dependent on the colonial economic system. Dispossessed black people meant a cheap supply of labour for settler farmers; for the colonial powers the process meant the systematic destruction of rival political powers; and for the missionaries it meant the opportunity to draw dispossessed blacks into mission stations, on the ground that this afforded them a measure of freedom from the restrictive influences of the chiefs.

The missionaries generally argued that a system of individual ownership of land under colonial law would do more than any other single innovation to disrupt the power of chief and chiefdom – a necessary development, they claimed, in freeing the individual to respond to the gospel. It would also, they argued, provide a basis for economic self-determination. Colonial policy on land sought at the same time to ensure the ongoing supply of labour to white-owned farms. De Kiewiet, for example, shows that the land allotted on individual tenure for blacks, in terms of the Glen Grey Act of 1894, was never intended as the sole means of family support. It was assumed that the women would cultivate the land while men laboured elsewhere, and soon many of those eligible for individual tenure were labouring on white farms in return for squatting rights and a small monetary reward roughly equivalent to the newly imposed hut tax. Africans who were, in turn, settled on mission farms at times experienced demands even more exacting than those made by farmers. 'Besides taxes to the state, tithes were usually required for church buildings, educational facilities, ploughs, new seed, symmetrically constructed villages, and European clothes.'[53] Lacking the sense of corporate responsibility and decision-making as practised in the African system from which they had been removed, and at the same time motivated by a sense of individual reward inculcated by the missionaries, many left these mission farms for more lucrative jobs in the colonial labour market. Whatever the complexity of causes involved, and in spite of the motives involved, the consequence was obvious. The traditional, communal, pastoral structure of African life gave way, for better or worse, to a dependent African peasantry and rural proletariat. The acquisition of manufactured goods became the accepted mark of civilisation and progress, often to the neglect of a sound economic and political infrastructure as the basis of self-reliance and esteem.

The other economic lever devised by the colonial authorities was the imposition of a wide-ranging tax system. 'Native taxation' formed an important part of the general taxation and economic policy of the time. It was also presented as a device to release the labour force imprisoned within an unproductive tribal society. The total package of 'native taxation' was wide-ranging. There were hut taxes, marriage taxes, labour taxes on the unemployed and a poll tax; and little of the income was returned to blacks in the form of services.[54] When one takes into account that many missionaries cooperated with the colonial authorities in collecting taxes and in other aspects of the hege-monic process, it is not possible to exonerate the missionaries from the charge of subjugating the black people.

Education

There is a further aspect to the role played by the churches in the develop-ment of the country: this concerns the establishment of hospitals, social ser-vices and schools. It is important to recognise that by locating these services outside of the existing tribal structures (on mission stations), in the very act of being philanthropic the churches further contributed to undermining African traditional society. In this sense, at times quite deliberately and at times by default, the churches were involved in the colonial process which marginalised Africans in the developing economy of the time. A more radical interpretation suggests that they were part of a systematic programme designed to 'under-develop' Africa.[55] Those adhering to this position suggest that during the colo-nial period, poverty and disease increased rather than diminished.

Of these services, missionary education in particular has generated a great deal of debate; questions have been asked about the extent to which it ulti-mately benefited and also undermined African development. This question must be posed in relation to a definite shift in educational policy which occur-red at mission schools like Lovedale and Zonnebloem in the 1860s. Earlier policy prescribed a classical curriculum which included science and mathe-matics, Latin, Greek and English, and at least one additional modern Euro-pean language. Then in the 1860s the emphasis shifted towards a more general and practical education aimed at a broader cross-section of the com-munity.

This transition was marked, for example, in 1869 when Dr James Stewart replaced Dr Alexander Duff as principal of the Lovedale Missionary Institute. The intention now was to produce black preachers and teachers equipped to meet 'the wants and conditions of Africans', many of whom 'were wholly illit-erate'. In the elementary and secondary schools the emphasis shifted from a classical curriculum designed for equivalent schools in Scotland to instruction in the vernacular tongue and as adequate an understanding of English 'as pos-sible'.[56] Janet Hodgson has shown how Zonnebloem College in Cape Town was established in 1858 to provide education for an African elite, a primary aim being to separate the sons of chiefs from the 'heathen and barbarous' influences of their traditional culture and equip them as enlightened (and anglicised) leaders of the future. With the passing of the Education Act of 1865, educational institutions in the Eastern Cape provided comparable facili-ties, and Zonnebloem was compelled to draw its student body from a wider constituency. In the process its character changed significantly.

Despite the limitations of an earlier elitism, the changes opened the way for a very different kind of mission education. In 1877 Dr Langham Dale, the Cape Superintendent General of Education, observed that the 'kid-glove era' had come to an end and 'the saw, plane, hammer and spade had taken its place'.[57] Mission schools had, of course, always been of a mixed quality, and after the change in policy this difference continued to be manifest. Control of schools was often heavy-handed, paternalistic and rejected by black leaders because the system promoted Western values and desires. It was only with the collapse of traditional African societies that mission education began to be sought instead of shunned. It is enough to indicate here that the glorification of mission education is not substantiated by careful analysis. By far the majority of black children received no education at all. The role of mission schools in the planned subversion of African power and the destruction of traditional values is something that needs to be fully researched.

Attention has been given to work, land, taxes and education. What conclusions about the social function of the missionary endeavour can be drawn from these developments? The success of missionary proselytisation was largely dependent on the collapse of the traditional social structure of African society. African chiefs particularly resented the missionary practice of dividing their people into 'converts' and 'heathens', which contributed towards breaking down the cohesion of the chiefdom and the traditional structures of authority. Not only, in the words of Colenso, did missionary demands 'fill their whole chiefdom with anarchy and confusion', but chiefs could no longer count on their subjects who had been converted to obey their commands or show loyalty in time of crisis or war.[58] Yet once the collapse of tribal cohesion was a reality, whether due to attacks from other chiefdoms, forced migration, or the deliberate disruption of tribal existence by the imperial administration, missionary help was often welcomed to assist with the transition to the emerging new order.[59] The problem is that having facilitated the disintegration of the old order, the missionaries could not provide the necessary resources to integrate blacks into the new.

Despite this ambiguous role of the missionaries, a few did act as the conscience of the settlers. Van der Kemp, Read, Philip and Colenso are among them. Colenso's condemnation of the British role in instigating the Anglo-Zulu War of 1879 stands in stark contrast with the spying on the Zulu undertaken by some missionaries for the British forces. Colenso stood alone in condemning vengeance in the wake of the British defeat at Isandlwana.[60] In the Eastern Cape, William Shaw appealed to the values of the settlers, relating these to their new environment and reminding them that 'they came from a land of freedom ... and that they had learned there that personal liberty is the birthright of every man'.[61] Yet he too, as already suggested, worked in co-operation with the imperial administration.

This framework of missionary loyalty to imperialist and capitalist interests would, in time, take on new dimensions with the discovery of minerals.[62] In brief, the missionary churches became increasingly influenced by the moneyed classes and were criticised for failing to attract working class members. The *Methodist Churchman* would lament that 'the sons of toil are mainly conspicuous by their absence from church worship', while the clergy were said to have 'no sympathy with [the worker] in his struggle for what he believes to be his rights'.[63] The *Anglican*, in turn, carried a letter condemning this church for failing to 'grasp or understand the working man's aims and ambitions'.[64]

When the General Missionary Conference met at the turn of the century, its concern was with 'heathenism' and 'Romanism' rather than the impact of the industrial age or the consequences of this development for black people.[65]

A further dimension of imperial loyalty emerged at the time of the outbreak of the Anglo-Boer War. Some English-speaking clergy and missionaries intervened as the conscience of the British, both in supporting the cause of the Boers and in counselling blacks to have no part in the war. The major preoccupation, however, was British supremacy, and the English clergy and missionaries were as imperialist in outlook as most other colonists. Cuthbertson argues that in this instance it was the LMS which did most to generate the myth that the Anglo-Boer War was waged on behalf of the black population. Even John Moffat, who championed African interests during the war, insisted that 'the preservation of British influence and civilisation in South Africa' was paramount.[66] It took J. A. Hobson, writing in the *British Weekly*, to make the point which the missionaries failed to comprehend:

> Let those who believe that this war is going to result in benefit to the natives read the avowals of native policy made by leading capitalists of the Rand, expressing their intention to reduce Kaffir wages, and to introduce hut and labour taxes, in order to compel natives to offer large quantities of labour to mining companies.[67]

When the war was over, some clerics saw fit to advocate that the former Republics be returned to the Boers but saw no reason to support black participation in the affairs of government. And during the war, missionaries who felt constrained to vacate their stations when war broke out often became chaplains to the British forces, reinforcing the popular imperial myth that the war against the Boer forces was the 'Lord's battle', fought by the 'soldiers of Christ', with the aim of bringing 'glory to his name'.[68]

The role of the missionaries

The debate on missionary activity in Southern Africa is a complex one. There are those who would argue that the missionaries were among the worthy and honourable pioneers who contributed to the quest for social justice in the development of the subcontinent. At worst, the argument goes, they were well-meaning, even if naive and misguided. Others contend that the missionaries were tacit and, on occasion, conscious agents of colonial subjugation, and apologists for white domination. 'Conquerors or Servants of God?' asks Monica Wilson.[69] Still others stress the difference between early missionaries of the London Missionary Society who promoted the cause of the indigenous people against the racial exclusivism of the settlers, and the mission activity of the white Dutch Reformed and Lutheran churches, which tended to promote settler interests overtly.

In trying to assess the social function of the missionaries in the colonial period, one can make several observations.

The English missionaries had little doubt about the superiority of their culture. There is a narrow line, however, between regard for the virtues of one's own religion and civilisation and disregard for the values and achievements of others. It was this second attitude which caused missionaries to dismiss the African way of life as evidence of religious and cultural depravity, and reason for it to be replaced by their gospel and their civilisation. Converting souls to Christ meant, for many missionaries, a complete rejection by blacks of the African worldview and a denial of traditional social custom. As Elphick argues, they sought to replace what they perceived to be the 'false consciousness' of the indigenous people with 'true consciousness', ensuring that the 'old order' would give way to a 'new order'. As a result, 'the kraal was becoming the scene of disagreement, of arguments, of indecision, where authority for patterned behavior was lost'.[70] It was this kind of systematic destruction of culture and political cohesion that was probably the most negative function performed by the missionaries in Africa. They 'condemned African customs and institutions and taught the social norms of nineteenth-century Europe as though these crystallised a moral code of universal validity'.[71] Ancestor veneration, polygamy and tribal solidarity were condemned by the missionaries, and converts were obliged to turn their backs on the corporate responsibility inherent in each of these cornerstones of African society.

Trapped within an imperialist cultural ideal, the missionaries' sense of superiority also left them indifferent to African religious ideas. The Methodist missionary Samuel Broadbent, working among the Barolong, spoke of their 'gross ignorance of spiritual subjects' and concluded that 'they had literally no God; and having had no intercourse with the colony, they had no knowledge of God'.[72] Robert Moffat of the LMS came to similar conclusions, arguing that 'a profound silence reigns on this awful subject' of salvation and God; the missionaries thus needed 'to prepare for the gracious distribution of the waters of salvation in that desert soil, sowing the seed of the word, breathing many a prayer, and shedding many a tear, till the Spirit of God should cause it to vegetate, and yield the fruits of righteousness'.[73] So uncompromising was the missionary attitude on these matters that P. W. Harrison, writing in the early 1900s, was constrained to redress this wrong: 'Missionary work', he told his colleagues, 'is no enterprise of pity in which we of the smug and self-satisfied West take a superior religion, and hand it down to poor miserable and degraded heathens.'[74]

Generally speaking, the missionaries were guilty of social paternalism. Peter Hinchliff points to a particular form of paternalism at the centre of the missionary structures of the churches. The ecclesiastical authorities in England were of a different social class and, as a rule, enjoyed a higher education than the rank-and-file missionaries sent to the colonies. The result was the imposition of English structures onto the emerging African church: missionaries in the field were treated with firm, benevolent paternalism by their superiors at home. The missionaries were obliged to account for every decision made and every item of expense incurred. The outcome was that when missionaries dealt with their black converts, they tended to respond to them with the same paternalism prevalent in British society. When indigenous leaders and ministers began to emerge, they were treated in the familiar paternalistic manner, and in turn learned that this was the manner in which they were to treat their parishioners. Hence an authoritarian and paternalistic ecclesiastical structure emerged that relegated the grassroots members to a servile status. 'My own view', says Hinchliff, 'is that it was this paternalism, developed originally by the English churches with regard to their own missionaries which rubbed off, as it were, on the whole colonial church.'[75] This condescending attitude toward the indigenous people led in part to the establishment of the Ethiopian Order within the Anglican Church, and the emergence of a large number of African Independent churches.

Another feature of the English missionaries was (with a few notable exceptions) the sense of missionary deference to civil authority. The point has been made earlier: the Anglican Church was the state church in England, and in the British colonies of the Cape and Natal it was the church of the government, showing political support for and conformity with the *status quo*, at least until the time of political union between the British colonies and the Boer Republics in 1910.[76] In spite of Methodist involvement in the causes of the working class in England, Methodists tended, with the notable exception of trade-union activity, not to become involved as an institution in political affairs. In nineteenth-century Southern Africa, Methodists were not actively engaged in political dissent. When John Ayliff was in conflict with the Grahamstown magistrate about chaplains visiting prisons, he was told by his superiors in the Methodist Church that 'preachers have been tried before conference for saying so much'.[77] Yet, it is also clear that Ayliff worked in active cooperation with the authorities to impose their 'native policy', and William Shaw, the superintendent of the Wesleyan Mission, was instrumental in depriving the Basotho chief Moshoeshoe of parts of his land.[78] Scottish missionaries similarly abstained from overt criticism of the government. Hinchliff argues that the one exception to this deference was the LMS missionaries who, he suggests, acted in keeping with their Nonconformist heritage in responding less submissively to the authorities.

Certainly Van der Kemp, Philip and others laid the blame for racial friction and the frontier wars on the settlers. And there is much evidence to support the view that the intentions of these missionaries were good. Van der Kemp had, for example, intended to work among the Xhosa but turned to assist the Khoikhoi only because he felt their immediate needs to be so much greater. The need Van der Kemp witnessed was socio-economic, not evangelical, and he committed himself to striving for the political and economic rights of the oppressed. The LMS settlement established at Bethelsdorp was intended to give the Khoikhoi a measure of economic independence from the settlers and to ensure their economic advancement. The hostility Van der Kemp engendered among the colonists, in turn, needs to be attributed to his apparent success in diverting their labour, and to the poignancy of his contention that the Khoikhoi had the same rights as the settlers. Seeking to locate himself on the side of the oppressed, he found himself locked in conflict with the Dutch Governor, Janssens, writing: 'I could not forbear to warn him of the displeasure of God who most certainly would hear the cries of the oppressed.'[79] John

Philip found himself every bit as unpopular with the white community as Van der Kemp, being criticised by fellow LMS missionary Robert Moffat for being too political. Reference has also been made to the controversy between Philip and Wesleyan missionaries – more particularly William Shaw.

Despite the concern of Van der Kemp and Philip for the weak in their conflict with the strong, there is little evidence to suggest that they were ultimately less enamoured of the virtues of imperialism than some other missionaries. Indeed, to fail to allow for this internal conflict within the most dedicated missionaries is to fail to understand the pathos of the early missionary movement. It is a pathos that finds the noblest of missionaries, rejected by their own colleagues and churches, being trapped within the very structures which those whom they sought to help needed to overcome. As already indicated, Van der Kemp cooperated with the colonial authorities in certain situations.[80] There is also evidence that while Philip promoted the cause of the indigenous population, he remained loyal to imperial economic interests. He argued that 'in adopting a more liberal ... policy', not only would the African population be more productive, providing a better market for British goods, but that 'taxes will be paid and the farmers will have no cause to complain of a lack of labour'.[81]

Uzoigwe, in turn, shows how Moffat, who became assistant commissioner for what was then Bechuanaland, assisted Cecil John Rhodes in persuading Lobengula, the hitherto uncooperative king of the Ndebele, to sign documents forbidding him to enter into treaty obligations with any other foreign powers and to cede the mineral rights of his land to Rhodes.[82] It was on the basis of this agreement that Rhodes eventually occupied Mashonaland, Lobengula was driven into the wilderness and the Ndebele kingdom was effectively destroyed. The long rule of white supremacy in what was to be known as Rhodesia had begun and was to last until the birth of an independent Zimbabwe in 1980.

It would be quite wrong to suggest that through their involvement in imperialist designs these missionaries were not committed to their evangelical task. On the contrary, it would appear that their romantic and naive understanding of evangelism led many among them to believe that the gospel was the immediate answer to all socio-economic and political problems. As a result they were inclined to sanction almost anything that was necessary to convert souls, including the colonial subjugation of indigenous people. It has already been shown that for the missionaries, evangelical conversion was subsumed into the imperial socio-economic and political transformation process. Uzoigwe, in fact, argues that even those political protests in which the missionaries engaged were usually motivated by fear that government policy towards the indigenous people would hamper their evangelical task.[83] Etherington concurs, showing that 'many missionaries believed that the future stability of their societies, and the ultimate success of their work of evangelisation depended on more positive action by the British government to prevent exploitation in Africa'.[84]

The missionaries needed the support of the government to succeed in their work, and the government, in spite of periodic quarrels with the missionaries, soon realised that the missionaries were essentially allies in their cause, able to act as intermediaries, motivating blacks to play their part in the emerging economic order and incorporating them into the social milieu of the Empire.

Little is to be gained in the search for motives and intent. It is enough to note that the missionaries seldom stopped to question their own values, the long-term effect of their endeavours, or to take seriously the African voices of protest. Cochrane sums up the situation as follows:

> Missionary enterprise, remaining always beyond radical self-criticism, could do no other than transmit the values and structures embodied in British imperial colonialist expansion without sufficient awareness to distinguish firmly between what was intrinsically worthwhile and what could lead to long-term destructive consequences for precisely those people whom they believed themselves to be championing.[85]

NOTES

1. Martin Hall, *The Changing Past: Farmers, Kings and Traders in Southern Africa, 200–1860.* Cape Town: David Philip, 1987, p. 58.

2. A comprehensive social history of Christianity in this period, together with primary missionary and other documentation, is contained in Charles Villa-Vicencio and John de Gruchy (eds.), *The Social History of Christianity in South Africa,* vol. 1, forthcoming.

3. C. G. Botha, *The French Refugees at the Cape.* Cape Town: Cape Times Limited, 1919, p. 27.

4. A. Dreyer, *Boustowwe vir die Geskiedenis van die Nederduits Gereformeerde Kerke in Suid-Afrika,* Part 1: *1804–1836.* Cape Town: Council of the Nederduitse Gereformeerde Kerke of South Africa, 1936.

5. Robert Shell, 'From Rites to Rebellion: Islamic Conversion in the Cape Colony', in Abukader Tayob and Muhammed Haron (eds.), *Islam in South Africa,* forthcoming.

6. Johannes Marais, *The Cape Coloured People, 1652–1937.* London: Longmans, 1957, p. 168.

7. R. L. Watson, *The Slave Question: Liberty and Property in South Africa.* Johannesburg: Witwatersrand University Press, 1990, p. 172. See also R. W. Cope (ed.), *Journals of the Rev. T. L. Hodgson.* Johannesburg: Witwatersrand University Press, 1977, p. 44.

8. J. du Plessis, *A History of Christian Missions in South Africa.* Cape Town: Struik, 1965, p. 93.

9. *Ibid.*

10. A. Moorrees, *Die Nederduitse Gereformeerde Kerk in Suid-Afrika.* Cape Town: S.A. Bybelvereniging, 1937, pp. 375, 528–9.

11. See C. Villa-Vicencio, *Civil Disobedience and Beyond: Law, Resistance and Religion in South Africa.* Cape Town: David Philip, 1990.

12. Ido H. Enklaar, *Life and Work of Dr. J. Th. Van der Kemp 1747–1811.* Cape Town: A. A. Balkema, 1988, p. 113.

13. *Ibid.,* p. 177.

14. Christopher Saunders, 'James Read: Towards a Reassessment', in *Collected*

Seminar Papers on the Societies of Southern Africa in the 19th and 20th Centuries. London: Institute of Commonwealth Studies, University of London, 1976.

15. Quoted in *ibid.*, p. 20.

16. Enklaar, *Van der Kemp,* p. 106.

17. Quoted in Eddie Roux, *Time Longer than Rope: A History of the Black Man's Struggle for Freedom in South Africa.* Madison, Wisconsin: University of Wisconsin Press, 1964, p. 13.

18. Janet Hodgson, *Ntsikana's Great Hymn: A Xhosa Expression of Christianity in the Early 19th Century Eastern Cape.* Cape Town: Centre for African Studies, University of Cape Town, 1981.

19. J. B. Peires, *The House of Phalo: A History of the Xhosa People in the Days of Their Independence.* Johannesburg: Ravan Press, 1981, p. 73.

20. Roux, *Time Longer than Rope,* p. 16.

21. J. Philip, *Researches in South Africa,* vol. 1. London: Duncan Books, 1828, p. 359.

22. See R. L. Watson, *The Slave Question.*

23. B. Shaw, *Memorials of South Africa.* Cape Town: Struik, reprint, 1970.

24. Watson, *The Slave Question,* chapters 10 and 11.

25. G. M. Theal, *Basutoland Records,* vol. 1. Cape Town: Struik, 1964, pp. 99f.

26. Philip, *Researches,* vol. 2, pp. 206–7.

27. N. A. Birtwhistle and W. Threlfall, *A Study in Missionary Vocation.* Cape Town: Struik, 1966, pp. 133–4.

28. C. P. Groves, *The Planting of Christianity in Africa.* London: Lutterworth Press, 1948, p. 248.

29. Philip, *Researches,* vol. 2, pp. 239–40.

30. W. Shaw, *A Defence of the Wesleyan Missionaries in Southern Africa: Comprising Copies of Correspondence with the Reverend John Philip, D.D.* London: Mason, 1839, pp. xvi-xvii.

31. Quoted in A. Ross, *John Philip 1775–1851.* Aberdeen: Aberdeen University Press, p. 109.

32. V. C. Malherbe, *What They Said, 1795–1910.* Cape Town: Maskew Miller, 1971, pp. 33–5.

33. J. Kitchingman, *The Kitchingman Papers: Missionary Letters and Journals, 1817–1848,* ed. by B. Le Cordeur and C. Saunders. Johannesburg: Brenthurst Press, 1967, p. 98.

34. See William Shaw, *A Defence of the Wesleyan Missionaries in Southern Africa.*

35. Du Plessis, *History of Christian Missions,* p. 432.

36. W. B. Boyce, *Notes on South African Affairs from 1834–1838.* Cape Town: Struik, reprint, 1971, pp. vii-x.

37. G. M. Theal, *Documents Relating to the Kaffir War of 1835.* Pretoria: Union of South Africa, 1912, p. 152.

38. G. W. Eybers (ed.), *Select Constitutional Documents Reflecting South African History, 1795–1910.* London: Routledge, 1918, pp. 143–5.

39. D. J. Kotze (ed.), *Letters of the American Missionaries: 1835–1838.* Cape Town: Van Riebeeck Society, 1950, p. 98, n13.

40. Jeff, Guy, *The Destruction of the Zulu Kingdom.* Johannesburg: Ravan Press, 1982, p. 58.

41. J. B. Peires, *The Dead Will Arise: Nongqawuse and the Great Xhosa Cattle-killing of 1856–7.* Johannesburg: Ravan Press, 1989.

42. *Ibid.*

43. See Donovan Williams (ed.), *The Journal and Selected Writings of the Reverend Tiyo Soga*. Cape Town: A. A. Balkema, 1986.

44. Roux, *Time Longer than Rope*, p. 78.

45. First published in *Imvo Zabantsundu*, September 1896. Quoted in Glenda Kruss, 'Religion, Class and Culture: Indigenous Churches in South Africa, with Special Reference to the Zionist Apostolic Church.' MA thesis, University of Cape Town, 1985, p. 80.

46. Selope Thema, 'Thinking Black: The African Today', *Advance* (April 1929), quoted in James Cochrane, *Servants of Power: The Role of English-speaking Churches 1903–1930*. Johannesburg: Ravan Press, 1987, p. 4.

47. A. D. Martin, *Doctor Van der Kemp*. Westminster: The Livingstone Press, 1931, p. 138.

48. James Wells, *Stewart of Lovedale*. London: Hodder & Stoughton, 1908, p. 216.

49. Philip, *Researches*, vol. 1, pp. ix–x; vol. 2, p. 227.

50. Greg Cuthbertson, quoting Gladwin and Saidin, *Slaves of the White Myth*, in 'The English-speaking Churches, Colonialism and War' in C. Villa-Vicencio (ed.), *Theology and Violence: The South African Debate*. Johannesburg: Skotaville, 1987, p. 17.

51. *Christian Express*, 8, 95 (1 August 1878), pp. 1–2.

52. C. W. de Kiewiet, *The Imperial Factor in South Africa*. Cambridge: Cambridge University Press, 1937, p. 159.

53. Cochrane, *Servants of Power*, p. 25.

54. De Kiewiet, *Imperial Factor*, pp. 190, 194; D. Welsh, *The Roots of Segregation: Native Policy in Natal: 1845–1910*. Cape Town: Oxford University Press, 1971, p. 77.

55. Walter Rodney, *How Europe Underdeveloped Africa*. Washington, DC: Howard University Press, 1974, pp. 205–81.

56. R. H. W. Shepherd, *Lovedale South Africa: 1824–1955*. Lovedale: Lovedale Press, 1971, pp. 27–32.

57. Janet Hodgson, 'Zonnebloem College and Cape Town: 1858–1870', in C. Saunders (ed.), *Studies in the History of Cape Town*, vol. 1. Cape Town: UCT, 1979.

58. Welsh, *Roots of Segregation*, p. 44; T. R. H. Davenport, *South Africa: A Modern History*. Johannesburg: Macmillan, 1977, p. 247.

59. Gabriel Setiloane, *The Image of God among the Sotho–Tswana*. Cape Town: A. A. Balkema, 1979, p. 133.

60. J. Guy, *The Heretic: A Study of the Life of John William Colenso 1814–1883*. Johannesburg: Ravan Press, 1983, pp. 256–75.

61. A. de Villiers, *English-speaking South Africa*. Cape Town: OUP, 1976, p. 221.

62. See C. Villa-Vicencio, *Trapped in Apartheid: A Socio-Theological History of the English-speaking Churches*. Cape Town: David Philip, and Maryknoll: Orbis Books, 1988, pp. 65–92; Cochrane, *Servants of Power*.

63. Quoted in Cochrane, *Servants of Power*, p. 113.

64. *Ibid.*, p. 214.

65. Villa-Vicencio, *Trapped in Apartheid*, p. 72.

66. R. U. Moffat, *John Smith Moffat: Missionary. A Memoir*. New York: Negro Universities Press, 1969, p. 330.

67. *British Weekly*, 12 April 1900, cited by Cuthbertson in Villa-Vicencio, *Theology and Violence*, p. 25.

68. Cited by Cuthbertson in Villa-Vicencio, *Theology and Violence*, p. 26.

69. Monica Wilson, 'Missionaries: Conquerors or Servants of God?', *South African Outlook* (March 1966).

70. R. Elphick, 'Africans and the Christian Campaign in Southern Africa' in

H. Lamar and L. Thompson (eds.), *The Frontier in History: North America and Southern Africa Compared.* New Haven: Yale University Press, 1981.

71. Leonard Thompson, 'The Subjection of African Chiefdoms, 1870–1898', in M. Wilson and L. Thompson (eds.), *The Oxford History of South Africa*, vol. 2. Oxford: Oxford University Press, p. 251.

72. Samuel Broadbent, *A Narrative of the First Introduction of Christianity Amongst the Baralong Chiefdom of the Bechuanas, South Africa.* London: Wesleyan Mission House, 1865, p. 811.

73. Robert Moffat, *Missionary Labours and Scenes in South Africa.* London: John Sow, 1842, pp. 243–4.

74. P. W. Harrison, 'Instructing Missionaries Misleading Natives', *South African Outlook* (November 1925).

75. Hinchliff in De Villiers, *English-speaking South Africa*, p. 173.

76. Peter Hinchliff, *The Anglican Church in South Africa.* London: Darton, Longman & Todd, 1963, pp. 10–11, 28–9; De Villiers, *English-speaking South Africa*, p. 174.

77. Peter Hinchliff (ed.), *The Journal of John Ayliff: 1797–1862.* Cape Town: A. A. Balkema, 1971.

78. N. Majeke, *The Role of the Missionaries in Conquest.* Johannesburg: Society of Young Africa, 1952, p. 52.

79. A. Hastings, *Mission, Church and State in Southern Africa.* London: Society for the Propagation of the Faith, 1985, p. 5.

80. Majeke, *Role of the Missionaries*, p. 52.

81. *Ibid.*

82. G. N. Uzoigwe, *Britain and the Conquest of Africa.* Ann Arbor: University of Michigan Press, 1974, p. 186.

83. *Ibid.*, p. 27.

84. N. Etherington, *Preachers, Peasants and Politics in Southern Africa, 1835–1880.* London: Royal Historical Society, 1978, p. 10.

85. Cochrane, *Servants of Power*, p. 26.

5

The Impact of White Settlement on African Traditional Religions

JIM KIERNAN

It would be a mistake to suppose that San, Khoikhoi and Bantu-speaking communities, with their distinctive religious perspectives, were inertly awaiting the missionary tentacles of Dutch and British colonisation and that nothing of much significance had happened to them before then. Certainly, indigenous societies were adversely affected by white settlement and expansion, ultimately to the point of succumbing to white dominance and control. But, aside from this far-reaching external influence, they also fell victim to internal transformations brought about by demographic pressures. Even while white settlement was steadily encroaching from the south, in the northeast the mounting internal strains long experienced by pastoral farming communities erupted into an explosion of such dimensions that it sent powerful shockwaves across the whole spectrum of black society. Indeed, it was where these two sets of forces, internal and external, appeared to operate in conjunction that the effect was most destructive. Black societies, their way of life and religious outlook were affected in different ways.

The fate of Khoisan religions

The most irrevocable effect was the virtual disappearance of the Khoikhoi. Unlike the San, who were mobile and could withdraw from unfavourable circumstances, the Khoikhoi were unable to avoid confrontation with the Cape settlers and were ill equipped to withstand them. Reduced by settler wars and ravaged by imported diseases such as smallpox, they were crushed against the expanding Bantu-speaking population along the Fish and Orange rivers. More telling, perhaps, was their absorption into other societies by widespread miscegenation. As a result, their distinctive way of life totally disintegrated, and only small pockets of Khoikhoi descendants still survive on reserves in Namaqualand and Namibia. These communities have been Christianised but, in varying degrees, maintain continuity with their religious past enshrined in myth, legend and belief. The twin supernatural principles of good and evil in Khoikhoi religion easily blended into the Christian opposition between God and the Devil, particularly emphasised in the Calvinist tradition, although the Christian God adds omnipotence to the omnipresence of the Khoikhoi deity. Yet God exercises his omnipotence in a manner reminiscent of the ancestor of Bantu-speaking society in that, if he feels like it, he can allow misfortune to take its course, even though he can prevent it. Moreover, the retention of sorcery as a latent explanation of misfortune serves to reinforce the individualism promoted by the Protestant ethic. However, belief in the ancestral hero, Heitsi Eibib, the purveyor of individual good fortune, has entirely disappeared. We might say that, in the bleakness of the reserve, the Khoikhoi have ceased to believe in the windfall principle and emphasise the competitiveness and striving for advantage that are expressed in sorcery. Finally, there is further evidence of Bantu-speaking influence in the accommodation of two other mystical agents, the snake and the *tokoloshe*, but with different meanings. Instead of a real snake representing an ancestor, an enormous mythical snake bespeaks sexual possessiveness and jealousy of outside intrusion. The *tokoloshe*, by contrast, is shorn of its sexual connotation as companion to Nguni witches, and stands for malicious aggressiveness on the part of strangers. Thus Khoikhoi Christianity is adapted to express religiously the problems of living in closely confined, beleaguered and deeply divided communities.

As for the San, unable to contend with successive invasions of their preferred ecological domain by white and black alike, they gradually retreated to the waterholes of the Kalahari Desert, secure in the knowledge that no other form of social organisation could successfully compete with theirs in the exploitation of these sparse resources. Though severely circumscribed and much reduced numerically, they were able to maintain their way of life virtually intact, until South African military excursions in Namibia and Angola sucked some of them into the South African military apparatus. Though many of them entered of necessity into client relationships with Tswana cattle-keepers, few attempted to make the transition to a sedentary way of life and fewer still were successful. Because of this firm adherence to their distinctive lifestyle and because of their relative inaccessibility, they were but faintly touched by missionary Christianity, and the protracted but isolated missionary presence among them was unable to overcome their resistance to conversion.

Today there is a diversity of religious expression among the 50 000 San living in Botswana, Namibia and Angola, so that no consistent and common body of belief can be discerned. We can attempt the construction of a general outline only, but it differs significantly from that presented in chapter two, whether because San religion has undergone change or because we have access to a more complete picture of what it always was, we cannot tell. The belief in a creative higher being endures, though he is accompanied by a subordinate fellow deity. Nevertheless, both are humanly equipped with wife and children, they enjoy a typically human jocular relationship with each other, redolent of trickery, and they give vent to characteristically human desires and passions, though unbridled by any social restraints. For the most part, the San approach them on the level of human interaction, alternating between deference and ridicule, even to the extent of parodying the ineptness of the creative act. But more seriously, they are credited with being the cause of misfortune and suffering, employing spirits as their agents. The deities, it is feared, can level a whole camp for no other reason than to demonstrate uncontrollable power. Yet the San frequently pray to and plead with the gods, voicing their hopes and anxieties, in an attempt to tap this source of power for compensatory benefits in the harsh Kalahari environment. At the same time, the San continue to have recourse to their old healing techniques to redress the difficulties of their situation. Although a rain dance is still performed, as also a giraffe, eland and buffalo dance, the object is not to anticipate rainfall or to secure success in hunting, which has become more peripheral to the economy, but to invoke the powers of divinity indwelling in natural things to promote the curing of people. All people have within them a curative capacity, though not all choose to activate it by becoming entranced. In the state associated with this capacity they hold off impending evil and struggle with the gods to take back the evil they have inflicted. Paradoxically, these healers draw upon a god-given capacity to rid others of afflictions induced by the gods themselves. As noted in chapter two, the nature of divinity is whimsical, both supportive of and antagonistic to people, making healing possible, but also on occasion opposing it.

Consequences for Bantu-speaking African societies

Among the Bantu-speaking population, white invasion was preceded by internal social upheaval. The steady southerly expansion of these pastoral farmers, through the segmentation and multiplication of independent chiefdoms, had been arrested by white settlement. Thereafter, expansion was by a process of conquest and aggregation of weaker neighbours, which was intensified in the narrow eastern corridor and, ultimately, culminated in the formation of a large state dominated by the Zulus. Those resisting assimilation and escaping the turmoil erupted outwards in all directions. Schooled in the techniques of a new and merciless warfare, they plundered and uprooted communities in their path, causing each to fall back on its neighbours, spreading ripples of disorder to the verges of the Kalahari and as far north as Mashonaland. The results of this great convulsion and dispersion (known as the Mfecane, or Difaqane) were the consolidation of the powerful Zulu kingdom, the formation of fledgling militant offshoots, and a pervasive condition of social disruption and unsettled violent relations over a very wide region. It was against this background that the northward incursions of whites into Natal and the Highveld interior took place. However, there is a strong emergent body of opinion that whites were agents, and not merely witnesses, of these events and that Africans were being squeezed between Boer and British advance from the south and the raiding parties of Portuguese slavers in the northeast.[1]

It would be strange if the religious system were left unmarked by a social upheaval of this dimension. Population displacement and resettlement resulted in the acceptance in the west of elements of Nguni religion. This is particularly noticeable in the borrowing of divining techniques, which now coexist with the throwing of bones or dice. Such borrowed methods include that of interrogating the patient's party and, by means of their responses, narrowing down the possibilities until the location of stolen articles can be 'smelt out'. A further possibility is that of divining intuitively by means of direct spiritual contact with the ancestors. A general tendency has also been noted of adopting medium divination by female practitioners. Even the name for such divining mediums retains the same root, *-goma* (meaning drum), across all Bantu-speaking societies in which the divining dance is accompanied by drumming.

A different kind of religious development occurred in the east as a consequence of the emergence of the nation-state. The first fruits ceremony, which was widely held annually by individual chiefdoms to mark the beginning of the ritual cycle, was elevated to a state ritual notably among the Swazi and the Zulu. The Swazi *Incwala* is still mounted today. The ritual held at the capital was militarised and served to strengthen the monarch and his regiments and, while it allowed the divisions and oppositions within the realm to be given expression in formalised criticism of the ruler, this was in order to seal them within an acclamation of unity and loyalty.

The organised attempt to extend Christianity into these African communities began at much the same time among the Xhosa in the east and the Tswana to the west, well before the Mfecane had run its course. The fact that in most cases the long-established social organisation of these communities was in disarray actually favoured the missionaries. It is inconceivable that people should abandon their religious system for another as long as it is anchored in a stable and satisfying way of life. An alternative religious outlook exercises attraction only when social organisation is severely disrupted or individuals become dislocated from it. That is why, in the early stages of missionary contact, only a handful of refugees, outcasts and the discontented of African societies went over to Christianity.

While African societies in the west were attempting to re-establish their settled, orderly way of life, a task at which they eventually proved to be relatively successful, their leaders welcomed the missionaries as an opportunity from which they might wrest advantage. The literacy they brought with them was highly prized but they were also pressed into the roles of political envoy, mediator and adviser, and were at times called upon to provide superior firepower. In the east, even the cohesively organised Zulu nation saw the wisdom of exploiting the missionary relationship for political and material gain. In this common reaction, Africans were quick to discern and seize upon the distinction between the spiritual and material dimensions of mission Christianity, their alleged inability to distinguish sacred from profane to the contrary. Unwilling to accept the Christian God and his salvational dispensation, they were eager to avail themselves of the secular services and technological benefits which the missionaries could provide. Among these, literacy, as a means of storing and transmitting knowledge, was to prove to be the most irresistible attraction. Missionary success attended progressive investment in schools and printing presses and was to a lesser extent related to the provision of healing services and hospitals. The pattern was the same to east and to west, but the pace was different. Missionaries in the west enjoyed early success, entering the very heart of the Tswana polity by converting the sons or brothers of reigning chiefs. But missionary progress was greatly delayed in the east, where it encountered intractable organised resistance from the Zulu in particular, who initially gave token hostages to Christianity but later regarded conversion as tantamount to treason and devised strategies to gain the benefit of education without a religious commitment.

However, while over time missionary Christianity put education within the grasp of Africans and introduced useful innovations in agriculture and construction, the cost was the ineluctable erosion of customary economic and political relationships. And as they gained a secure foothold, the missionaries, true to their 'civilising' impulse, set out deliberately to destroy essential institutions of African society such as polygamy, bridewealth, leviratic marriage,[2] circumcision, sorcery, rain-making, drinking and even festive dancing. Unable to eradicate these practices entirely, they succeeded in driving deep wedges into the cohesion of African cultures. The ambivalent relationship between the missions and encroaching white settlement further promoted the demise of African society, and the missionaries were not averse on occasion to resolving their difficulties by falling back on colonial support. While on one level they were intent on creating an independent black Christian peasantry, they nevertheless cultivated in those whom they influenced a predisposition for entering white employment. Colonial legislation purposely weakened the control of chiefs over their subjects and compelled an increasing number of men to supply their labour to the colonial economy and, later on in even greater numbers, to become migrant workers on the mines and in the burgeoning industrial centres. The cumulative result of these combined missionary and colonial interventions in African life was to demolish the political, social and moral foundations of African society and to propel its occupants into a way of life not recognisably their own, patterned on categories and values embedded in Christianity. Not surprisingly, the majority of Africans who were forced or persuaded to make this social transition embraced Christianity; today, more than 75 per cent of the African population of South Africa professes to be Christian.

Continuity and discontinuity

It would appear, then, that African religion has largely succumbed to Christianity. Yet it would be untrue to say that it has been supplanted or crushed out of existence, for, besides its survival in its own right among about 25 per cent of the population, it endures as a skein threaded into the weft of Christianity. Some elements have been deeply incorporated, while others blend imperfectly and uneasily with Christian teaching. This mixture of continuity and discontinuity between the two religious forms means that the African Christian or Christian African has a more formidable range of religious resources to draw upon in the explanation and resolution of human problems than does his or her counterpart among white Christians, or among those retaining a purely African religious outlook.

The idea of identifying and exploiting common ground between the two religious systems was a fundamental principle of mission methodology. If some area of resemblance could be found to exist between them, then a Christian meaning could be fittingly transferred to and impressed upon the corresponding feature of African religion. To this end, the missionaries fastened on to the notion of uNkulunkulu or Modimo. We have seen (p. 26) that Africans used these terms to refer to 'first human of our kind' or 'original settler of this region', conceived as the most remote of ancestral spirits. And since these references were enshrined in what appeared to be accounts of creation, the missionaries took these terms to mean the 'Creator Spirit' or 'Great Spirit', a semantic receptacle into which they could pour the attributes of Christian divinity, supernatural, omnipotent, omnipresent, punitive and forgiving, not at a distance from creation but intervening decisively in human development. In their zeal, they took resemblance for near-identity and dissimilarity for opposition.

In hindsight we have a better grasp of what constituted the resemblance. It resided in the notion of 'encompassment'. In societies organised on the principle of descent, the founding ancestor would socially encompass all his living descendants; the God of Christianity spiritually encompasses all of humanity within his creation. What they had in common was a wide fan of social reference, although in the case of the primal ancestor, reference did not necessarily mean relevance or influence. These differences were overlooked. The missionaries transposed a spirit of human origin, whose connection to the living was by a distant human act of reproduction, into a superhuman deity involved with humanity through a mystical act of creation. This accounted for the confusion that attended their early attempts to capture the names uNkulunkulu and Modimo and enlist them in the service of Christianity.

A further source of confusion, at least for the Zulus, was their belief in a mystical counterpart of the highest secular authority of the chief or the king, which was rendered as 'the Lord of the Heavens' and which the missionaries identified with their derived meaning of uNkulunkulu. The Zulus swore to an agreement by invoking the name of an ancestor or of their chief. When they were required to take an oath in their dealings with whites, this was not acceptable. A compromise was reached, whereby they swore by 'the Lord of the Heavens', referring obliquely to their chief, whereas whites accepted it within missionary usage to mean uNkulunkulu, that is God. But used in this context and detached from their culture, the phrase took on a life of its own. 'The Lord of the Heavens' came to mean 'the Supreme Being', and in this guise became an innovation in Zulu culture, an invention of traditional religion. While generations of Christian converts learned to accept the missionary meaning of uNkulunkulu and Modimo, they found common ground with the adherents of traditional religion, who now also professed a belief in a Supreme Being. So complete has been the Christian takeover of these African notions that it is commonly assumed that African societies always acknowledged the existence of a Supreme Being or God.

The ancestors and the impact of Christianity

Once the idea of an all-pervasive deity, intimately attentive to the needs of his people, had become firmly entrenched in African Christianity, the religious role of the ancestors was rendered uncertain. In fact, the assault on the ancestors came from more than one quarter and, to appreciate the manner of their survival as mystical agents, we need to unpack the several capacities which they exercised on behalf of the living and for which they were held in high esteem. In the first place, ancestors functioned as symbolic markers to divide one social group from another, the basis of association within such groups being, of course, common descent. Secondly, they were the guardians of the moral order, which was articulated primarily in norms regulating kinship behaviour. Thirdly, ancestors were the key element in the explanation and management of shifting fortune. Under their protection their descendants prospered but, if their displeasure was aroused, their descendants suffered the consequences. Thus instances of sickness, affliction and adversity were accounted for. Moreover, in the same capacity, the ancestors commissioned diviners who, with ancestral enlightenment, could determine the cause of a misfortune and point out the remedy.

With the collapse of descent group organisation, undermined by the withdrawal of migrant workers and the progressive urbanisation of the African population in conjunction with the declining carrying capacity of the land, the ancestors were deprived of their salience as boundary markers. Though descent has not disappeared as a reference point, it is rare for whole descent groups to act collectively or to meet to celebrate their common descent in a commensal sacrifice presided over by the lineage head. The effective unit of social organisation is the small domestic group of at most three generations, in which ritual remembrance of the dead addresses parents and grandparents only. Thus ancestors are reduced to the level of the Roman household gods. Kinship, that is the range of relationships based on marriage and procreation in which the individual is encased, is durable, despite the fact that kin are usually dispersed over great distance. As moral guardians, ancestors (parents and grandparents) patrol the kinship network and, in their capacity as dispensers of varying fortune, can move between city and countryside to attend upon and influence their wards. There are three significant changes resulting from the stress on kinship. In the first place, ancestors may be acknowledged as much on the maternal as on the paternal side. Furthermore, female ancestors may assume as much importance as male ancestors, or even greater importance; thus mother and maternal and paternal grandmothers may emerge as influential figures. Finally, there is an element of choice in selecting ancestors to whom to entrust one's protection and providence, depending on how close and rewarding the living relationship had been.

Now, these are developments which equally affect Christian and non-Christian Africans, but, for Christians, there was the additional strain of reconciling the now diminished range of ancestral influence with the predominance of a caring God. The operations of the one would seem to trespass on the competence of the other. It is a fact that a great proportion of African

Christians keep faith with ancestors in their third capacity as the purveyors of ill or good fortune. To them, the explanation of an affliction as being caused by a virus is perfectly acceptable as far as it goes. But why has the virus picked on this individual in a particular set of circumstances? To say it is God's punishment for wickedness has limitations, especially if one has not been particularly iniquitous. In any case, one is invoking the most universal of agents to account for the most specific of events. The particularity now enjoyed by ancestors, and of course that was always accorded to sorcerers, makes an explanation along these lines more satisfying. Moreover, as long as sorcery endures, neither God nor Christianity supplies an effective counter to it; thus the only insurance is the protective mantle of an ancestor. Instances abound of committed Christians, even of ecclesiastical rank, being pulled back from the brink of death in the course of a serious illness by the intervention of an ancestor in a vivid dream, of others strenuously resisting an ancestral call to the divining profession, and it is an everyday occurrence for Christians to turn to a diviner for help in their distress. In such cases, people operate a dual religious system, compartmentalised in order to avoid contradiction. Depending on their needs and the occasion, they can appeal separately to God or the ancestors, but it is in times of personal mental and physical crisis that they bring their ancestors into the foreground.

Yet there is much evidence to indicate that attempts are also made to reconcile the two and to see them as complementary aspects of a single integrated religious system. From this perspective, ancestors may be regarded as lesser agents of the divinity. They continue to supervise the welfare of descendants but in subordination to God's design for humankind. The concept of ancestor thus resembles that of angel, at least as regards an assumed common function inclusive of messenger, guardian and mediator. Like angels, ancestors can counsel and warn in dreams, can watch over the interests of the living and can be approached in prayer to petition God for favours. On the other hand, this spiritual hierarchy can cast God in the role of super-ancestor, all the more so since Christianity enshrines the principle of quasi-human descent in the Godhead itself and elaborates it in the doctrine of incarnation. Christian saints, too, resemble the ancestors, being fully human and credited with powers of intercession and patronage, a concept that can readily be extended to include all the dead who are presumed to dwell in God's presence. The honouring of the Christian dead can therefore provide a vehicle for the expression of piety towards immediate ancestors. Thus the provision and unveiling of a tombstone some time after burial can be as much an African as a Christian rite.

Consequences for belief in sorcery

While the influence of ancestors has contracted as the range of effective kin has dwindled, the belief in sorcery, the other principle in the explanation of misfortune, has scarcely wavered. Sorcery or witchcraft is conceived as human malice (anger, jealously, envy) activated on the mystical plane, and arising from strained relationships, originally between neighbours and co-residents.

To be more precise, sorcery runs in such relationships only to the extent that their competitive character breeds an uncertainty which is not open to resolution by other means.

The entry of Africans into a commercialised, industrialised and urbanised milieu, which stresses individual ambition and achievement, has not by any means released Africans from the burden of this type of relationship. Indeed, it has had the effect of exacerbating the difficulty by multiplying the incidence of such strained relationships and by increasing their intensity. People are involved in new forms of personal competition for houses, jobs, qualifications and so on; they are introduced to new social situations of doubtful and uncertain outcome almost daily. Not surprisingly, even among Christians sorcery thrives on this condition of augmented competition and uncertainty. It follows from the continued salience of ancestral influence and of sorcery-yielding relationships that diviners and herbalists retain a useful function in the diagnosis and curing of affliction. Christians often have recourse to these services for the resolution of their problems.

Other results of contact with settler populations

African religion has undergone further changes as a result of contact with settler populations, and new elements have been incorporated within it. Modern developments have led to the recognition of several different types of novel spirit existence, more prevalent among the coastal population. Some of these spirits emerge indirectly from the ancestral cult and, like ancestors, are of human origin. They are referred to as *indiki* spirits, first recorded among the Zulu at the turn of the century.

It will be recalled that a deceased person does not become an ancestor until he or she has been formally installed by the living through the performance of a first sacrifice to end the mourning period (see p. 21). Between interment and the sacrificial rite, the deceased is wandering about without status or purpose and is deemed to be harmful to the living. If for some reason the rite is never performed, the period of aimless wandering is indefinitely extended and the spirit becomes permanently and capriciously harmful, in a word an *indiki*. This can happen when Christian children refuse to sacrifice for a non-Christian father, but is more commonly attributed to the migrant labour system. It is believed that the more dangerous *indiki* are of foreign extraction, the spirits of migrants who have died without returning to their native Mozambique, Malawi and so on, and have been left to roam unwanted, without being formally joined to the aggregate of their ancestors. Unanchored in the social structure and uncontrolled by the system of sacrificial appeasement, these spirits are undomesticated and wild, hence anti-social and evil.

Ufufunyane spirits were added more recently, but represent something more sinister than *indiki* because of their connection with sorcery. Sorcerers, it is believed, are able to capture the spirits of the dead and employ them in their nefarious designs against others. Even when the sorcerer's victim has been released from their clutches, they swell the ranks of roaming spirits which can by chance batten on the weak and unsuspecting. *Ufufunyane* spirits attack in legions and are of mixed cultural derivation, typically thousands of whites and Indians, hundreds of Sotho and Zulu. The *indiki* victim cries and shouts in a frenzy, while those possessed by *ufufunyane* give vent to uncontrolled hysterical behaviour verging on the suicidal, and both utter snatches of a foreign language.

Special expertise attached to the divining role has been developed for treating cases of *indiki* and *ufufunyane* possession. Over a period of time, the invading *indiki* spirit is replaced by a protective male ancestor; the patient becomes an adept of the *indiki* cult to which the diviner already belongs and may even proceed to become a diviner herself. The *ufufunyane* hordes must be driven out by the infusion of regiments of benevolent spirits drawn from the diviner's store. Furthermore, the weakest members of society, the newly born, are given special ritual treatment by a diviner to engage the closest protection of a male ancestor as a safeguard against the random attacks of wandering spirits.

Although by no means enough is known about these novel manifestations of spirit activity, the general pattern is clear enough. As African societies were drawn into interaction with workers and settlers of foreign extraction and suffered severe social disruption as a consequence, certain maladies and nervous disorders were identified as flowing from the stresses and deprivations of this social disorder. Granted the principle of mystical causation of illness, these afflictions were logically attributed to alien, intrusive and aggressive spirits, and these echelons of new spirits had to be accommodated within the religious system dominated by the ancestors. It can thus be seen that, even as African religion was making its compromises with Christianity, it demonstrated its resilience in another way by adjusting and extending its spiritual repertoire to new developments and changing conditions.

NOTES

1. For an introduction to this debate see John Wright, 'A. T. Bryant and the Wars of Shaka', *History in Africa*, 18 (1991).
2. The custom of compulsory marriage with a childless brother's widow.

SELECT BIBLIOGRAPHY

Carstens and Hoernlé consider religion under modern conditions among Khoikhoi remnants, while Katz, Marshall and Van der Post deal extensively with religious healing still practised by the San. Hammond-Tooke's recent edition on the Bantu-speaking people contains three chapters, written by Pauw and himself, on religious topics. Several other works by Pauw focus on the interpenetration of Christian and African beliefs among the Xhosa and the Tswana. Comaroff provides detailed information on the response to missions by Tswana, and Etherington performs a similar task for the Zulu. Ngubane's account of Zulu healing shows that Zulu religion endures even while it absorbs new experiences. Vilakazi has a useful chapter spanning traditional Zulu religion and Christianity. For those interested in the related Shona religion, Bucher will serve as an up-to-date guide. Finally, Hexham is a little-known but impressive contribution to the contentious issue of belief in a Supreme Being.

Bucher, Hubert, *Spirits and Power. An Analysis of Shona Cosmology*. Cape Town: Oxford University Press, 1980

Carstens, Peter, 'Some Implications of Change in Khoikhoi Supernatural Beliefs' in M. G. Whisson and M. West (eds.), *Religion and Social Change in Southern Africa.* Cape Town: David Philip, 1975

Comaroff, Jean, *Body of Power: Spirit of Resistance. The Culture and History of a South African People.* Chicago and London: University of Chicago Press, 1985

Etherington, Norman, *Preachers, Peasants and Politics in Southeast Africa, 1835–1880.* London: Royal Historical Society, 1978

Hammond-Tooke, W. D. (ed.), *The Bantu-speaking Peoples of Southern Africa.* London: Routledge and Kegan Paul, 1974

Hexham, Irving, 'Lord of the Sky, King of the Earth: Zulu Traditional Religion and Belief in the Sky-God'. *Sciences Religieuses/Studies in Religion,* 10, 3 (1981)

Hoernlé, Winifred and Carstens, P. (eds.), *The Social Organisation of the Nama.* Johannesburg: University of Witwatersrand Press, 1985

Katz, Richard, *Boiling Energy.* Cambridge, Mass.: Harvard University Press, 1982

Marshall, Lorna, '/Kung Bushman Religious Beliefs'. *Africa,* 32, 3 (1962)

Ngubane, Harriet, *Body and Mind in Zulu Medicine.* London: Academic Press, 1977

Pauw, B. A., *Religion in a Tswana Chiefdom.* London: Oxford University Press, 1960

Pauw, B. A., *Christianity and Xhosa Tradition.* London: Oxford University Press, 1975

Van der Post, Laurens and Taylor, Jane, *Testament to the Bushmen.* Harmondsworth: Penguin, 1984

Vilakazi, A., *Zulu Transformations.* Pietermaritzburg: University of Natal Press, 1965

Wright, John, 'A. T. Bryant and the Wars of Shaka'. *History in Africa,* 18 (1991)

6

Christianity in Twentieth-Century South Africa

JOHN W. DE GRUCHY

Christianity has been integrally related to the social and political development of South Africa from the beginning of the colonial period. This relationship has continued throughout the twentieth century. While other major world religions have also played an important role in shaping modern South Africa, Christianity has become *the* dominant *world* religious tradition in the region. Approximately 77 per cent of the total population regard themselves as members of one of the many Christian denominations, with blacks comprising the vast majority of church membership.[1]

The transformation of Christianity, from a white, European-dominated settler religion, with expatriate missionaries engaged in evangelising the indigenous people of the country, to a black-majority religion rooted in African culture and engaged in the struggle against white social, political and ecclesial domination, is undoubtedly the most significant development of twentieth-century Christianity in South Africa. It is also the central theme of this chapter and thus the focus for understanding other developments in South African Christianity.[2] This struggle has developed in distinct stages since the end of the Anglo-Boer War,[3] and is now entering a decisive new phase with the end of apartheid, the establishment of a non-racial democratic government, and the task of reconstruction and development.

From the Anglo-Boer War to Union

The relationship between Christianity and the European colonisation of Southern Africa has been described in chapter three. That chapter ended with the Anglo-Boer War (1898–1902) in which the Afrikaner descendants of Dutch colonialism struggled to preserve the independence of their Republics from British imperialism. Both sides were Protestant in their religious affiliation, legitimating their respective claims and actions by calling on the name of the Christian God.[4]

Although the Anglo-Boer War was a 'white man's war', blacks were inevitably drawn into the conflict, many believing that a British victory would result in their own emancipation from Boer domination. For this reason many black leaders, invariably missionary converts to Christianity, expressed considerable loyalty to the British crown and were willing to suffer for its cause in anticipation of their own liberation.[5] The Treaty of Vereeniging signed in 1902 seriously undermined any such hopes, however, and led to the formation of the South African Native Congress in the Eastern Cape that same year.

In 1903 the executive of the South African Native Congress addressed their post-war hopes and grievances in a lengthy letter to the British Colonial Secretary, Joseph Chamberlain. The opening section of the letter expressed their 'indebtedness ... to the Government and people of Great Britain' and loyalty to the colonial churches. The executive went on to point out, however, that the missionary movement had given rise to reformist expectations, particularly in education, and expressed concern at the conservative reaction of whites to such impulses. The executive also commented on the emergence of secessionist black Christian groups, saying that these should not be regarded as undermining either the authority of the state or that of the church. Indeed, they declared:

> The black races are too conscious of their dependence upon the white missionaries, and their obligations towards the British race, and the benefits to be derived by their presence in the general control and guidance of the civil and religious affairs of the country to harbour foolish notions of political ascendency.[6]

Nothing could better express the extent to which missionary Christianity and Cape liberalism had influenced the values and perspectives of black elite leadership at the turn of the century.[7] There were, of course, other more radical black leaders whose views had been shaped by an already long history of struggle. Some were avowedly Christian but anti-white, like the later eccentric preacher and nationalist, Wellington Buthelezi. Also of significance was the influence of the African American struggle in the United States,[8] mediated in large measure through contact with the American Methodist Episcopal Church.[9] This had contributed directly to secession within the mission churches, or what was then referred to as the Ethiopian movement,[10] towards the end of the nineteenth century under the leadership of Nehemiah Tile, Mangena Mokone and James Dwane.[11]

The first of many General Missionary Conferences to be held in South Africa was convened in 1904. All the major missionary societies were present, and their concern was the consolidation of what had been achieved during the previous century as well as planning for the future. Of major importance to the delegates was the need to ensure the Protestant character of the country against the inroads of Roman Catholicism, the conversion and education of the heathen, polygamy, and 'Ethiopian' secessionism.

The government-commissioned Lagden Report on 'Christianity and Civilisation', published in 1906, expressed concern that the secessionist 'Native Churches' had established their own schools, and that they were even sending young people to America to study in 'Negro colleges'.[12] Seeing that neither government policy nor the Lagden Commission favoured compulsory education for blacks, and that the Report preferred an education which generally kept them subservient to white interests, it is not surprising that many Africans sought alternative forms of education. In a very paternalistic spirit, the Commission recommended that the growing desire for education could and should not be suppressed, but that nothing other than the existing missionary education should be undertaken. The churches themselves believed, moreover, that the best education for the majority of Africans was that which equipped them for manual labour. Thus the missionary societies and churches warmly received the Lagden Report. Yet hindsight enables us to see that so much that was to characterise South Africa's discriminatory racial policies in the future was embodied or implied within it.[13] It should be added, however, that the Second General Missionary Conference of 1906 supported the view of the Cape liberals that 'the rights of the Natives' be secured in the framing of the constitution for the proposed Union of South Africa.

Articles and correspondence of the period indicate considerable apprehension about the Ethiopian movement on the part of the colonial authorities. Secession not only fragmented further the unity of the church, already seriously divided by European denominationalism, but more especially it created social ferment. Proof of this came, so it was argued, in the Bambatha Rebellion which shook Natal in June 1906. Also blamed for the rebellion was the missionary education given to blacks. Needless to say, this was denied by the missions, and the churches supported the suppression of the rebellion, in which 3 000 Africans were killed.

Alongside the Ethiopian separatist churches was another movement soon to be described as Zionism. The origins of Zionism are complex. While the first Zionist congregation was established in Johannesburg in 1895 by an American missionary, the most important development can be traced back to Petrus Le Roux, a white Dutch Reformed missionary in the rural Transvaal town of Wakkerstroom. Le Roux, a student of Andrew Murray, jun., the renowned Dutch Reformed leader, was greatly influenced by the teachings of John Alexander Dowie of Zion City, Illinois, who stressed the importance of divine healing. Shortly after the Anglo-Boer War, Le Roux was forced to leave the Dutch Reformed Church because of his newly adopted views, but his Zulu congregation in Wakkerstroom agreed with him and established the first Zulu Zionist church. The war had been particularly hard on such rural black communities, and they found in the somewhat apocalyptic message of Zion a means of coping with their situation and rebelling against white domination.[14]

Zion at Wakkerstroom laid the foundations for a movement which was to grow widely and rapidly during the rest of the century. It was at Wakkerstroom that the characteristic language, symbols, dress and worship of Zionism in South Africa were first established. Le Roux eventually became disenchanted with Dowie, and he also developed reservations about what he regarded as the syncretism of his Zionist flock. This led him to move to the Witwatersrand, where he helped form the Apostolic Faith Mission (AFM) in 1908. The founding of the AFM, followed by the establishment of the Assemblies of God in 1914, which brought together various independent missions, signalled the birth of Pentecostalism in South Africa.

While the leaders of the South African Native Congress protested to the colonial authorities against accusations of disloyalty, there was rising discontent within black Christian ranks that was as much political in character as ecclesiastical.[15] From the beginning Ethiopianism, with its built-in rejection of European control, fostered militant political action at the grass-roots level, providing many of the leaders within the broader emergent African nationalist movement.[16] The bulk of the leadership came, however, from the more educated, Westernised African Christians who remained within the established churches and missions, though they were more inclined to petition the colonial authorities than engage in militant protest.[17]

There was considerable discussion within the 'mainline' churches on the evangelisation and education of 'the Natives' in the immediate post-war years. The 1904 Provincial Synod of the Anglican Church stated clearly that it regarded the evangelisation of the 'Native Races' as a priority, though it also declared that the acceptance of Christianity did not imply social equality or political enfranchisement.[18] Although there were some more enlightened prophetic voices in the churches, this view was widely shared amongst all the English-speaking churches[19] and missionary societies. The Afrikaans Reformed churches[20] were invariably more conservative in their opinions.

The English-speaking churches saw their task as threefold. Firstly, they sought to consolidate their denominational structures, with control firmly in the hands of the white membership. Secondly, though segregated at the local level, they adopted a more liberal, paternalistic stance with regard to the 'native question', and sought to speak on behalf of blacks, especially those who were 'civilised' as a result of missionary education. Thirdly, they attempted to engender a spirit of reconciliation and unity between English and Afrikaner. This dovetailed with the conciliation policy of the British colonial authorities after 1905 and decisively affected the way in which the English-speaking churches developed.[21]

Reconciliation between English and Afrikaner was fostered in 1906 when the ecumenical pioneer, John R. Mott, visited South Africa. His visit was sponsored in part by the Student Christian Association (SCA), formed in 1896 as a means of ministry amongst white students. Mott held evangelistic campaigns around the country, putting special emphasis on the need for reconciliation between Afrikaner and English through their shared Christian commitment. Reflecting on a Student Missionary Conference in Cape Town, he wrote: 'for the first time since the terrible Boer War most of the differing Christian forces of the country had been brought together, a feat that could possibly be accomplished only by the Christian student movement ...'[22] Yet it must be noted that no black students were members of the Conference, though some students from Zonnebloem College in Cape Town put in an appearance.

During the decade that separated the end of the war from the establishment of the Union of South Africa in 1910, black socio-political aspirations were thus sacrificed on the altar of white unity with the support of the churches. This was despite the many pleas by black Christian leaders to the British authorities for a significant say in the shaping of the new country. Leaders within the established churches, such as the Congregationalist Dr Walter Rubusana, the first African to win a seat in the Cape Provincial Council, played key roles in fighting for the entrenchment and extension of black political rights. The rejection of their increasingly anguished attempts to achieve even this limited objective meant that black reaction to the formation of the Union of South Africa was one of intense disappointment, anger and growing resistance. The legislative programme which ensued during the next few years confirmed the very worst fears of black leaders. Not only were they excluded from the political process, but racially discriminatory legislation became the order of the day.

From Union to Apartheid

The government census in 1911 revealed that more than a quarter of the African population was now Christian.[23] As this number included the majority of those who had received a Western-style missionary-based education, it is not surprising that much of the black political leadership at that time was Christian. Black church leaders of both the mission and the Ethiopian churches played a major role in protesting against the racial discrimination that was built into and flowed from the constitution of the Union. This link between African nationalist aspirations and Christianity, while in evidence elsewhere, found further expression when the South African Native National Congress was inaugurated in Bloemfontein in 1912, to be renamed the African National Congress (ANC) in 1923. The principles adopted by the Congress affirmed the liberal Christian values as taught in missionary schools.[24]

This close relationship between African Christians and African nationalism elicited cautious rather than wholehearted support from the Missionary Conference, the English-speaking churches and their respective missions. Understandably this aroused considerable cynicism among blacks, making Christianity, as the first president of the ANC and Congregationalist leader, John Dube, complained, 'an offensive smell to a large number of Natives'.[25] Nonetheless, Christianity was expanding rapidly amongst the African population, both within the established churches and missions, and within the independent church groups. Despite denominational loyalty and fragmentation, it provided a unifying moral basis for African nationalism, and for this reason the ANC encouraged unity amongst the churches.[26] Many years later, however, James Calata, an Anglican priest and ANC leader, would bemoan the fact that the missions had contributed, by their divided state, to the disintegration of African national life.[27]

The introduction of land and labour legislation (the Mines and Works Act of 1911, the Natives Land Act of 1913, the Native Affairs Act of 1920, and the Natives (Urban Areas) Act of 1923) effectively reduced blacks to the role of serfs. The official response of the established churches to this legislation was mixed, though there was no doubt in the minds of black Christian leaders such as the Methodist Z. R. Mahabane that it was unredeemably evil.[28] In a paper read before the Natal Missionary Conference in July 1920, Dr D. D. T. Jabavu, a Presbyterian layman from Fort Hare University College, castigated the NGK for helping to pilot 'through parliament in the teeth of glaring heterodoxy an act calculated to stamp herself indelibly as an anti-Native Church'.[29] In a far more scathing critique of the NGK at a conference held in Johannesburg in 1923 to discuss Christianity as the basis for 'native policy', James Thaele rejected such nonsense as blatant hypocrisy, the reason why so many blacks were turning to Islam, and accused the NGK of simply being part of white political domination.[30]

A tragic illustration of the desperation of religiously inspired black protest and rebellion against government land policies came in 1921 when a millenarian movement called the Israelites established an 'independent' communal settlement near Bulhoek in the Eastern Cape. This was ruthlessly destroyed in the 'Bulhoek Massacre' by colonial troops because of the perceived threat to colonial authority and order.[31] The fourth South African Missionary Conference held that same year took a strong and critical position against the Land Act, but apart from adopting appropriate yet cautious resolutions the Conference was unable to do anything about it.[32]

The position adopted by the English-speaking churches was more ambiguous than that of both the NGK and the Missionary Conference. This was because they tried to serve the interests of white congregations while also seeking to adopt a more liberal approach to the 'native question'. Being thus allied to the dominant colonial ideology of the time, they were unable and usually unwilling to act in solidarity with blacks.[33] On the whole the white church leadership had little grasp of the plight of either the black rural communities or the black workers during this period of rapid urbanisation and industrialisation. With some notable exceptions, missionaries spent much effort in evangelising rural peasants or urbanised mine labourers, but were often far less concerned about their material conditions. Referring to the missionaries, Jabavu bemoaned the fact that those of his day no longer had the courage and compassion of their predecessors.[34]

The defeat of the Afrikaners in the Anglo-Boer War strengthened their sense of nationhood and desire to control their own destiny. Despite attempts by the former Boer generals Louis Botha and Jan Smuts to foster a broad white South African nationalism, a rift within Afrikanerdom resulted in the formation of the National Party in January 1914. For Afrikaner nationalists the party was soon regarded as more than an ordinary political organisation; it was a national movement grounded in a sense of divine calling.

By the 1920s many Afrikaners had migrated from the farms to the cities and towns, especially in and around Johannesburg, in search of work. Often reduced to poverty, especially during the Depression, they formed a growing white working class increasingly alienated from the church. In response to this 'poor white' problem the Afrikaans Reformed churches provided material, spiritual and cultural support. This concern for the poor did not extend to the black community, which was even more devastated by the Depression. On the contrary, the NGK helped build an alliance between party, church, and *volk* which ultimately enabled Afrikaner nationalists to achieve power in 1948 on the platform of apartheid.

The Afrikaner Broederbond was established in 1918 as the ideological think-tank which coordinated Afrikaner nationalism's rise to power. The Broederbond became a secret society in 1921 and exerted influence in every sphere of society. It was committed to ensuring that Afrikaner nationalism achieved total control over the country, and that its brand of Protestant Christianity would shape social norms. Many *dominees* were members of the Broederbond, and through their influence the NGK's support for Afrikaner nationalist aspirations and programmes was assured in all areas of public life. The policy of Christian National Education (CNE) advocated by the Broederbond ensured that Afrikaner children were educated in their mother tongue and according to the religious convictions and cultural traditions of the *volk*.[35] Afrikaner nationalism was thus able to withstand the attempt to anglicise the Afrikaner and ensure the emergence of a generation of Afrikaners imbued with its religious and cultural spirit. By extension of the principle, CNE later became the dominant educational ideology in implementing Bantu Education, a cornerstone of the policy of apartheid.

Integral to these developments was the reinterpretation of Afrikaner history as 'sacred history'. President Paul Kruger of the Transvaal Republic, a founding member of the Gereformeerde Kerk, made powerful rhetorical use of this theme in his speeches in the years preceding the Anglo-Boer War.[36] During the 1920s and 1930s, however, the notion of Afrikaner history as 'sacred history', with the *volk* as the Chosen People, became the normative filter through which Afrikaners as a whole interpreted their history. The Great Trek was the Exodus from the bondage of British rule at the Cape; it led to the years of struggling in the wilderness against all odds, en route to the promised land of the Boer Republics.[37] There, like Israel of old, the Afrikaner nation fulfilled a divine mandate to remain separate from and rule over the heathen nations in the interests of Christian civilisation.

Although the majority of Afrikaner ideologists claimed to be Calvinists, they were more imbued with the spirit of racial superiority and romantic nationalism than with Reformed theology.[38] The myths and symbols which they drew from the Old Testament became 'Calvinised' largely because the vast majority of Afrikaners belonged to the Afrikaans Reformed churches, and because of the role which the ministers of these churches played in fostering the spirit of Afrikaner nationalism.

During the 1920s the question of racial segregation began to predominate in Afrikaner political and church circles. In 1927 a conference sponsored by the NGK was held in Cape Town to discuss black representation in parliament at a time when the limited franchise of some blacks in the Cape Province was being reconsidered. White English-speaking as well as black Christians attended, but there was considerable disagreement on the main issues, with most Afrikaner delegates supporting segregation.[39] No consensus was possible, and from this period onwards the Afrikaans Reformed churches, particularly the NGK, provided the theological rationale for what was to become the policy of apartheid.

Racial segregation also characterised the development of the three main Pentecostal denominations, the Apostolic Faith Mission, Assemblies of God, and the Full Gospel Church (which was established in 1920). While each of these churches was multi-racial at the outset, they soon conformed to the prevailing social norms within white society.[40] In the case of the AFM, racial segregation was reinforced by the fact that by the 1930s it had a preponderance of white Afrikaner members, many of them dissidents from the NGK who were in search of a Christianity which was more emotionally satisfying.

Although the English-speaking churches continued to maintain good relations with the NGK, the latter's alignment with the narrow interests of Afrikaner nationalism and of racial segregation made this increasingly difficult. The English-speaking churches were, in fact, caught in the middle between Afrikaner and African interests, unable to identify fully with either for conflicting reasons. Nevertheless they sensed that the church could not remain Christian and be divided by race. Significantly, then, and in contradiction to the racial segregation built into the NGK's missionary policy, the English-speaking churches cautiously took steps which, sometimes unintentionally, moved them in a multi-racial direction. This was partly the significance of the union of the three branches of Methodism in 1931 to form the Methodist Church of South Africa.[41] Moreover, the English-speaking churches also opposed legislation which they regarded as unjust. In 1932, for example, the Baptist Assembly expressed 'its strong indignation at the Government's apparent policy of repression towards the Native Peoples, especially in the matter of replacing native labour by European labour ...'[42]

The English-speaking churches found it relatively easy to pass such resolutions, and to relate to those formally educated blacks who had begun to share their middle-class values, but there is little evidence of their 'forging a close relationship to labour as such, either black or white'. On the contrary, their 'connections to sections of capital and to the small but influential bourgeoisie were deepened'.[43] With respect to the English-speaking churches of the period 1903–30, James Cochrane concludes:

> The Victorian tradition, a colonial mentality, the structures of the Church itself, the material interests of its white members, and the impact of European immigrants – all played a part in determining the theory and the practice of the Church along lines prejudicial to the colonised indigenous people and the working class in particular.[44]

Although the English-speaking and Afrikaans Reformed churches were gradually growing apart instead of providing a means of reconciling the white groups, there was a degree of contact between some of their leaders, particularly in the Cape and Transvaal. Ever since the first South African Missionary Conference, both English and Afrikaner had regularly met to discuss common problems and issues. When John R. Mott returned to South Africa in 1934, at a time when the ecumenical movement was gathering momentum throughout the world, leaders of both groups caught something of the vision. As a result, the Christian Council of South Africa was formed in 1936, with the Cape and Transvaal Synods of the NGK as members alongside all the established churches and missionary societies. Some NGK leaders played a key role in the work and development of the Council.

This spirit of cooperation was, however, gradually undermined by Afrikaner nationalism and racial issues. In 1941, in the midst of the Second World War, the NGK synods withdrew from the Council. Dr Willem Nicol, who was both the moderator of the NGK and president of the Council, gave three reasons. Firstly, the Council was insufficiently bilingual; secondly, there were fundamental differences of opinion on the 'native question'; and thirdly, the other NGK synods refused to join.[45] It is undoubtedly true that the Council was not particularly relevant to Afrikaner needs and that few of its members could speak Afrikaans. It is also true that agreement on racial matters was impossible as the NGK, along with the National Party, became more and more firmly committed to the new dogma of apartheid. And the reason why the other synods (Natal and Orange Free State) refused to join was a profound rejection of anything that would liberalise the church or lead in some way to flirtation with the Roman Catholic Church. This suspicion of ecumenism was to prevail throughout the forthcoming years.

Afrikaner nationalism and the Afrikaans Reformed churches perceived several major threats to their existence and success. English liberalism was one, Roman Catholicism and 'godless' communism were others, and always in the background loomed the 'native problem'. Suspicion of the Roman Catholic Church, *die Roomse gevaar*, had always been in evidence within Protestant circles in South Africa.[46]

In 1922 Pope Pius XI established the Apostolic Delegation in South Africa, the first step away from the church as a mission under direct control of the papacy, and thus a significant step towards the eventual establishment of the Southern African Catholic Bishops' Conference in 1947, and finally the erection of the hierarchy (dioceses and diocesan bishops) in 1951.[47] Although the hierarchy remained totally white, the laity was by now predominantly black. The rapid growth in membership marked by these developments, partly a result of increasing European immigration, but even more the result of successful missionary work among Africans, increased Afrikaner nationalist fears of Roman Catholic influence.[48] Ironically, the Roman Catholic Church, while universal in its orientation, was as anti-communist as the Afrikaner nationalists and remained aloof from the ecumenical movement until the Second Vatican Council in the 1960s.

In 1942 the Christian Council of South Africa convened a conference to discuss the task of the churches in 'Christian reconstruction' after the Second World War. Although the war was to last a further three years, there was already a spirit of optimism in the air. There was also the hope, at least amongst liberal English-speaking and more moderate black Christians, that the end of the war would result in an attempt to build a more just South Africa. After all, Afrikaner nationalism's flirtation with Nationalist Socialism seemed to imply that the defeat of Germany would lead to the discrediting of the former. But the end of the war, when it eventually came, did not result in the end of Afrikaner nationalism; it heralded the dawning of a new era in which the National Party became the ruling power with apartheid as dominant ideology. In anticipation of an intensification of the struggle, younger, more militant members of the ANC, such as Peter Mda, Jordan Ngubane, William Nkomo, Nelson Mandela and Walter Sisulu, had formed the Youth League in 1943. This had a decisive impact upon the future direction of the ANC itself, especially after 1949, when a new phase of black resistance began.

The beginning of the church struggle

The National Party came to power in 1948, the same year in which the World Council of Churches was founded in Amsterdam. In 1949 the Christian Council convened at Rosettenville for another conference, this time focusing on the theme 'The Christian Citizen in a Multi-racial Society'. By now the mood was far more sombre than at the hopeful 1942 Fort Hare conference. Instead of the dawning of a new era of enlightened racial policies, the Nationalist government had immediately begun to plot and implement its apartheid vision.

Rosettenville was the first of a series of post-1948 conferences convened to deal with the 'race problem'. It strongly condemned apartheid, as did the subsequent conferences which followed in regular succession.[49] However, conferences convened by the NGK, to which English-speaking church representatives were sometimes invited, were far more cautious, and staunchly supportive of government policy. While a few NGK leaders, notably B. B. Keet, professor of theology at Stellenbosch, spoke out against apartheid, the NGK invariably supported each piece of apartheid legislation as it was proposed and adopted by the government.[50] Indeed, significant aspects of apartheid policy originated within the Afrikaans Reformed churches.

While church opposition to racial discrimination predates 1948, it was generally muted until the implementation of apartheid forced the churches to take a clearer stand. Even then the churches were not always united or unequivocal in their criticism of apartheid. The Roman Catholic Church operated in isolation from the other churches. The Catholic hierarchy was traditionally cautious in relating to the state, and the bishops did not want to be identified with what they perceived as the more outspoken liberal stand of the English-speaking churches. But they were also divided amongst themselves on both the issues and strategy. While archbishops Owen McCann of Cape Town and Denis Hurley of Durban condemned apartheid from the beginning, the majority of bishops believed that a conciliatory approach would better protect Catholic interests and achieve some modicum of improvement in the situation. This posed serious problems for the black majority in the church, and led other, more liberal Catholic organisations to take the initiative in opposing apartheid.[51]

On the whole, the English-speaking Protestant churches took a clearer stand than the Roman Catholic. Generally, those with a larger black membership (Anglicans, Congregationalists, Methodists) were more outspoken, while those with a smaller black constituency (Presbyterians, Baptists) were more restrained. In the case of the Anglican Church there was also a sense in which its establishment mentality prevented it from confronting the state head on.[52] Nevertheless, all the English-speaking churches condemned apartheid in principle from the beginning and passed resolutions against it at their synods and assemblies. Their failure was not the passing of resolutions but their implementation. Furthermore, all the English-speaking churches, despite their protests, were compromised by their own life and structures. Although they were not racially segregated into different synods or denominations, as were the Afrikaans Reformed and Lutheran churches (amongst the traditionally English-speaking churches, however, the Baptists also had segregated denominational structures), there was considerable racial discrimination in their common life and practice, and their leadership was virtually all white. At its annual Conference in 1954 there was even an attempt to segregate the Methodist Church. This was narrowly avoided by the eventual acceptance by a slender majority of a counter-motion claiming that the church was 'one and undivided'. It is not surprising, then, that while black members tried to ensure that their churches kept up pressure on the government, they did not expect too much and pinned their hopes instead on the ANC.

A different situation prevailed in the black mission churches. As black resistance to apartheid gathered momentum and expressed itself in such action as the Defiance Campaign in 1952, the ministers and elders of the Bantu Presbyterian Church (formerly the Church of Scotland Mission), for example, issued a statement in which they declared their support for the campaign because it corresponded with the will of God. 'Aware as we are', they said, 'that our people are not in possession of the political instruments that make for peaceful change in a normal democratic society, we are compelled to see a certain necessity in their choice of passive resistance as the one way open to them.' They went on to caution, however, that the campaign should be conducted non-violently and without bitterness.[53] Similar positions were adopted by other black mission churches. In comparison, the Roman Catholic Church stressed the need for patriotism and specifically called on its black members to dissociate themselves from the movement and take a more moderate position.[54]

Within the Roman Catholic and English-speaking churches the divisive issue was not so much the condemning of apartheid legislation in principle, but the political role of the churches in actively opposing the government and its policies. This tension was highlighted in the case of the Anglican Church because of the role played by several forceful expatriate leaders in the decade after 1948, notably Michael Scott, Geoffrey Clayton, bishop of Johannesburg and later archbishop of Cape Town, Trevor Huddleston of the Community of the Resurrection, and Bishop Ambrose Reeves, Clayton's successor in Johannesburg.[55] Clayton was outspoken in his criticism of apartheid, but was equally certain that the church as an institution, and especially its priests, should not be actively engaged in politics. Scott, Huddleston and Reeves, after working closely with the black community, came to the opposite conclusion. It was insufficient to pass resolutions. The white minority government was illegitimate, they argued, and Christians were called to take sides in the black struggle for liberation by joining forces with the ANC.[56] Thus, while the churches generally stood aloof from the Congress of the People at Kliptown in June 1955, when the 'Freedom Charter' was adopted, Huddleston and a few other clerics were present.

This solidarity with the African nationalist cause was deeply appreciated by the black community, and resulted in long-term relationships during the subsequent intensification of the struggle against apartheid. After they were forced to leave South Africa, Scott, Huddleston and Reeves played key roles in awakening the conscience of Christians in Europe to the evils of apartheid and the need to support the anti-apartheid movement.[57] Indeed, international opposition to apartheid, not least within church circles, was soon to become quite crucial in the struggle. Indicative of this was the position taken against racism by the second Assembly of the WCC held in Evanston, Illinois, in 1955.

Although these 'rebellious priests' and a few other ministers incurred the anger of many within their churches, as apartheid was implemented and generally opposed so relations between these churches and the government rapidly deteriorated. The churches were, in fact, trapped between a rock and a hard place. This was particularly so when legislation directly affected the life of the churches themselves, as was the case when the Bantu Education Bill came before parliament in the early 1950s.

In spite of their paternalism and lack of adequate resources, mission schools had a long and worthy tradition in South Africa. In normal circumstances it might have been appropriate for them to be taken over by the state at this stage, but the South African situation was abnormal. Bantu Education was designed to keep blacks subservient to white interests. The churches were caught in a cleft stick. Unless they handed over their schools to the state they would lose their government subsidy; if they lost their subsidy they would be forced to close. There were those, like Bishop Reeves, who advocated resistance and, if need be, closure under protest; there were others like the Roman Catholic hierarchy who sought to gain concessions through a more conciliatory approach;[58] and there were yet others like Dr J. B. Webb, president of the Methodist Church, who justified handing over the schools because, whatever the dangers, it would have certain benefits both for the churches and for black pupils. Even black opinion was divided and confused, not least within the ANC.[59]

In the end, with the notable exception of the Roman Catholics, who dug in their heels and sought ways and means to keep their many schools operative, the churches capitulated and thereby lost not only control of some of the finest educational institutions in the country, but also their influence in education. The Bantu Education Act was passed in 1953, leaving the field to the apartheid educational ideologists with increasingly tragic consequences for all concerned.[60] The moderate stance taken by the churches was indicative of their failure to understand the intentions of the government, and of an unwillingness to defy and resist in the interests of truth and justice.

A further critical moment of testing came in 1957 when the government promulgated the 'church clause' of the Native Laws Amendment Bill. This Bill made it very difficult for black people to attend worship in white residential areas. It was, in fact, an attempt to force apartheid upon the churches whether they liked it or not. There was an outcry from all the English-speaking churches as well as the Roman Catholics, and even the NGK was perturbed. Several church leaders, including Archbishop Clayton, called on their clergy to disobey the law. Eventually the Act became law, but its effect was minimal.[61] If anything, it had created a new unity amongst the English-speaking churches in opposing the government and, for the first time, led the Roman Catholic Church to cooperate ecumenically in protest against the government.[62] Indeed, 1957 marked a significant change in the Roman Catholic approach to the state and to apartheid. During that year, and in anticipation of a later debate, Archbishop Whelan of Bloemfontein declared that apartheid was nothing less than a heresy,[63] and the 'Statement on Apartheid'[64] issued by the hierarchy indicated that the more progressive bishops had finally taken the lead, recognising that the time for prevarication had passed.[65]

Sharpeville, Cottesloe, and 'The Message'

Black resistance to apartheid gained fresh momentum when the newly formed Pan Africanist Congress (PAC), a breakaway from the ANC led by a Methodist lay preacher, Robert Sobukwe, initiated the Anti-Pass Law campaign in the late 1950s. In the course of a protest march on the police station at Sharpeville on 21 March 1960, sixty-nine blacks, mainly women, were shot by the police. This massacre raised international anti-apartheid consciousness to a new level, and led to the gradual isolation of South Africa from the world arena. In the post-Sharpeville state of emergency thousands of blacks were arrested, many banned, and many went into exile. The ANC and PAC were banned in 1960 and forced underground,[66] and a year later the armed struggle was initiated by the ANC (*uMkhonto weSizwe*) and PAC (*Poqo*). White morale was at an all-time low as the economy plummeted, and increasing numbers of whites left the country.

Whereas the 'church clause' had evoked heated church reaction, Sharpeville required prompt action. Archbishop Joost de Blank, successor to Clayton, demanded that the World Council of Churches expel the Cape and Transvaal NGK Synods from membership for the sake of the future of Christianity in the country. The WCC refused to take such action but helped to organise a conference of all its South African member churches. The Cottesloe Consultation held in Johannesburg in December 1960 was one of the most significant events in the history of the church in South Africa. Eighty delegates of the South African member churches of the WCC, including eighteen black participants, debated their response to apartheid and, with the exception of the Nederduitsch Hervormde Kerk delegates, reached consensus. The Cottesloe Statement was not a radical document; it certainly did not go as far as the black and some English-speaking delegates wanted, but it did challenge the fundamental basis of apartheid.[67] Moreover, it had the support of the NGK delegates. Tragically, political pressure from Prime Minister Hendrik Verwoerd led to the rejection of Cottesloe by the NGK synods which met shortly afterwards, and in 1961, at the Third Assembly of the WCC held in New Delhi, the Cape and Transvaal Synods withdrew their membership. Thus began a process in which the NGK first isolated itself from the world-wide ecumenical community, and was later in turn excluded from participation.

Ecumenical relations between the English-speaking churches, especially the Congregational, Methodist and Presbyterian (PCSA), had grown considerably since the end of the Second World War, despite ongoing division and even competition between them. In 1947 these churches had cooperated in the establishment at Rhodes University of the first ecumenical Faculty of Divinity, though government policy insisted that it was confined to whites only and the churches had acquiesced. Ecumenical cooperation in black theological education had been in progress at Lovedale Bible Institute since 1885 and then, from 1920, at Fort Hare University. But the government take-over of Fort Hare in 1959, as well as its legislative action against other theological institutions, led the Methodists, Presbyterians, Congregationalists and Anglicans to establish the Federal Theological Seminary (FEDSEM) in 1960 at Alice near the Fort Hare campus for the training of black clergy.[68] The scandalous expropriation of the Alice FEDSEM campus by the government in 1975 led to the eventual establishment of its campus at Imbali near Pietermaritzburg. FEDSEM tragically closed in 1993.

As a direct consequence of the back-tracking of the NGK after Cottesloe, and the withdrawal of the NGK from ecumenical participation and contact, Beyers Naudé, moderator of the NGK Southern Transvaal Synod and a delegate at Cottesloe, established the Christian Institute of Southern Africa (CI) in 1963. Though its scope soon broadened, the initial aim of the CI was to provide ecumenical support for dissident NGK members and ministers in opposing apartheid and in furthering the Cottesloe resolutions. A further consequence of Cottesloe was the strengthening of ecumenical relations between the other participating churches. This found expression primarily through the Christian Council of South Africa, which began to take on a new lease of life. Both the CI and the Christian Council were, however, dominated by whites. Indeed, at this stage there were virtually no blacks in positions of national leadership within the structures of the English-speaking churches. The first black bishop within the Anglican Church, Alphaeus Zulu, became suffragan bishop of Zululand in 1960, the first black president of the Methodist Church, the Rev. Seth Mokitimi, was only elected in 1964, and as late as 1972 only one of the twenty-three Roman Catholic bishops was black. And, as in the case of the English-speaking churches, the theological education of Catholic priests was still largely segregated throughout the 1970s.

Two major international ecumenical events of the 1960s had a decisive impact on the church situation in South Africa. The first was the Second Vatican Council (1962–5), the second the Geneva Conference on Church and Society sponsored by the WCC in 1966. Vatican II brought the Roman Catholic Church in South Africa into much more direct contact with the English-speaking churches, and some dialogue began even with the NGK. Catholic observers now attended meetings of the Christian Council, thus strengthening the anti-apartheid ecumenical cause. Vatican II, in continuity with a growing social awareness this century within the Roman Catholic Church, encouraged a far stronger commitment to social justice than previously. This found expression in a succession of Pastoral Letters issued by the Catholic bishops in South Africa on matters relating to apartheid, though Catholic ability to implement resolutions was generally no better than in the case of other churches.

The Geneva Conference on Church and Society took an even more radical position than Vatican II, calling on Christians to participate directly in the struggle for justice in situations of oppression and revolution. It also led directly to the establishment of the WCC's Programme to Combat Racism (PCR), which was to have a decisive impact on the church situation in South Africa. Two of the South African participants, Anglican bishop Bill Burnett, newly appointed General Secretary of the Christian Council, and Beyers Naudé, returned home with a renewed commitment to the ecumenical struggle against apartheid. A series of conferences were held throughout the country to discuss the issues raised in Geneva and to plan the church's role. One result of this process was the drafting of what became known as *The Message to the People of South Africa.*[69]

In 1967 the Christian Council changed its name to the South African Council of Churches (SACC), and a year later, in cooperation with the CI, *The Message* was published. The central theme of *The Message* was the rejection of apartheid as a false gospel. There was immediate and bitter reaction to *The Message* from the government and its supportive churches. But in due course, and with some reservation, the English-speaking and the Roman Catholic churches endorsed *The Message*, as did several thousand individuals. The Baptist Union, which had distanced itself from the Council's growing political involvement for some years, reacted by resigning its membership and becoming an observer. This status was relinquished a few years later during the controversy on conscientious objection.

The Message initiated a new phase in the church struggle. The establishment of the Study Project on Christianity in Apartheid Society (SPROCAS) and related programmes of action, sponsored jointly by the CI and SACC, sought ways of implementing *The Message* within the various facets of South African life. Many of the ideas which were to be embodied later in political developments can be traced to SPROCAS.[70]

During the 1960s leaders within the SACC and the CI also became increasingly aware of the significance of the rapidly growing African Independent churches, and steps were taken to include them within the broader ecumenical movement. The CI in particular helped to establish the African

Independent Churches Association (AICA), as well as a theological college at Lovedale in the Eastern Cape. While these projects soon ran into considerable difficulties, they began a process whereby at least some of the indigenous churches began to cooperate with one other in new ways and have contact with the wider church. Although the Ethiopian-type churches provided much of the leadership, growth was particularly noticeable amongst the Zionists, who stayed outside AICA. The largest of the Independent churches, the Zionist Christian Church, whose strongly disciplined membership had reached several million by 1970, and the Nazarite Church founded in Natal by Isaiah Shembe, also remained distinct and separate.

Just as their origins were distinct, so the Zionists developed a very different ethos from that of the Ethiopians. Whereas the Ethiopian-type churches kept closely to the theology and practice of the missions from which they originally seceded, the Zionists synthesised Christianity and African tradition more fully. Moreover, while Ethiopianism was a largely black middle-class protest movement, Zionism was an adaptation of Christianity to the needs of an impoverished proletariat.[71] Avoiding any direct political involvement, and placing their major emphasis on a ministry of healing, they eventually outstripped the Ethiopian churches in growth and vigour.

While ecumenical cooperation in the sixties focused on the struggle against apartheid, there were also moves to foster church union. In 1967 the United Congregational Church of Southern Africa was formed out of the Congregational Union, the Bantu Congregational Church (formerly the American Board Mission) and the churches of the London Missionary Society (largely in Botswana and Zimbabwe). A far more ambitious attempt at church union was that which led the Anglican, Congregational, Methodist and Presbyterian churches (three Presbyterian churches were involved: the Presbyterian Church of Southern Africa, the Bantu Presbyterian Church, and the Tsonga Presbyterian Church) to form the Church Unity Commission (CUC) in 1967. The work of the CUC resulted in considerable ecumenical cooperation, including the establishment of united parishes and congregations as well as intercommunion. The goal of union remained elusive, however, because of the apathy of many church members and considerable opposition from denominational loyalists, but also because many blacks felt that church union was not a priority at the time. An attempt to unite the three Presbyterian churches faltered in 1971 largely because leaders in the two black churches felt uneasy about uniting with the PCSA, in which white members formed a majority. Negotiations between the PCSA and the United Congregational Church, which were re-started at this time after several attempts earlier in the century, also failed to produce a united church a decade later.

There was considerable growth during this period within the Pentecostal denominations in South Africa, as elsewhere in the world. Estimates are that by 1980 almost a quarter of the South African population was either Pentecostal or Zionist.[72] By 1973, for example, the membership of the black Apostolic Faith Mission in Africa numbered almost four hundred thousand.[73] The Assemblies of God, like the AFM, developed along segregated lines. Though its white membership grew rapidly, its real numerical strength was within the black population. While the Full Gospel Church also grew numerically and separately within each racial group, its most notable success was amongst the Indian population in Natal where they numbered far more than any other denomination.[74] The Pentecostal churches had extensive Bible-training programmes which reached tens of thousands of black church leaders and preachers, many of them becoming pastors in African Independent churches. In fact, Pentecostal influence also led to the emergence of a third strand amongst the African indigenous churches alongside the Ethiopian and Zionist, namely the Evangelical–Pentecostals.[75] While the Pentecostal Bible-training courses made little attempt to relate the biblical message to the major social and political issues facing South Africa, some young black Pentecostals were soon to be decisively affected by the eruption of black student protest which shook South Africa to the core in 1976.

Black consciousness, theology and resistance

If the first phase in the church struggle against apartheid was initiated by white leaders within the English-speaking and Roman Catholic churches, and ecumenically by the SACC and the CI, the next phase came as the result of a black political renaissance in the form of the Black Consciousness Movement (BCM).[76] Black Consciousness was inspired in part by similar developments in the United States. But far more, it was a black student response both to the intensification of apartheid repression and to the vacuum in black resistance politics which had followed the banning of the ANC and PAC. Ironically it emerged on the campuses of the black 'tribal' university colleges, which had been established by the government as a means of furthering its Bantu Education apartheid policies.

At the heart of Black Consciousness lay the conviction that white liberals, who had spoken on behalf of blacks especially since the banning of the ANC and PAC, could not truly represent the oppressed. Blacks had to take the initiative and direct their own struggle for freedom. This led black students to withdraw from the liberal National Union of South African Students (NUSAS) and form SASO, the South African Students' Organisation in 1969, with Steve Biko as its first president. The birth of SASO can be traced back to the emergence of a black caucus at the national conference of the University Christian Movement (UCM) held the previous year in Stutterheim.[77] Many BCM leaders were theological students or ordained ministers, or at least had some contact with the church.

The UCM was an ecumenical alternative to the segregated and theologically conservative Student Christian Association, the main student Christian organisation on university campuses in South Africa. Originally the SCA was multi-racial, but pressure from the NGK in the late 1950s and early 1960s led to its fragmentation along language and ethnic lines. As a result, the SCA catered for white English-speaking students, with parallel organisations for Afrikaners, blacks (SCM) and other groups. When the World Students' Christian Federation (WSCF) demanded that the SCA adopt a stronger stand against apartheid, the SCA refused and thus forfeited its membership in 1964. A few years later it adopted a conservative evangelical statement of faith. As a result of these developments, the English-speaking churches found it difficult to identify with the SCA and sought to establish an ecumenical student movement. In this they were overtaken by more progressive Christian students themselves, who took the initiative and, with the cautious blessing of the churches, established the UCM in 1967. Within a short time the majority of its membership was black and located on the campuses of the ethnic university colleges.

During the next few years the UCM lost the support of the churches as it adopted an increasingly radical style of life, worship and theology. While the UCM pioneered feminist forms of theology, its main contribution lay in the development of Black Theology. Inspired by the writings of the North American James Cone,[78] the General Secretary of the UCM, Basil Moore, and other members developed the Black Theology Project. Its aim was to stimulate theological reflection on the basis of the black experience of suffering, oppression and struggle. New black theological voices began to articulate a theology of protest against apartheid which was strikingly different from that of the liberal message of their churches.[79] In a scathing attack on the white-dominated multi-racial churches, Steve Biko, a Catholic and executive member of UCM, argued that despite their criticism of apartheid they had tacitly accepted the *status quo* and adapted themselves to the South African way of life.[80]

In 1971 the WCC launched its controversial Programme to Combat Racism (PCR). Central to the PCR was its grants to liberation movements struggling against racism in various parts of the world, notably in Southern Africa – the ANC, PAC, Frelimo (Mozambique), ZANU and ZAPU (Zimbabwe), and SWAPO (Namibia). The launching of the PCR and the announcement of its grants to liberation movements in Southern Africa caused considerable and ongoing controversy in South Africa. Generally speaking, blacks enthusiastically welcomed the PCR's programme while whites rejected it. This polarised reaction created serious tension within the churches, exacerbated by government propaganda which pressurised the churches to withdraw from the world body. Despite this pressure, none did so, but their ambiguous synodical statements reflected the conflict within their ranks. The PCR was to remain a contentious issue until well into the 1980s.

More and more, white Christians in the English-speaking churches found themselves on the defensive, forced into accepting decisions which alienated them from the wider white society. In response some members joined more conservative denominations, others turned towards an apolitical charismatic spirituality, and yet others, if they happened to be more liberal or progressive, looked for ways to identify with the black struggle. But such identification could no longer be paternalistic; the agenda was being set by blacks. There was some positive, though usually ambiguous, reaction by the churches to the radical challenge which Black Theology and the PCR presented. In 1972 the Roman Catholic hierarchy issued its *Call to Conscience*, and similar statements emanated from the SACC and its member churches. Most significantly, however, there was now an awakening of awareness amongst blacks within the churches, who began to determine policy and claim positions of leadership.

During the 1960s a remarkable phenomenon emerged within the 'mainline' churches throughout the world. Named the neo-Pentecostal or 'charismatic movement',[81] it began in the United States but soon penetrated South Africa and spread widely amongst ministers and lay people alike, particularly within the white and 'coloured' constituencies of the major denominations. While some members left their churches to join Pentecostal denominations, and others left later to form new independent charismatic-type congregations, the majority stayed within their own churches. By the 1970s there were significant charismatic groups within the Anglican, Methodist, Presbyterian, Roman Catholic, Baptist and Congregational churches and even some within the NGK. The charismatic movement was strengthened greatly when Bill Burnett, the Anglican bishop of Grahamstown and, later, archbishop of Cape Town, together with several other bishops, became part of the movement. Various reasons have been given for the emergence of the charismatic movement. One, to which we have already alluded, is that it was a negative reaction to the social and political activism of the mainline churches. Thus, while it had a significant impact upon the life and worship of many congregations, it also led to a spirituality of withdrawal from socio-political involvement, as well as to dissension and the formation of independent charismatic churches.

Charismatics together with conservative evangelicals in a variety of denominations concentrated their attention on evangelism and church growth, and generally stood apart from ecumenical cooperation, especially in the political arena. Although claiming political neutrality, white charismatics and evangelicals usually supported the *status quo* while blacks patiently accepted their oppression. In 1973 an attempt was made to relate 'evangelicals' and 'ecumenicals' at the Congress on Mission and Evangelism held in Durban, and to enable them to integrate their respective concerns. Jointly sponsored by the SACC and Africa Enterprise (an evangelistic organisation founded in the mid-1960s by an Anglican evangelical, Michael Cassidy),[82] the Congress brought together a wide range of church groups in the country, including Pentecostals and Roman Catholics, to address the issues facing the church. Although the Congress became an important milestone in preparing the way for future relations between groups that had previously not met together, it also revealed the extent of racial and theological polarisation. This was demonstrated in the response of many whites to black theologian Manas Buthelezi's address entitled 'Six Theses on Evangelism in the South African Context'.[83] Buthelezi argued that the time had arrived for blacks to take the initiative in the life of the church and in the church struggle against apartheid. Indeed, he declared, it was now necessary for blacks to evangelise whites and enable them to be set free from their racism.

Although there were members of the NGK present at the Congress, the Afrikaans Reformed churches officially refused to participate. A year later, in 1974, at its General Synod, the NGK continued to provide theological legitimation to government policy in its report on 'Human Relations in the Light of

Scripture'. The NGK believed that this report signalled an important reform-ist development in its understanding of the South African situation. While it did mark some progress, it was yet again an endorsement of government apartheid policies as these had developed at the time. Furthermore, it con-tinued to base its support for apartheid on dubious biblical foundations.[84] Any lingering hopes that the NGK could provide a prophetic lead in the struggle for justice and human rights were dashed.

When the SACC National Conference met at Hammanskraal in 1974 there was a mood of desperation in the air. Every attempt to resist apartheid by the BCM, the CI and SACC, as well as by the churches, had been severely coun-tered by state security action. Many church people had been arrested, banned or deported. Apartheid legislation was being implemented ruthlessly and speedily. To make matters worse, South Africa was already involved in action against SWAPO in Namibia and was about to become embroiled in the civil war in Angola, and was in the process of becoming heavily militarised. Dele-gates to the conference knew that the pot was boiling in the black townships and was going to burst sooner rather than later, with terrible effect.

In trying to determine what response white Christians could make to the growing conflict, some white delegates focused their attention on the issue of conscientious objection to military service. This was not an issue that directly affected blacks, simply because they were not subject to the draft. But it was a direct challenge to the moral authority and legitimacy of the state, and to the patriotic assumptions of most whites.[85] In adopting its controversial Resolu-tion on Conscientious Objection, in which it was argued that the war in Namibia was an unjust war and that Christians had an obligation not to par-ticipate in it, the member churches of the SACC were once more faced with a controversy which radically divided their constituencies and brought the wrath of the government upon their heads. By far the majority of white South Africans were supportive of the government and the military, whereas the majority of blacks opposed the war. Throughout the ensuing years this issue remained a major point of contention, heightened by the fact that increasing numbers of young people, both Christian and others, went to jail for their convictions.

A watershed in the struggle against apartheid was reached with the student uprising in 1976. This began in Soweto, strongly influenced by the BCM and SASO, and rapidly spread throughout the country. The immediate cause of the uprising was Bantu Education, but the real target was the whole edifice of apartheid. Within a matter of days South Africa was yet again plunged into social turmoil, and the hopes of many blacks, which had been shattered after Sharpeville and the banning of the ANC and PAC, were revived. Soweto marked the beginning of a new era in black resistance as a whole. Between five and seven thousand radicalised young black people went into exile, many of them committed to the armed struggle, and international pressure on South Africa began to increase significantly. Within the country a new generation of black leaders began to emerge, some of them with strong church connections. The churches in Soweto and other black townships often fulfilled a crucial, though sometimes reluctant, supportive role in the uprising, and as casualties mounted, funeral services became religio-political events in which the churches and community organisations cooperated. This marked the beginning of a new phase of church involvement in the struggle within the black community, which was to continue through the years ahead. It must continually be recognised that from the beginning of the apartheid era, the majority of Christians in South Africa were black and therefore the victims of government policy. Thus, while powerful sections of the church were compromised, the vast majority of church members suffered as a result of apartheid policies, and many died in the process.

Although the SACC filled an increasingly important role in support of black interests, a more radical part was played by the Christian Institute. From the time of *The Message* (1968) and the emergence of the BCM, the CI had consciously identified itself with black resistance.[86] This was at considerable cost: both the NGK and the government turned the screws on Beyers Naudé and his staff. Eventually, in the aftermath of the Soweto uprising and the murder of Steve Biko by the police in September 1977, the CI and its leadership, along with SASO and the Black People's Convention, were banned.

Soweto was the prelude to more than a decade of intensifying black resistance, state repression, church–state conflict, and struggle between reactionary and progressive groups within the churches. During this period the Afrikaans Reformed churches continued to consolidate and rationalise their support for apartheid and government policy,[87] while the English-speaking and Roman Catholic churches, torn apart by the conflict between white and black interests, sought ways to speak and act more prophetically.

In 1976 the Roman Catholic bishops decided to integrate their schools, and in February the next year, in calling for the fundamental restructuring of society, they affirmed that in the struggle for justice they were 'on the side of the oppressed', and committed themselves 'to working for peace through justice in fraternal collaboration with all other churches, agencies and persons dedicated to this cause'.[88] At the same time the bishops issued a 'Declaration of Commitment on Social Justice and Race Relations within the Church', which tackled the whole problem of racial injustice within the life of the church itself.[89]

While church opposition to the government was also voiced by the member churches of the SACC in a plethora of synodical and conference resolutions, this increasingly became the domain of the Council, especially after the banning of the CI and the appointment of the Anglican bishop Desmond Tutu as the SACC General Secretary in 1978. By this time the predominantly black staff of the Council had grown considerably, and its programmes had diversified and extended to meet the urgent needs created by apartheid and the struggle against it. Moreover, the SACC took the lead in calling for an intensification of international sanctions against South Africa as the only peaceful strategy remaining in the struggle against apartheid. All of this meant that the SACC was continually under state surveillance and regularly the target of state security action.

Throughout this period it became clear that the church in South Africa was divided not only into different denominations, or divided by race, or by the traditional separation of the Afrikaans and English-speaking churches, but by different perceptions of social reality and different understandings of the task of the church. While the SACC and other more progressive Christian organisations confronted the state and the structures of apartheid prophetically, other initiatives concentrated on the renewal of the church and on programmes of evangelism and reconciliation. There were also right-wing Christian organisations which vociferously attacked progressive church leaders, the SACC and its member churches as communist, and which did everything possible to undermine their witness. The Information Scandal, which rocked South Africa in 1978, revealed that several of these right-wing groups had been funded by the state.

In 1979, in continuity with the Congress on Mission and Evangelism held in Durban in 1973, Africa Enterprise made a further attempt to bring the various church constituencies together at the South African Christian Leadership Assembly (SACLA) held in Pretoria that July. More than six thousand Christians from a vast array of cultural, language and denominational backgrounds met to consider ways of responding to the crisis in the country. SACLA undoubtedly made an important contribution to the life and witness of the church. Indeed, partly in reaction to the dominant role played by charismatics and conservative evangelicals, it helped generate a more radical evangelical witness especially amongst student participants. Like the Durban Congress, SACLA revealed the extent to which the church had become even more polarised by politics and especially by the question of appropriate political action. For some, the way to overcome apartheid was by a gradual process of changing people's hearts and minds through spiritual conversion and the renewal of the church; for others, apartheid had to be opposed by direct political action and, if need be, by participation in African nationalist armed struggle, which, since the Soweto uprising, had taken on new vigour.

Apartheid as a heresy

Like the NGK, the Lutheran churches in Southern Africa had developed into segregated synods. Several black synods, largely ethnic in composition, emanated from a variety of European Lutheran missions, and a white, predominantly German-speaking synod embraced settler congregations. In 1966 the Federation of Evangelical Lutheran Churches of Southern Africa (FELCSA) was established to bring Lutherans together, though white Lutherans remained outside or on the periphery. Subsequent attempts were made to create a united Lutheran church, but after long and protracted negotiations the white synod voted to stay out. In 1975 the black synods could wait no longer, and united to form the Evangelical Lutheran Church of Southern Africa (ELCSA).

The failure of white Lutherans to reject apartheid structures was foremost in the minds of the South African delegates to the Lutheran World Federation (LWF) meeting in Dar es Salaam in 1977. Together with the post-Soweto crisis in the country, this led Manas Buthelezi, now a bishop within ELCSA, to argue that a *status confessionis* had arisen in South Africa.[90] This Reformation insight meant that a stage had been reached where the church had to reject apartheid not only as sinful but as a heresy which undermined Christian faith at its core. There could be no compromise or cooperation with apartheid, least of all in the structures of the church. Consequently, the white Lutheran synod could no longer be part of the LWF or in fellowship with ELCSA.

Although racism was most obvious in the structures of the Afrikaans Reformed churches, and demonstrated in the failure of white and black Lutherans to achieve unity, it also prevailed in most other denominations as well. Methodists, though claiming to be 'one and undivided', had been trying for several years to establish geographical circuits which would bring white and black congregations together, and while some success was achieved there was considerable opposition from both sides. In the meantime the SACC, now under the leadership of Bishop Desmond Tutu, was fully identified with the black struggle for liberation, and it provided the prophetic leadership which was too often lacking within the churches themselves. In February 1980 the SACC convened a Consultation on Racism at Hammanskraal, which in turn issued an ultimatum to 'all white Christians to demonstrate their willingness to purge the church of racism'. The black delegates went on to declare that 'if after a period of twelve months there is no evidence of repentance shown in concrete action, the black Christians will have no alternative but to witness to the Gospel of Jesus Christ *by becoming a confessing church*'.[91]

The formation of a black confessing church was a logical outcome of Black Theology, but it did not come about in precisely the way proposed at Hammanskraal. Instead, a 'black church' within the churches had emerged which increasingly united black Christians and theologians across denominations in a common struggle against apartheid in society as well as in their respective denominations. Indicative of such developments was the birth of the Alliance of Black Reformed Christians in South Africa (ABRECSA) in 1981. ABRECSA took up the *status confessionis* issue originally raised by black Lutherans and ensured that it was on the agenda of the World Alliance of Reformed Churches (WARC) meeting in Ottawa, Canada, the following year.[92]

During the 1970s the relationship between the NGK and its so-called daughter churches (NG Sendingkerk, NG Kerk in Afrika, and the Reformed Church in Africa) became a significant issue. Whereas previously the 'daughter' churches had been relatively content with their status, the situation now began to change dramatically. In 1975 the NG Kerk in Afrika became an observer member of the SACC, to be followed by the Sendingkerk in 1978 and the Reformed Church in Africa in 1980. This was a rejection not only of the paternalistic control of the NGK, but also of its alignment with government policy. Of crucial importance in these unfolding events was the role played by Dr Allan Boesak, who was elected moderator of the WARC at its Assembly in Ottawa in 1982.

Relations between the NG black churches and the NGK came to a head when the WARC resolved to suspend the membership of both the NGK and the Nederduitsch Hervormde Kerk.[93] While the Hervormde church subsequently withdrew its membership rather than change its 'whites only' church policy, there was more at stake in the case of the NGK. The NGK had become increasingly isolated from the ecumenical church since its rejection of Cottesloe in 1961 and because of its ongoing legitimation of apartheid. From an NGK perspective, however, all was well as long as Afrikanerdom retained its monolithic unity. This situation was soon to change with the advent of P. W. Botha to power in 1978. From the beginning Botha's policy was determined by a concern to consolidate power while at the same time widening his power-base and improving international relations. As previously, the NGK tried to keep in step with state policy, and therefore it now sought to strengthen its ecumenical relations and play down its theological legitimation of apartheid. Ottawa was therefore a set-back leading to even further isolation.

Later, in 1982 the NG Sendingkerk synod took a major step in response to the *status confessionis* by drafting *The Belhar Confession,* in which the unity of the church was confessed over against apartheid. *The Belhar Confession,* finally adopted in 1986, was an historic document.[94] Not only was it the first time since the Reformation period that a Dutch Reformed church had adopted a new confession, but it was also a confession which made ethical commitment to justice central to Christian faith and church unity. The legitimation of apartheid by those within the NG family of churches was no longer tenable; it had finally lost any moral or theological grounding which it had previously claimed. Moreover, the black NG churches had now established their own identity over against the NGK. No longer were they 'daughter' churches; they, rather than the white NGK, were setting the pace and the agenda.

Quite apart from the challenge which the black NG churches and the WARC now presented to the NGK, the NGK had to reckon with a major rift within Afrikanerdom brought to a head by Botha's 'reformist' policies. This was exacerbated by the government's decision to change the constitution and establish a tricameral parliament in which whites, 'coloureds' and Indians, but not blacks, would participate. Even though whites would retain control, this move was too much for a significant section of Afrikanerdom. Thus the Conservative Party (CP) was launched in 1983 under the leadership of Dr Andries Treurnicht. Treurnicht had long represented the right-wing of the National Party and the NGK. As an NGK minister he was responsible for the break-up of the SCA years previously; as editor of the NGK's mouthpiece, *Die Kerkbode,* he had kept the church faithful to the policies of apartheid; as a Cabinet Minister, he was largely responsible for the mishandling of education in Soweto, which sparked off the uprising in 1976; and now, with considerable support from within the NGK, he led the break-up of the National Party in defence of apartheid. All of a sudden the unity of the NGK was threatened as never before, as its members and ministers were forced to take different political sides. This led to a growing reluctance of the NGK to commit itself on social and political issues in a way contrary to the principled position it had previously adopted in its promotion of apartheid legislation. At its General

Synod in 1986 the NGK finally gave up the attempt to provide biblical and theological justification to apartheid in its report entitled *Church and Society* (*Kerk en Samelewing*).[95]

While the tensions within Afrikanerdom and the NGK signalled the beginning of the end of Afrikaner unity in church and state, the reaction to the Botha 'tricameral reforms' from the black oppressed and the more progressive sections of the population was even more vociferous and significant. Botha's reforms were a patently obvious attempt to retain control by broadening his political power-base amongst 'people of colour' and gain much-needed diplomatic and economic help. But his plans badly misfired. In 1983 the United Democratic Front was launched, and South African politics entered a new phase of resistance and repression. Botha's 'reformist' plans now became secondary to the massive strengthening of state security in the struggle against the revolutionary 'total onslaught', which it was claimed was threatening to destroy the country.

End of the old order, beginning of the new

The escalation of resistance and repression in protest against the government's new constitution overtook the 'apartheid is a heresy' debate. The church struggle now became focused specifically on the struggle for the liberation of South Africa.[96] Central issues of church debate and action were international pressure through sanctions and disinvestment, and participation in revolutionary violence and the armed struggle.[97] During 1985–6, as the war in Angola and Namibia was intensifying, a new wave of resistance and protest erupted in the black townships, often spearheaded by the trade unions. The government responded by declaring states of emergency (the second of which, declared on 21 July 1985, lasted until Botha's demise) and used its massive security power to crush all opposition at enormous cost. An undeclared civil war was in progress, forcing Christians and the churches to indicate clearly where they stood.

Christian leaders such as Desmond Tutu (who became archbishop of Cape Town in 1986) and Allan Boesak, who, together with Archbishop Denis Hurley, were patrons of the UDF, played a crucial leadership role in the absence of recognised black political leaders. On 16 June 1986, the tenth anniversary of the Soweto uprising, the SACC called on the churches to pray for the end to unjust rule.[98] In its rationale for this call, it declared:

> The considered judgement of every synod, assembly and conference of the Roman Catholic and mainline Protestant Churches (with the exception of the Afrikaans Reformed Churches), has been that the present regime, together with its structures of domination, stands in contradiction to the Christian Gospel to which the churches of the land seek to remain faithful. We have continually prayed for the authorities, that they may govern wisely and justly. Now, in solidarity with those who suffer most, in this hour of crisis we pray that God in His grace may remove from His

people the tyrannical structures of oppression and the present rulers in our country who persistently refuse to heed the cry for justice, as reflected in the Word of God as proclaimed through His Church within this land and beyond.[99]

Despite white apathy within the churches to this call, there was widespread response. In retrospect it was a decisive moment in the church struggle. The SACC had now publicly declared the state to be a 'tyrannical regime' and prayed for its removal. The die was cast. It was in this context that the internationally celebrated *Kairos Document* was published by the Institute for Contextual Theology (ICT).[100]

ICT had been formed in 1982 as a means of fostering the development of progressive or liberating theological responses to the unfolding social and political situation. Its first director, Frank Chikane, a minister of the Apostolic Faith Mission, had been in the forefront of black student politics since the Soweto uprising in the mid-1970s. Now, with his ministerial licence withdrawn by his own church because of his political activities, Chikane, together with Fr Albert Nolan, a Catholic theologian involved with ICT, became responsible for helping to formulate a theological response to the issues facing the church and society.

The Kairos Document was a response to the crisis situation which then prevailed in South Africa. At the heart of the crisis, as perceived by the 'Kairos theologians,' was the spiral of violence caused by years of unjust rule implemented by police and military force. Its dominant theme was the illegitimacy of the government in South Africa, indeed its tyrannical nature, which had to be resisted through acts of civil disobedience. While *The Kairos Document* did not overtly justify the armed liberation struggle, it was a radical rejection not only of the 'state theology' which supported the *status quo*, but also of the more liberal response to apartheid which had characterised the English-speaking churches through the years.

Government reaction to *The Kairos Document* was sharp and immediate. Many of its signatories were detained and suffered for their convictions. In countering its claims, the state once again worked in tandem with right-wing religious organisations which, despite the Information Scandal, continued to flourish.[101] Some of them even became involved in covert support for the Renamo movement, which, with the aid of the South African security forces, was involved in the destabilisation of Mozambique. *The Kairos Document* and those who supported it were dismissed as part of the anti-Christian revolutionary 'total onslaught' being waged against South Africa. In this way the government sought to regain its Christian legitimation and obtain the support of members within the English-speaking churches.

All of this heightened the tension within these churches that had been growing in pitch since the WCC initiated its Programme to Combat Racism, and widened the gulf between those who were committed to the struggle against apartheid and those who were supporters of the *status quo*. Indeed, the English-speaking churches found it difficult to accept the challenge presented to them by *The Kairos Document*, though some recognised the need to respond positively. The tendency within these churches was to identify more fully with the National Initiative of Reconciliation, which had been established to provide a 'third way' approach to the issues. But it was *The Kairos Document* which gave theological direction and impetus to those progressive political activists who were seeking to be Christian in the struggle against apartheid, including a growing number of 'radical evangelicals'.[102]

While the state of emergency enabled the government to keep a tight control on the security of the country, it was becoming clear that it could only continue to rule on this basis. The black townships were increasingly ungovernable, the economic situation in the country was critical, and the human, financial and diplomatic cost of the war in Angola was becoming unsustainable. The emergence of the Mass Democratic Movement, a broad alliance of progressive organisations, including church-related groups, which increasingly coordinated protest and resistance, indicated that the struggle against apartheid was reaching its climax. Despite efforts by the government to prop up its authority and maintain control, it was clear that it could not resist both internal and international pressure for much longer. Eventually State President Botha was forced to resign and was replaced by F. W. de Klerk in the closing months of 1989.

However history will finally evaluate the presidency of De Klerk, his speech in parliament on 2 February 1990 and especially the unbanning of the ANC, PAC and the South African Communist Party, and shortly thereafter the release of Nelson Mandela and other political prisoners, set in motion a train of events which were to transform the social and political life of South Africa. These events also brought about a change in the role of the churches and of church leaders in the political arena. The time had come to give way to political leaders who were released from prison or who returned from years of exile. Nonetheless, the churches continued to play a vital role, not least because of the eruption of violence which tore the townships apart during the ensuing months. Church leaders, particularly those whose anti-apartheid record was unquestioned, now found themselves in the forefront of efforts to mediate between warring factions.

Two events signalled the beginning of a new phase in the political involvement of the churches in South Africa. The first was the National Conference of Church Leaders held at Rustenburg in November 1990. This conference brought together leaders from across the whole spectrum of the church, from Roman Catholic to NGK and African Independent, from the English-speaking to the Pentecostal and independent charismatic churches. For the first time Christian leaders of such diversity, many of whom had been in strong political opposition to one another during previous years, sought to reach a common mind on the witness and role of the church in the shaping of a new South Africa. While tensions remained, the conference moved towards consensus on some key issues which had previously polarised the churches. This was reflected in *The Rustenburg Declaration*, which was adopted at the conclusion.[103]

The second significant event was the Consultation organised by the SACC and the WCC for their member churches and held in Cape Town in October 1991. This was the first time since the Cottesloe Consultation that a WCC delegation visited South Africa and that such a meeting was held. While it had been hoped that the Consultation might have coincided with the birth of a new South Africa, the political process, largely because of the violence wracking the country, had still not reached such a conclusion. But the fact that such a consultation was possible was a further sign that the end of apartheid was in sight.[104] It was also an indication of the need for the Christian church in South Africa to consider again its task in the building of a post-apartheid nation, and of expressing its own unity.

As the twentieth century enters its final decade, it is sobering to recall that the century began with a war which tore the country apart, and that for the remainder of the century black South Africans increasingly suffered at the hands of white racism. For much of this period blacks struggled for political rights using non-violent means, but to no avail. In the end they were forced to embark on an armed struggle and on widespread mass political action aimed at overthrowing the state. Now apartheid as a legal system is at its end, but its legacy will continue to haunt all those who seek to build a new non-racial nation.

It is equally sobering to recall the ambiguous role which the church has played through these years in the fight for justice and equality. With this in mind, any hopes for the future must be qualified by caution, for there is no inevitable progress towards a truly reconciled new nation. Yet the Christian gospel remains a message of hope, and in its more faithful and better moments the church believes, lives and acts in the light of the coming of God's kingdom of justice and peace. In doing so, the church is called to continue its prophetic witness against everything which dehumanises society and destroys community, and at the same time to care for and uphold the rights of the victims and the poor. In this way alone will the church remain faithful to its task and play a major role in the twenty-first century. It is safe to assume, however, that just as the church in South Africa is very different in many ways from what it was at the beginning of the century, it will inevitably change significantly in the decades that lie ahead.

High on its agenda, as it seeks to participate in the creation of a new nation, will be the need not only to help overcome the legacy of apartheid but also to enable the creation of a non-sexist culture. Moreover, the church will have to come to terms with an increasingly plural society in which, while it may remain the majority religion, it will no longer necessarily have the same status or even influence as it has had since the beginning of the colonial era.

NOTES

1. Government census 1980. See J. J. Kritzinger, *'n Statistiese Beskrywing van die Godsdienstigte Verspreiding van die Bevolking van Suid-Afrika.* Pretoria: HSRC, 1984.

2. Christianity in South Africa in the twentieth century is a highly complex and differentiated subject. This chapter does not attempt to deal with it in all its manifold

variety but specifically in relation to this theme. For that reason, many developments in the life of the church and of particular denominations, which may have significance in other respects, have been omitted or are only referred to in passing.

3. For a periodic typology of Christian resistance in South Africa see James Cochrane, 'Christian Resistance to Apartheid: Periodisation, Prognosis' in Martin Prozesky (ed.), *Christianity in South Africa*. London: Macmillan, 1990, p. 93.

4. See G. C. Cuthbertson, 'The Nonconformist Conscience and the South African War, 1899–1902'. Doctoral dissertation, University of South Africa, 1986.

5 Peter Walshe, *The Rise of African Nationalism in South Africa*. Berkeley: University of California Press, 1971, pp. 19f.

6. T. Karis and G. Carter (eds.), *From Protest to Challenge: A Documentary History of African Politics in South Africa 1882–1964*, vol. 1. *Protest and Hope, 1882–1964*. Stanford, Calif.: Hoover Institution Press, 1993, p. 18.

7. See Walshe, *Rise of African Nationalism*, p. 7f.

8. See Charles Villa-Vicencio, *Civil Disobedience and Beyond: Law, Resistance and Religion in South Africa*. Cape Town: David Philip, 1990, p. 2.

9. *Ibid.*, p. 14.

10. Bengt G. M. Sundkler, *Bantu Prophets in South Africa*. London: Lutterworth, 1948, pp. 38f.

11. Karis and Carter, *Protest and Hope*, p. 7.

12. South African Native Affairs Commission, 1903–5, p. 67.

13. See James Cochrane, *Servants of Power: The Role of English-speaking Churches 1903–1930*. Johannesburg: Ravan, 1987, p. 65.

14. B. G. M. Sundkler, *Zulu Zion and Some Swazi Zionists*. Oxford: Oxford University Press, 1976, p. 43.

15. André Odendaal, *Vukani Bantu! The Beginnings of Black Protest Politics in South Africa to 1912*. Cape Town: David Philip, 1984, p. 9.

16. *Ibid.*, pp. 82f.

17. Leo Kuper, 'African Nationalism in South Africa, 1910–1964', in Monica Wilson and Leonard Thompson (eds.), *The Oxford History of South Africa*, vol. 2. Oxford: Clarendon Press, 1971, pp. 433f.

18. Report of Synod in the *Provincial Synod Scrapbooks, 1898–1904 Synods*.

19. By 'English-speaking churches' is meant those churches of Anglo-Saxon origin, for whom English is the main language of discourse, even though it is not the first language of the majority of members. The main English-speaking churches in South Africa are the Anglican (Church of the Province), United Congregational, Methodist, and Presbyterian who have forged a common identity during the twentieth century. The Baptist Union has located itself on the periphery of this grouping. There are other English-speaking churches, such as the Church of England in South Africa and the Seventh Day Adventists, but these are not normally included within this designation. See John W. de Gruchy, *The Church Struggle in South Africa*. Grand Rapids: Eerdmans, and Cape Town: David Philip, second edition, 1986, pp. 85f.

20. The Afrikaans Reformed churches comprise the Nederduitse Gereformeerde Kerk (NGK), the Nederduitsch Hervormde Kerk, and the Gereformeerde Kerk. The largest of the three is the NGK, often referred to as the Dutch Reformed Church. The three churches refer to themselves collectively as 'sister churches'. See De Gruchy, *Church Struggle*, pp. 18f, 69f.

21. See for example Walter Carey, *Dutch and British in South Africa: An Appeal to the British Section*. Bloemfontein: Nasionale Pers, n.d.

22. C. Howard Hopkins, *John R. Mott: 1865–1955*. Grand Rapids: Eerdmans,

1979, p. 298.

23. See Kuper, 'African Nationalism', p. 434.

24. Walshe, *Rise of African Nationalism*, pp. 38, 158f.

25. *Ibid.*, p. 163.

26. *Ibid.*, p. 39.

27. Presidential Address to the Interdenominational African Ministers Federation of South Africa (IDAMASA), National Conference, Durban, 25 May 1950.

28. See, for example, the address on 'The Exclusion of the Bantu' by the Rev. Z. R. Mahabane, President of the Cape National Congress, 1921, in Karis and Carter, *Protest and Hope*, pp. 290ff.

29. D. D. T. Jabavu, 'Native Unrest ; Its Causes and Cure', in his *Papers and Addresses on Various Native Problems.* Lovedale Book Depot, 1920–1, p. 4f.

30. James S. Thaele, 'Christianity, Basis of Native Policy?', *Workers' Herald*, 21 December 1923, quoted in Karis and Carter, *Protest and Hope*, pp. 214f.

31. A full account of this event from the perspective of the authorities is given in the government Native Churches Commission Report, 1925, Section 2, which exonerated the police. For a very different black perspective see Z. K. Mahabane, 'The Evil Nature of the Colour Bar', Presidential Address delivered at the Annual Convention of the Native Congress, 18 May 1922.

32. Minutes of the South African Missionary Conference, 1921, p. 24. See *The Good Fight: Selected Speeches of Z. R. Mahabane.* Evanston: Program of African Studies, Northwestern University, n.d.

33. This is the major theme of Charles Villa-Vicencio, *Trapped in Apartheid.* New York: Orbis, 1988; see for example pp. 65ff.

34. Jabavu, 'Native Unrest', pp. 12f.

35. Irving Hexham, 'Religious Conviction or Political Tool? The Problem of Christian National Education', *Journal of Theology for Southern Africa*, 26 (March 1979).

36. T. Dunbar Moodie, *The Rise of Afrikanerdom: Power, Apartheid, and the Afrikaner Civil Religion.* Berkeley: University of California Press, 1975, pp. 22f.

37. F. A. van Jaarsveld, *The Afrikaner's Interpretation of South African History.* Cape Town: Simondium Publishers, 1964; Moodie, *Rise of Afrikanerdom*, chapters 1–2.

38. John W. de Gruchy, *Liberating Reformed Theology.* Grand Rapids: Eerdmans, and Cape Town: David Philip, 1991, pp. 21f.

39. Karis and Carter, *Protest and Hope*, Document 42b, pp. 233f.

40. C. R. de Wet, 'The Apostolic Faith Mission in South Africa, 1908–1980: A Case Study in Church Growth in a Segregated Society'. Ph.D. thesis, University of Cape Town, 1989.

41. Leslie A. Hewson, *An Introduction to South African Methodism.* Cape Town: Methodist Publishing House, 1950, p. 89.

42. Minutes of the Assembly, *Baptist Union Year Book*, 1932, p. 102.

43. Cochrane, *Servants of Power*, p. 133.

44. *Ibid.*, p. 183.

45. See E. Strassberger, *Ecumenism in South Africa: 1936–1960.* Johannesburg: SACC, 1974, pp. 157ff.

46. John W. de Gruchy, 'Catholics in a Calvinist Country', in Andrew Prior (ed.), *Catholics in Apartheid Society.* Cape Town: David Philip, 1982, pp. 74f.

47. *The Catholic Church and Southern Africa.* Cape Town: Catholic Archdiocese of Cape Town, 1951. For a summary of these developments see Garth Abraham, *The Catholic Church and Apartheid: The Response of the Catholic Church in South Africa to the*

First Decade of National Party Rule 1948–1957. Johannesburg: Ravan, 1989, pp. 3f.

48. Between 1911 and 1951 Roman Catholics increased by 378 per cent compared with the total population growth of 81 per cent.

49. See De Gruchy, *Church Struggle*, p. 55.

50. See Johann Kinghorn (ed.), *Die NG Kerk en Apartheid.* Johannesburg: Macmillan, 1986, pp. 90ff.

51. Abraham, *Catholic Church*, p. 26ff.

52. Michael E. Worsnip, *Between Two Fires: The Anglican Church and Apartheid, 1948–1957.* Pietermaritzburg: University of Natal Press, 1991, pp. 45f.

53. *Statement on the Present Non-European Passive Resistance Campaign*, October 1952. Mimeographed document.

54. Abraham, *Catholic Church*, pp. 49f.

55. See R. G. Clarke, 'For God or Caesar: An Historical Study of Christian Resistance to Apartheid by the Church of the Province of South Africa, 1946–1957'. Ph.D. thesis, University of Natal, 1983.

56. *Ibid.*, pp. 94ff.

57. See Trevor Huddleston, *Naught for Your Comfort.* London: Collins, 1956.

58. Abraham, *Catholic Church*, pp. 62ff.

59. See Thomas Karis, 'The Congress Movement', in Thomas Karis, Gwendolen M. Carter and Gail Gerhart (eds.), *From Protest to Challenge*, vol. 3. Stanford: Hoover Institution Press, 1977, p. 30.

60. See Charles Villa-Vicencio, *Trapped in Apartheid*, pp. 95–107.

61. De Gruchy, *Church Struggle*, pp. 60f.

62. Abraham, *Catholic Church*, p. 111.

63. *Ibid.*, p. 114.

64. De Gruchy and Villa-Vicencio, *Apartheid is a Heresy*, p. 144.

65. Abraham, *Catholic Church*, p. 116.

66. The South African Communist Party had disbanded shortly before the Suppression of Communism Act was passed by Parliament in 1950.

67. De Gruchy and Villa-Vicencio, *Apartheid is a Heresy*, pp. 148f.

68. On black theological education in South Africa see Simon Gqubule, 'An Examination of the Theological Education of Africans in the Presbyterian, Methodist, Congregational, and Anglican Churches in South Africa from 1860–1960'. Ph.D. thesis, Rhodes University, 1978.

69. De Gruchy, *Church Struggle*, pp. 115ff.

70. *Ibid.*, pp. 115f.

71. James Kiernan, 'African and Christian: From Opposition to Mutual Accommodation', in Prozesky, *Christianity in South Africa*, p. 23.

72. S. Grossmann, *Stewards of God's Grace.* Exeter: Paternoster, 1981, p. 39.

73. See De Wet, 'Apostolic Faith Mission'.

74. G. C. Oosthuizen, *Pentecostal Penetration into the Indian Community in Metropolitan Durban, South Africa.* Pretoria: HSRC, 1975; Gerald Pillay, 'A Historico-Theological Study of Pentecostalism as a Phenomenon within a South African Community'. Ph.D. thesis, Rhodes University, Grahamstown, 1983.

75. For a description of the various types of African Independent churches by a leader within the movement, see Paul Makhubu, *Who Are the Independent Churches?* Johannesburg: Skotaville, 1988, pp. 5ff.

76. See Robert Fatton, Jr., *Black Consciousness in South Africa: The Dialectics of Black Resistance to White Supremacy.* Albany: State University of New York Press, 1986; N. Barney Pityana, Mamphela Ramphele, Malusi Mpumlwana and Lindy Wil-

son (eds.), *Bounds of Possibility: The Legacy of Steve Biko and Black Consciousness.* Cape Town: David Philip, 1991.

77. On the connection between UCM and SASO see Basil Moore, 'Black Theology: In the Beginning', *Journal for the Study of Religion*, 4, 2 (1991), p. 23.

78. See Basil Moore (ed.), *The Challenge of Black Theology in South Africa.* Atlanta: John Knox, 1973. On the relationship between Black Theology in the United States and South Africa, see Dwight N. Hopkins, *Black Theology USA and South Africa: Politics, Culture, and Liberation.* New York: Orbis, 1989.

79. During the next two decades Black Theology developed in a variety of different ways. See for example, Itumuleng Mosala and Buti Tlhagale (eds.), *The Unquestionable Right to be Free.* Johannesburg: Skotaville, 1986.

80. S. Biko, 'The Church as Seen by a Young Layman', in A. Stubbs (ed.), *Steve Biko: I Write What I Like.* London: Bowerdean Press, 1978.

81. Richard Quebedeaux, *The New Charismatics.* New York: Doubleday, 1976; René Laurentin, *Catholic Pentecostalism.* London: Darton, Longman & Todd, 1977.

82. See Michael Cassidy, *The Passing Summer.* London: Hodder & Stoughton, 1989.

83. 'Six Theses on Evangelism', *Journal of Theology for Southern Africa*, 3 (June 1973), p. 55.

84. See De Gruchy, *Church Struggle*, pp. 70f; Douglas Bax, 'The Bible and Apartheid 2,' in De Gruchy and Villa-Vicencio, *Apartheid is a Heresy*, pp. 112f.

85. De Gruchy, *Church Struggle*, pp. 138f.

86. Peter Walshe, *Church Versus State in South Africa: The Case of the Christian Institute.* Maryknoll: Orbis, 1983.

87. Kinghorn, *NG Kerk*, pp. 117ff.

88. *The Bishops Speak*, vol. II, *Pastoral Letters and Statements 1967–1980.* Pretoria: SACBC, p. 41.

89. *Ibid.*, pp. 42f.

90. See De Gruchy and Villa-Vicencio, *Apartheid is a Heresy*, p. 160.

91. *Ecunews*, 27 February 1980, p. 11.

92. See De Gruchy and Villa-Vicencio, *Apartheid is a Heresy*, pp. 163ff.

93. *Ibid.*, pp. xvi, 172.

94. See G. D. Cloete and D. J. Smit (eds.), *A Moment of Truth: The Confession of the Dutch Reformed Mission Church 1982.* Grand Rapids: Eerdmans, 1984.

95. For a discussion of later developments within the NGK see Douglas Bax, 'The Vereeniging Consultation: A Perspective on What Happened', *Journal of Theology for Southern Africa*, 68 (September 1989); see also Johann Kinghorn, 'On the Theology of Church and Society in the NGK', *Journal of Theology for Southern Africa*, 70 (March 1990).

96. John W. de Gruchy, 'The Church and the Struggle for South Africa', in Buti Tlhagale and Itumuleng Mosala (eds.), *Hammering Swords into Ploughshares.* Johannesburg: Skotaville, 1986.

97. See Charles Villa-Vicencio (ed.), *Theology and Violence: The South African Debate.* Johannesburg: Skotaville, 1987.

98. See Allan Boesak and Charles Villa-Vicencio (eds.), *When Prayer Makes News.* Philadelphia: Westminster, 1986.

99. 'A Theological Rationale and a Call to Prayer for the End to Unjust Rule, 1985', in Charles Villa-Vicencio (ed.), *Between Christ and Caesar: Classic and Contemporary Texts on Church and State.* Grand Rapids: Eerdmans, 1986, p. 249.

100. *The Kairos Document: Challenge to the Church.* Johannesburg, Skotaville,

second edition, 1986.

101. *Journal of Theology for Southern Africa,* 69 (December 1989).

102. *Evangelical Witness in South Africa.* Dobsonville: Concerned Evangelicals, 1986.

103. Louw Alberts and Frank Chikane (eds.), *The Road to Rustenburg: The Church Looking Forward to a New South Africa.* Cape Town: Struik Christian Books, 1991.

104. 'The Cape Town Statement', *Journal of Theology for Southern Africa,* 77 (December 1991).

SELECT BIBLIOGRAPHY

Cochrane, James, *Servants of Power: The Role of English-speaking Churches 1903–1930.* Johannesburg: Ravan, 1987

De Gruchy, John W., *The Church Struggle in South Africa.* Grand Rapids, Eerdmans, and Cape Town, David Philip, second edition, 1986

Kinghorn, Johann (ed.), *Die NG Kerk en Apartheid.* Johannesburg: Macmillan, 1986

Mosala, Itumuleng J. and Tlhagale, Buti (eds.), *The Unquestionable Right to be Free: Black Theology from South Africa.* Johannesburg: Skotaville, 1986

Prozesky, Martin (ed.), *Christianity in South Africa.* London: Macmillan, 1990

Villa-Vicencio, Charles, *Trapped in Apartheid: A Socio-Theological History of the English-speaking Churches.* New York: Orbis, and Cape Town: David Philip, 1988

Villa-Vicencio, Charles, *A Theology of Reconstruction: Nation Building and Human Rights.* Cambridge: CUP, 1992

7

The African Independent Churches

JIM KIERNAN

Chapter five outlines the process whereby, after initial rejection, the bulk of the African population accepted Christianity, without entirely abandoning the deep-seated religious orientation of a distinctive way of life. What remains to be seen is how a large proportion of Africans, after prolonged exposure to mission Christianity, rebelled against it. The revolt took two directions: a sundering of the bonds of white ecclesiastical control; and an exploration of new religious forms around a core of Christian teaching. Both departures were rooted in a society organised on the divisive and exploitative principles of apartheid.

Apartheid has been ingrained in the social edifice of Southern Africa for much longer than its proclamation as official Nationalist policy in the mid-twentieth century would suggest. The apartheid state was simply the outcome of antecedent social forms grounded in colonial history. It had its origins in the colonial conquest of the land and the appropriation of its mineral wealth. Racial segregation was a manifestation of the assumed superiority adopted by the conquerors in their relations with the conquered, and began with the carving out of special and limited enclaves for occupation by Africans. At first, only seven per cent of the total land-space, revised later to a still meagre thirteen per cent, was considered sufficient to support an economy that was entirely land-based. The imbalance of power, manifest also in burdensome legislative measures such as discriminatory taxation, led to the exploitation of black labour and the further consolidation of white control over the country's natural resources. By being squeezed off the land and impelled into the system of migrant labour, black countrymen were forced into supporting the institutions of their own oppression and into ever-greater dependence on them.

While the bases of the black farming economy, land and labour, were thus undermined, controls were imposed to prevent Africans from fully engaging in the emerging urban industrial economy on their own terms. The object was to create a labour force of transients which the urban centres would suck in and spit out again, without making provision for the acquisition of skills or the inevitability of permanent urban settlement. Apartheid merely entrenched these prevailing tendencies within an explicit political programme. Of course, the sheer unmanageability of the system made a mockery of influx control and led to the steady emergence of a vast settled urban population, a reality which more recent bureaucratic legerdemain, unrealistically redefining these people as rural for political purposes, did little to alter.

The early migrant experience gave rise to a distinctive religious expression, which has been called Zionist. It radiated from the industrial cities into the countryside through the migrant networks, but its strongest social support is still within the urban working class.

At the same time, missionary Christianity was pursuing a divergent course, one of upliftment rather than of exploitation. By the start of the present century, the missions were producing a significant educated elite. The intention was to create an enlightened and self-sufficient peasantry on the land, the realisation of which was so successful that Christian cultivators of the land thrived as entrepreneurs, by supplying a surplus of produce for sale to the mines and by setting up business as transporters of grain to these markets, until white farming interests hit back with repressive legislation. Unwittingly, however, the missionaries were preparing their adherents for entry into the urban industries, communicating to them Western values and attitudes, giving them the opportunity of acquiring useful skills and educating them to levels of literacy and numeracy exceptional among a pre-literate people. This equipped Christian Africans to come to terms more proficiently with urbanisation, and to extract better incomes from industry and commerce. Some of them gained the status of exemption from Native Law, though this concession was later discontinued.

Paradoxically, this progressive push by Christian Africans encountered obstruction from missionaries within the churches themselves. The white missionaries promoted the principles of democratic participation and self-determination in their convert communities, ultimately with a view to making these communities self-sufficient. Yet they were slow to ordain African pastors, reluctant to give them full responsibility and admit them as equals, and generally refused to grant any relaxation of ultimate white control. However justified this guarded paternalism was in missionary eyes, it effectively blocked the realisation of expectations engendered among Africans by the missionaries themselves. In a number of cases, the resultant frustration spilled over into defection and the formation of separatist or schismatic African churches, commonly labelled Ethiopian.

Each of these departures from Christianity, the Ethiopian and the Zionist, dates from the beginning of the present century. The foundation of Ethiopian churches was the less drastic, as they were content to break the shackles of white dominance while retaining the form of organisation, mode of worship and the denominational identity of the parent body, for example 'African Methodist' and 'African Congregational'. Nonetheless, it stemmed directly from the practice of an undeclared apartheid where it was least expected, from an insistence on segregation and white superiority on the part of missionaries.

These churches were African replicas of Christian denominations and were an explicit response to racial inequality.

The Zionist development was the reverse of this. These churches grew directly from the harsh experience of a displaced urban proletariat, with parallels elsewhere in the world, although these conditions were aggravated by specific manipulations in a racially stratified society. The organisation of Zionist churches and their order of service are quite distinctive, without being uniform. These churches were not cut in the missionary mould and were concerned with alleviating the conditions of impoverished workers. There is, therefore, a class distinction within African ranks to be discerned between the membership of both of these two religious types: the Zionist church serves the social and religious needs of the poor and illiterate by attempting to transcend their sense of deprivation and inadequacy; the Ethiopian church caters for the educated and somewhat better-off who have rebelled against a form of Christian discrimination.

Both of these departures have produced a multiplicity of offshoots, partly influenced by the spirit of rampant denominationalism, and partly continuous with the segmentation of lineal descent groups, a basic principle of social organisation in the African past. The result is that there now exist close to an estimated four thousand of these churches across a wide range of religious forms, claiming a combined membership of about thirty per cent of the total African population. By any standards, this is a significant and considerable body of adherents, so that it is not unrealistic to depict the spread and growth of these churches as phenomenal. It is certain that the bulk of this proliferation and increase is Zionist, one estimate placing their preponderance as high as eighty per cent, and there are several known instances of Ethiopian churches gravitating towards the Zionist model. Moreover, this religious phenomenon, particularly in the case of the Zionist majority, has spilled over geographically and is well established in neighbouring countries, notably in Swaziland, Zimbabwe, Zambia, Malawi and even in Zaire.

Attention can now be directed to a consideration of these developments in turn, giving due weight to the dominance of the Zionist strain.

Ethiopian churches

'Ethiopian' is a classificatory term which covers all churches, and their subsequent offshoots, that broke away from mission control chiefly on grounds of racial disparity; it does not mean that 'Ethiopia' will necessarily appear in their titles. And while there is a tendency among them to follow the pattern of mission churches, there are degrees of conformity such that, at the extreme of divergence, the distinction between Ethiopian and Zionist is not easy to discern.

In order to understand fully the complexity of the Ethiopian movement as a whole, it is necessary to re-examine the reasons advanced for breaking out of the missionary shell, namely the segregation of white leadership from African membership and the disinclination to advance Africans to positions of responsibility within the church. These reasons did not simultaneously prevail with equal force, and the second, in particular, must be unpacked and modified. The reluctance to ordain African pastors did not simply stem from a contempt for African ability, though this was at times an influential consideration. Some missionaries thought so highly of African capability that they preferred to await its full realisation as a prerequisite for ordination. There were also instances of enthusiastic and qualified men being deliberately overlooked because they would not temper their zeal and submit to the curbs of missionary discipline. Missionary motives for adopting a conservative position on this issue were, therefore, very mixed.

On the other hand, it is an undeniable fact that, despite the paucity of white pastors on the ground, Christian communities of Africans clearly saw the advantages of being represented by a white minister and were averse to having a black substitute outsider foisted on them. Much more telling is the consideration that the most suitable candidates were seldom tempted to enter the ministry. These were the natural leaders in Christian communities, men of undoubted intelligence, ability and drive, but they were attracted by ample opportunities of a secular kind for advancement, which existed in agriculture, commerce and education rather than within the church. Weighed against these prospects, the alternative of a poorly paid and time-consuming pastoral occupation was not a realistic choice. For such men the question of the suppression of upward mobility within the church was scarcely an issue. But it did become an issue when the opportunities for engaging in trade, property transactions and public affairs, generally, were quickly snuffed out by the mobilisation of white influence to counteract the economic challenge of African commercialism and the political threat revealed by the Anglo-Zulu War. It was then that the ablest of Christians began to consider a career in the church and found their aspirations blocked. The point is that, whereas racial discrimination and segregation were a constant feature of missionary churches from the beginning of evangelisation, the reservation of leadership to white missionaries became a matter of contention only from the 1880s onwards. This helps to explain why the formation of the Ethiopian churches was preceded by secessions of a very different kind.

The first Ethiopian church, a Wesleyan offshoot, actually called 'The Ethiopian Church', was established on the Witwatersrand in 1892. But, ten years earlier, Nehemiah Tile had broken away from the Wesleyans to found the 'Tembu Church' and, within a space of seven years, tribal churches of this kind had also emerged among the Tswana and the Pedi. This was an assertion of tribal autonomy against missionary rule and, because the chief of the tribal group was made head of the splinter church, it could not be seen as a bid to increase the personal influence of the instigators. 'The Ethiopian Church' on the other hand arose, not only out of resentment of missionary autocracy, but also out of indignation on the part of defecting ministers at the belittlement of their capacity for leadership. In rapid succession, the Congregational and Presbyterian churches experienced Ethiopian schisms, and this was to be the fate of all the Protestant mission churches.

A second factor that promoted the emergence of Ethiopian churches was the support they enlisted from churches of a similar character among black American Christians. The basis of their cooperation, and for a time their amalgamation, was their comparable experience of racial domination and manipulation in white-controlled societies. While the influence and support of these American churches were initially very strong, the connection gradually weakened and lapsed, not least because the South African separatists came to recognise that black Americans were as much foreigners and outsiders to their struggle for independence as were the missionaries, and equally failed to accord them parity in leadership.

Of more lasting consequence was the adoption of the term 'Ethiopian' for the title of the first of these churches. This was essentially a biblical reference to the text 'Ethiopia shall soon stretch out her hands to God' (Ps. 68:31), the meaning of which for Africans had been honed and refined within the mission churches. The Ethiopian reference was significant in two ways. Associated with Ethiopia in the Bible was the cognate term Cush, son of Ham, who, according to white supremacist interpretation, was an outcast and the precursor of all black Africans. The separatists turned this around. By identifying themselves as the descendants of Cush, they asserted a claim to an independent route into the Bible, free from white tutelage. They could also claim a relationship with the moral teaching of a society whose organisation resonated with parallels to their own, and from which the societies of Western Protestantism greatly differed. This 'theological' coup provided the legitimacy for their bid for ecclesiastical independence.

Secondly, it follows from this that Ethiopia, the land of Cush, was a microcosm of Africa as a whole. Ethiopia could thus be translated as Africa; hence the adoption of the political slogan 'Africa for the Africans', which reverberates with a call to nationalism on a very broad scale. The emphasis was no longer on the tribe but on Africa, and on being African, a form of unity that transcended tribalism. This emphasis reflected the non-tribal composition of dissident membership at the beginning. It could scarcely have been otherwise, because the mission churches themselves had by then drawn together a very mixed and mobile membership. Nowhere was this more evident than in the congregations on the Witwatersrand. In other words, the provision of separate black churches for a composite multi-tribal membership could scarcely have led anywhere else than to an appeal to common denominators, summed up in the word 'African'. This commonality also informed the apolitical drive of Ethiopian churches towards evangelisation. At the outset, at least, many of them entertained visions of converting the African masses beyond the borders of South Africa.

But it was the political edge of apparent nationalism and the potential threat of an opposition unified and charged with religious fervour which unsettled the government of the period and gained these churches a certain notoriety among whites in general. The climate of suspicion resulted in official investigations of the Ethiopians. Although several government commissions completely exonerated the separatist churches of political intrigue, it has to be said that many of their leaders, acting no doubt from personal conviction, supported the Bambatha Rebellion of 1906 in Natal and later promoted the formation of the African National Congress. But by the time the commission of 1921 sat down to write its report, it must have been abundantly clear that the separatists posed no collective threat. Far from generating a purposeful unity, they were already experiencing the inexorable process of internal fission, which has since divided and subdivided them into a multiplicity of small fragments (a fate which, it will be seen, also overtook the Zionists).

To unravel the complexity of these subdivisions is a task too daunting to be undertaken here. However, the reasons most likely to account for them are, on the basis of available evidence, the rivalry for positions of leadership (however cloaked in accusations of moral turpitude and monetary mismanagement), and the creation of new openings for those denied access to influence and recognition in apartheid society. A further aspect of this fragmentation was the reassertion of provincial, regional and tribal divisions. This, coupled with the desire to meet conditions laid down by government which would merit them the security and perquisites of official recognition, explains why the Ethiopians largely surrendered to the impress of apartheid. Few indeed managed to capture the seal of approval, fewer still succeeded in retaining it, and the practice has in any case been discontinued. What can be said with certainty, however, is that the Ethiopians have long lost whatever political aspirations they may at one time have harboured and have become the tame disciples of the doctrine of separate nationalisms. How they will place themselves within the post-apartheid state remains a matter of conjecture.

South Africa's Zionist Churches

Like the Ethiopian churches, the Zionists have had their points of resistance, notably in the Bulhoek 'Israelites' under the leadership of Enoch Mgijima. This man entertained visions to the effect that blacks would prevail over whites and destroy them. His visions led to his expulsion from an Ethiopian church but enabled him to build up a large body of followers, attracted by the promise that Jehovah would release them from the bondage of Europeans, and to settle them at Bulhoek, near Queenstown. He had no title to the land occupied by his village and, when he failed to heed numerous orders to disband, police action was resorted to in 1921. The outcome was a massacre, the 'Israelites' going up against the police guns in the firm belief that they were immune to bullets, which they were assured would turn into water. It was this tragic incident which gave some urgency to the setting up of a commission of inquiry in that year to report on the character of the Independent churches.

The 'Israelite' phenomenon was a spontaneous eruption of prophetism, borne upon the personal inspiration of a charismatic individual. Elsewhere in Africa, outbreaks of religious prophetism have occurred, without the benefit of Christianity, as a means of uniting a structurally divided society to meet an outside threat. But it has also recurrently manifested itself throughout the history of Christianity, beginning with the troublesome Corinthians. In the context of Christianity it has often been associated with social dissent voiced by charismatic leaders. At the very least, it has always had the character of popular religious effervescence, as against a religion of fixed doctrine, religion thrusting up from below rather than being imposed from above (above and below being references to social level only). In Zionism, no less than at Bulhoek, we encounter an expression of community religion, as opposed to bureaucratically organised religion, in which personal revelation is at least as important as a sacralised text. This is a distinction which arises in all literate religions and serves to set Zionists apart from Ethiopians.

While the Ethiopians exhibit an African Christianity, the African aspect is virtually limited to the exercise of authority. In the Zionist churches it applies also to religious content. It is a truism to say that Zionism is a blend of Christianity and African religion; this is neither odd nor derogatory, for it can be argued that all known religions have originated from a syncretic matrix. Sundkler first gave currency to the claim, though he later abandoned it, that Zionist syncretism was a bridge over which Christians returned to paganism. In the light of what has transpired in the development of these churches since then, it is much more likely that traffic is heavier in the opposite direction and that these churches operate as a means whereby those born into African religion are drawn towards exposure to Christianity, to a greater or lesser degree. What is important, of course, is the differing proportions of the admixture that underlie the bewildering variety presented in the full range of Zionism, so many being more or less Christian than others. It will not do, however, simply to think of Zionism as a combination, as if each of the components, African and Christian, was merely grafted onto the other. Their fusion has produced a true synthesis, and the result is the creation of something new.

While it is difficult to generalise across such a diverse range of churches, the Zionist phenomenon can be reasonably comprehended as a refinement of Christianity in relation to African experience. In effect, Zionism harnesses the distilled spiritual energy of Christianity to respond to modern African needs and channels it through African categories of thought and action, though without denuding it entirely of Christian categories. Thus, there is a retention of some African religious methods and techniques but these draw from a new source of power – the Holy Spirit rather than the ancestral spirits. The displacement of ancestors is often imperfectly realised while, in other cases, the role of the Holy Spirit is scarcely more than adumbrated; in between, ancestors can be accorded a status complementary to the Holy Spirit.

The emergence of the Zionist churches

Historically, the first Zionist church among Africans took shape under the direction of a disaffected Dutch Reformed minister, Rev. P. Le Roux, in the heart of the 'Boer Republic' close to the northern border of Natal in 1903, although it was predated by a Zionist congregation of Europeans in Johannesburg; both became centres of African evangelisation. In fact, the advent of Zionism in South Africa owed much initially to the efforts of a handful of local whites and to the influence of some white American churches. The major American influence radiated from 'Zion City', Chicago (hence Zionism), later to be refreshed by a missionary stream emanating from Pentecostal or Apostolic churches. From these two sources, African Zionism derived its twin emphases on divine healing (by prayer) and on the effusion of the Holy Spirit respectively. In the course of time, particularly as it incorporated migrant workers on the Witwatersrand, it generated additional characteristics of its own such as prophecy, white robes, coloured accessories, and 'holy' staves.

The many Zionist churches today which belong to the mainstream of that early foundation still vindicate their Christian pedigree, not least by insisting on the centrality of the Bible in all their work. However, they do not encompass the whole of Zionism in South Africa. If we think of them as 'core' Zionists, then the margins of the movement have been swollen by the inclusion of churches of quite a different provenance. These correspond more closely to the 'Bulhoek' model in which a charismatic African, filled by the urgency of a personal revelation or vision, compulsively preaches it, so attracting disciples whose lives he proceeds to organise along religious lines. The churches which have emerged from this prophetic impulse tend to lean more heavily towards the traditional pole of the Zionist spectrum, giving ancestors a more prominent role. Like Enoch Mgijima at Bulhoek, their founders have had some prior experience of Christianity, or of Zionism proper, and this, too, influences their outlook and organisation. In general, however, it can be said of these churches that prophecy is less constrained by biblical norms than in mainstream Zionism, and that they provide better opportunities for women to achieve prominence as leaders. And it is a fact that the largest and the most spectacularly successful of churches, such as Lekganyane among the Sotho–Tswana and Shembe among the Zulu, to mention only the better known, are to be found within this broad category.

This distinction between Zionist core and periphery can be variously rendered. Recently, Sundkler has set it between 'Zionists in the strict sense' and 'Zionists in the loose sense'. Core or mainstream Zionists are themselves conscious of it; their self-perception is that they are rightfully 'Christian Zionists' and, because they have a sense of history, they label others 'New Zionists' (with the connotation of 'upstart') or, more neutrally, 'Jerusalem Zionists'. The distinction may best be conceived by seeing core Zionists as evolving from within a Christian framework of ideas, and others as raiding Christianity from without, capturing some of its features selectively.

Zionists and urban challenges

Whatever the origin of different strains of Zionism, Zionist churches principally function to address the problems confronting those initially drawn into the cities as migrant workers. The migrant experience is predominantly one of dislocation and disorientation. Uprooted from a close-knit homogeneous community, the worker is transferred to a large-scale heterogeneous urban society. Social stress and uncertainty result from being thrown into relatively close and protracted association with outright strangers in work and residence. A sense of inadequacy and alienation is also produced by the industrial emphasis on efficiency, on the regulated control of time, and on the achievement of productive targets. Furthermore, as more people were pushed from the countryside to avail of urban resources, the limitations of accessible opportunities were soon exposed, and this brought a spirit of competitiveness and insecurity into urban employment. Among the poor and illiterate, lacking an intellectual grasp of the operation of market and political forces, these stresses were translated by means of pre-existing categories of thought into the widespread incidence of sorcery. Squeezed between the diminishing productivity of the land and the meagreness of urban wages, the impoverished working class fell prey to malnutrition and its consequent manifold maladies. Within the accepted mode of explanation, which attributed misfortune to the action of mystical agents, the prevalence of physical disorders gave substance to the conviction that sorcery had become rampant. None of these considerations were markedly affected by the gradual transformation of migrants into settled and domesticated townspeople.

The Zionist churches supplied answers to these problems. They provided intimate and supportive communities, they gave concentrated attention to healing, and they mobilised spiritual reserves to counter the aggression of sorcery. In all of these ways – organisational, supportive, therapeutic and protective – they formed coping institutions which aimed at the delivery of benefits in the here and now. It should be very clear that Zionists are not engaged in a programme of social reform under a religious guise. Their objective is not to undo the system or redress the conditions which produce the social sores that preoccupy them. Rather, their concern is with the rescue and salvage of individuals on a voluntary basis, and with supporting them economically, socially and spiritually. Their solution is not the reconstruction of an unjust society but the formation of refuges for the socially battered. To this end, they eschew all worldly pursuits, with the exception of the necessity to work, and cultivate an ascetic approach to life which stresses diligence, sobriety, frugality and savings. This self-contained and conservative outlook rules out any involvement or even interest in matters political. They are not merely politically neutral but intensely anti-political, another way in which they have always differed from the Ethiopians.

Organisational characteristics

In scale of organisation, a typical Zionist church would consist of less than twenty ministers (considerably less, usually) who are loosely supervised by a bishop or president, who may or may not be the founder. A minister may have several congregations, though one is the norm, membership varying from six to forty, not counting children. Few churches succeed in developing beyond this scale; constant fragmentation sees to that. The scramble for independent leadership is as much a reality for Zionists as it is for Ethiopians, and the only way an ambitious subordinate can become supreme is by hiving off from his bishop to establish his own church. This means in structural terms that whenever a church expands beyond the effective control of the leader, it will be riven into similarly manageable units.

At congregational level, groups are strongly cohesive and exclusive. Zionists severely limit their interaction with outsiders, though they cultivate those who are susceptible to conversion, and expend most of their free time and energy in associating with fellow Zionists. Discipline is exercised by the minister in conjunction with subordinate evangelists and preachers (who are all men), but the intimate size of the group ensures that to some extent each person monitors the behaviour of others. The unity and cohesion of the congregation is, therefore, based on the principles of shared responsibility and mutual support.

One way in which responsibility is shared is through the proliferation of minor offices, mainly among men but to some extent also among women, and support is expressed as much in economic as in social form. In this respect, it has been said that the Zionist congregation caters for the individual in much the same way as the kinship group once did, although it is manifestly not a kinship unit. The kinship group relied on marriage and descent for its continuity. The Zionist congregation largely fails to retain the allegiance of its children, and finds recruits from among adults troubled by misfortune in the population at large. It is here that links established by and through women become crucial conduits to conversion. It is perhaps for this reason that women are ordained along with their husbands and are accorded the corresponding status, but without the right to exercise any part of the office except in relation to women only. It must be remembered that Zionism has a barely literate, uneducated and untrained ministry, eligibility for which is not the acquisition of approved knowledge but the demonstrated capacity to attract adherents. The part played by women in attracting followers is acknowledged by joint ordination.

Healing activities

In its healing activities, the culmination and climax of all regular meetings, the congregation draws on its prophetic flair rather than on its ministerial faculty. In healing, it is believed that the power of the Holy Spirit is being brought to bear on human frailty. This extraordinary power is not freely available to anybody. It has to be carefully tapped and nurtured. The context for doing this is the constitution of a human gathering as a Christian congregation. Once this has been accomplished, the power of the Spirit is engaged by communal prayer, which is in part an expression of collective concern for the sick, and is further generated by the delivery of the scriptural Word reinforced in preaching. Healing thus always presupposes prayer and Christian revelation.

More than this, the precondition as well as social correlate of amassing spiritual power is a surge of congregational effervescence and enthusiasm. The more fervent the expression of collective solicitude, the more it evinces belief that the Spirit is present, and the more confidently the work of healing can be undertaken. In this way, the congregation can be regarded as a lens which relays, focuses and concentrates the effulgence of the Spirit on afflicted individuals. But the prophet is especially effective in sharpening and giving greater accuracy to that focus.

Zionist prophets

Prophecy is not an office but a personal gift which is technically open to all. In practice, it is the preserve of those men and women of visionary disposition who can cultivate interior states of heightened awareness. This is largely achieved by practising abstinence and an ascetic style of living. It is commonly believed that if a prophet were to lapse into self-indulgence, particularly in the area of sexual relations, such a prophet would be bereft of his or her powers. To be a precise conduit of the Spirit such people must be exceptionally pure; only then can they enjoy the enlightenment and clairvoyance afforded by the Spirit to find reason and remedy for an illness. The prophet is therefore poised between the Spirit and human suffering, and is the most important link between the two. Some prophets are more important and more effective than others; in general, men take precedence over women, and experience takes precedence over youth.

A number of commentators have noted the similarities between Zionist prophet and African diviner. Without our going into these similarities here, it can be said that they derive from the fact that within the Zionist order, the prophet holds a position roughly equivalent to that of the diviner, who relays ancestral potencies to the living. But this should not be taken to mean that a prophet is a thinly disguised diviner. The task of the Zionist prophet is two-fold. Firstly, it is to diagnose the cause of particular illnesses, which are usually located in sin or sorcery or some combination of these, in a departure from Zionist norms of behaviour; or in involvement in an envy-ridden relationship with an outsider. Secondly, the prophet's task is to prescribe suitable treatment for the alleviation of the disorder. Included in the repertoire of cures is immersion in clear water, the imbibing of water, the drinking of a purge consisting of water with additives of salt and ashes, and the adoption of an item of apparel. None of these is deemed to be effective unless blessed and imbued by prayer. They may indeed be viewed as material extensions of prayer and are thus linked to the ultimate remedy, namely an increase in the patient's recourse to prayer within the congregation, and thereby to renewed treatment. Not the least attractive aspect of Zionist healing is that it is inexpensive. The anticipated pay-off for Zionists is the capture by cure of a fresh convert, and it is a fact that most Zionists have entered the fold through an experience of healing.

To win a convert by healing is to snatch someone from the field of sorcery. In most cases, Zionists will have little difficulty in convincing the would-be convert that he or she is the victim of sorcery. Sorcery is born of human malice which can be mysteriously translated by means of specially primed substances ('medicines') into physical damage. And the malice is to be found in relationships which get out of control. Zionists would hold that the cities harbour too many uncontrolled relationships; therefore malice flourishes and sorcery abounds. At another level, this is a statement about the degree and intensity of social strain and uncertainty within a society, and especially about the experience and tolerance of these conditions by low-income earners. But for Zionists, among others, sorcery is a malign reality to be repulsed at all costs.

They are encircled by sorcery, which, in their eyes, is the scourge of urban living and the distillation of all their troubles. Ultimately, that is why they form relatively closed communities of the saved, bounded by a protective barrier or mystical *cordon sanitaire*. Zionists are, obviously, prohibited from active engagement in sorcery, and they move purposefully to neutralise any deliberate and unwitting contact with its agents.

Zionists unavoidably lose members from time to time for a variety of reasons, but the more they succeed in conserving and swelling membership, the more evident it is that they are winning in the battle against sorcery. Every convert is a victory over sorcery, a step in pushing back the frontiers of sorcery, proof of having cleared a bit more space that is free from sorcery. To fall back on a helpful analogy, Zionists are creating and extending Christian clearings in what is seen as the societal jungle, oases in a moral desert, pockets of social order in the midst of disorder.

It is difficult to predict what the future holds in store for the Ethiopian and Zionist churches. It seems inevitable that the Zionists will continue to expand in the immediate future. An economic miracle might arrest this trend, provided that the resultant prosperity is sufficiently distributed to uplift the very poor into a higher economic and social bracket. In such unforeseen circumstances the appeal of Zionism might well be diminished, but it is doubtful if it would be snuffed out or that its socio-economic preconditions would be eliminated. As for the Ethiopian churches, with their assertion of black independence in the religious sphere, the evidence from Zambia and elsewhere shows that the achievement of political autonomy does not result in their disappearance, although their popular appeal and social importance may be diminished. There might be some advantage in a return to their parental stock, but there is no reason to expect that they could not function independently in the manner of any of the missionary churches.

SELECT BIBLIOGRAPHY

Sundkler's early pioneering study of Ethiopian and Zionist churches among the Zulu, packed with empirical data overlaid with sociological analysis, is a scholarly opening approach to the subject. His later volume concentrates in a more directly descriptive style on Zionist leaders and on developments in Swaziland. It also incorporates an excellent historical chapter on the beginnings of Zionism. West's large survey of churches in Soweto, supplemented by a detailed anthropological investigation of three of these, is a valuable complement to Sundkler's rural work. Etherington, an historian, devotes two chapters of good quality to the reasons for the emergence of Ethiopian churches among the Zulu, and Johnson provides a useful description and analysis of the growth and decline of one of the better known of these churches in Zambia. On the Tswana, Pauw surveys a wide range of church associations, including Zionist and Ethiopian, and Comaroff concentrates on two groups, one a congregation of the massive Zion Christian Church of Lekganyane. Jules-Rosette and Dillon-Malone deal with popular churches of a Zionist kind in Zaire and Zambia respectively. I have included my own published work on 'Christian' Zionists in an urban setting, from which the reader may select, and this can be compared and contrasted with

Fogelquist's recent study of an atypical Zionist church on the fringes of the movement, located in Swaziland. Finally, Oosthuizen endeavours to place these South African churches along the theological spectrum, depending on their distance from or proximity to Christianity or traditional African religion.

Comaroff, Jean, *Body of Power: Spirit of Resistance. The Culture and History of a South Africa People*. Chicago: University of Chicago Press, 1985

Dillon-Malone, Clive, *The Korsten Basketmakers*. Manchester: Manchester University Press, 1978

Etherington, Norman, *Preachers, Peasants and Politics in Southeast Africa, 1835–1880*. London: Royal Historical Society, 1978

Fogelquist, Anders, 'The Red-dressed Zionists. Symbols of Power in a Swazi Independent Church'. *Uppsala Research Reports in Cultural Anthropology*, 5 (1986)

Johnson, Walter R., *Worship and Freedom: A Black American Church in Zambia*. London: International African Institute, 1977

Jules-Rosette, Bennetta, *African Apostles. Ritual and Conversion in the Church of John Maranke*. Ithaca, New York: Cornell University Press, 1975

Kiernan, J. P., *The Production and Management of Therapeutic Power in Zionist Churches within a Zulu City*. New York: Edwin Mellen Press, 1990

Kiernan, J. P., 'The Role of the Adversary in Zulu Zionist Churches'. *Religion in Southern Africa*, 8, 1 (1987)

Kiernan, J. P., 'The Other Side of the Coin: The Conversion of Money to Religious Purposes'. *Man*, NS 23, 3 (1988)

Kiernan, J. P., 'Wear 'n Tear and Repair: The Colour Coding of Mystical Mending in Zulu Zionist Churches'. *Africa*, 61, 1 (1991)

Kiernan, J. P., 'The Herder and the Rustler: Deciphering the Affinity between Zulu Diviner and Zionist Prophet'. *African Studies*, 51, 2 (1992)

Oosthuizen, G. C., *Post-Christianity in Africa*. London: C. Hurst, and Grand Rapids: Eerdmans, 1968

Pauw, B. A., *Religion in a Tswana Chiefdom*. Cape Town: Oxford University Press, 1960

Sundkler, B.G.M., *Bantu Prophets in South Africa*. Cape Town: Oxford University Press, 1961

Sundkler, B.G.M., *Zulu Zion and Some Swazi Zionists*. Cape Town: Oxford University Press, 1976

West, Martin, *Bishops and Prophets in a Black City*. Cape Town: David Philip, 1975

8

Islam in South Africa

EBRAHIM MOOSA

THE EARLY HISTORY

Islam in Africa

Some ten years after the death of the Prophet Muhammad, the Arab general 'Amr bin al-'As snatched Egypt away from Byzantine control in 642 CE. This was the first significant political and cultural impact Islam had on Africa. Prior to that, and perhaps more dramatically, the Prophet Muhammad had sent a small band of his persecuted Arab followers in 615 CE to seek asylum in the Christian kingdom of Abyssinia (Ethiopia). In other words, Islam reached Africa long before it even reached the vital centres of Arabia, such as Madinah and Taif.

'The faith and culture of Islam', says the historian Robin Hallett, was '... Asia's last major contribution to the development of Africa. Islamic culture implied far more than a religion: a new language, new concepts of law and government, and new standards of dress and architecture accompanied the new faith.'[1] Today, Islam has become more indigenised than any other immigrant culture on the continent.

Across North Africa, Islam spread dramatically, mainly by conquest; but the spread of Islamic influence south of the Sahara has tended to occur primarily through economic means. It was mainly the movement of nomads and pastoral migrations that carried Islam towards the equator. Travel on horseback and economic traffic between the different sections of the continent brought Islam to West Africa. Arab maritime trade on dhows during the monsoons carried Islam to East Africa. Trade and proselytisation went hand in hand, since Muslim traders were also part-time missionaries of the faith.

White conquest and European settlement in Southern Africa halted the southward drive of Islam from the seventeenth century onwards. Recent studies, however, show that Islamic penetration from the north into regions beyond the Soutpansberg in modern South Africa may have occurred as early as the fifteenth century or possibly in the late eighteenth century. Indications are that Swahili-speaking Arabs may have reached as far south as the St John's River on the Pondoland coast in the Transkei. This is further confirmed by accounts of 'Islamic' Africans, members of broken tribes who flourished among the Shona in southern Zimbabwe and the Venda, Sotho and Thonga peoples in the Transvaal. These Islamic Africans are called by various names such as Lemba, Varemba or Balemba, while variations of this name are used in other regions. Historians of religion have found among the Lemba certain religious and cultural practices which unmistakably resemble Islamic rituals, and there are reflections of Arabic in their language.[2]

Early Islam at the Cape

Ironically, it was colonisation that brought Islam to the Cape and later to other parts of South Africa. While it is disputed whether there were Muslim slaves in the party of the first coloniser, Jan van Riebeeck, when he set foot at the Cape on 6 April 1652, six years later free Muslims from the Moluccan Islands are known to have arrived. Called Mardyckers, they were employed as mercenaries to protect the Dutch settlement against marauding indigenous groups, and as servants of the Dutch settlers.

The Dutch policy of subjugation of the Muslim populations of the East Indies was also applied in the Cape. As early as 1642, the Dutch governor, Van Diemen, issued a proclamation which prohibited the public practice of Islam in the Cape on pain of death. It was reinforced in 1657. This repressive policy prevailed for nearly one and a half centuries, until 1804 when religious freedom was granted to all people. This liberalisation stemmed from the fact that Governor Janssens and Commissioner De Mist were influenced by the ideals of the French Revolution.

Freedom of religion for non-Christians, such as Muslims or Chinese, was not tolerated. While Catholics and Lutherans were also subject to prejudicial treatment by the Dutch Reformed colonial authorities, it was not as severe as that shown to non-Christians. Non-Christian religions could only be practised in public to the extent that white Christian authorities tolerated them.

It would be no exaggeration to say that Islam struck root in the Cape under extremely difficult circumstances in the seventeenth and eighteenth centuries. The level of repression produced unique social formations, which in turn shaped the type of religion and religious institutions that emerged within these contexts. This had a bearing on the psychology and attitude of its adherents. In East Asia, the increasingly fierce resistance shown to the Dutch in places like Amboyna, Batavia and the Moluccas produced a steady flow of political prisoners who were banished to the Cape. Among the political exiles were not only rank-and-file anti-imperialist activists and some petty criminals, but also senior leaders of the resistance in the Dutch East Indies. Some of these leading figures can be counted among the founders of Islam at the Cape.

Early founders

The spiritual father of Islam at the Cape was 'Abidin Tadia Tjoessoep, respectfully known as Shaykh Yusuf of Macassar (1626–99). He was born in

Macassar, in the region known today as the Malay Archipelago. He was educated in Java, but later visited several Islamic capitals such as Makkah and Madinah, the two holy cities of Islam, where he performed the pilgrimage (*hajj*) and became a pupil of several learned authorities. From Arabia he went to Damascus and Istanbul, two of the leading intellectual capitals of Islam at the time. In Damascus he became a disciple of the Khalwatiyyah spiritual order.[3] Later in life, this Sufi affiliation strengthened his role as a leading figure in the Bantamese independence movement, and contributed to the charismatic qualities which helped him lay the spiritual foundations of the Muslim community in the Cape.

As he was married to the daughter of the Prince of Bantam, Sultan Ageng, the Shaykh was inevitably drawn into the conflict between the Sultan and his son, 'Abd al-Qahhar. The conflict involved Dutch and British colonial interests in the region. The local royalty supported opposing sides, the father being on the side of the British and the son aiding the Dutch.[4] In support of the older Sultan, Shaykh Yusuf showed heroic defiance, eluding the Dutch authorities in a guerrilla war for nearly a year. When he gave himself up on the promise of pardon, the Dutch reneged on their undertaking. He was at first sentenced to death, but an appeal to the Dutch authorities by the Mogul Indian ruler, Aurangzeb, resulted in the sentence being commuted. Fearing his influence on the populace in Java, the Dutch exiled him to Ceylon in 1684. Then in 1694, Shaykh Yusuf and his retinue of wives, children and attendants arrived at the Cape aboard the *Voetboog*, still a political prisoner.

He came to be admired by both friend and foe, and legend has it that Governor Willem Adriaan van der Stel in the end befriended him. As a political prisoner with royal connections, the Shaykh was afforded certain privileges. He was allowed to settle at Faure, near Eerste River in the Cape. Most of the surviving members of his retinue who originally accompanied him were repatriated to Macassar after his death. At the request of the Sultan of Goa, the Shaykh's remains were taken to his native land, where they were reburied at Lakiung on 23 May 1703.

Shaykh Yusuf's impact on Islam at the Cape was perhaps more symbolic than real, largely because, as a prisoner of war, albeit one with a special status, his movement was restricted. Yet it is undeniable that he did manage to transmit knowledge of religion and spirituality to the slaves and free blacks.[5] The momentum derived from his work sustained the nascent Muslim community for at least a century. Some sources even suggest that he may have clandestinely provided religious instruction to the slaves in Cape Town in defiance of his restrictions.

Tuangs in exile

Towards the end of the eighteenth century several other important Muslim figures, such as Shaykh Madura (d. 1754) and Tuang Sayyid (d. *c*. 1760), helped establish Islam in South Africa. Their first pupils were fellow prisoners and slaves who in turn taught others. One important function was to write copies of the Qur'an either from memory or from manuscript and to circulate copies of the sacred text and divine word in the emergent community.

A semblance of community organisation can be detected with the coming of Imam 'Abd Allah ibn Qadi 'Abd al-Salam (1712–1807), better known as Tuang Guru. He could well be described as the second spiritual father of Islam at the Cape. Tuang Guru was born on the island of Tidore in the Moluccan Sea. Details of his background are unknown. Towards the close of the eighteenth century, anti-Dutch resistance was strong in the Southeast Asian islands, and Tuang Guru appears to have been one of those who opposed foreign rule. He was brought to the Cape in 1780, during a phase of tough Dutch action against rebellious colonies. Since Tuang Guru had no royal connections to procure privileged treatment for him, he was imprisoned on Robben Island for some thirteen years.

On his release, he devoted himself to the task of establishing a religious community. One of his first goals was to establish a mosque, the symbolic expression of Islamic *communitas*. For in its traditional role, a mosque has a dual function as a place of worship, sanctuary and spiritual retreat on the one hand, and as a space for social and political organisation on the other. Although Tuang Guru's first application to the Dutch authorities for a mosque site was turned down, his efforts led to the founding of the first mosque in Dorp Street in about 1804, although some believe it could be as early as 1798.

Tuang Guru's zeal was far from dampened by political exile. After the authorities refused him a mosque site, he defiantly led an open-air Friday (*Jumu'ah*) congregational prayer in a disused quarry site in what is today known as the Bo-Kaap. His action was a veiled threat to use his status as chief imam to mobilise his community if their rights were ignored. This was the first of a series of organised Muslim political activities opposing colonial rule at the Cape.

Mosques and imams: the rise of institutions

In a period of fourteen years on the mainland, Tuang Guru laid the foundations of an enduring educational tradition. In the Muslim heartlands from as early as the ninth century, educational institutes had grown up, known as mosque–madrassah (mosque–school) complexes. Over the centuries, leading mosques in the Muslim world developed extensive educational programmes which concentrated on religious curricula and other disciplines preparing students as teachers, judges, lawyers, secretaries or religious functionaries (imams). It was Tuang Guru who implemented a similar system, though on a reduced scale, at the Cape in the late eighteenth century.

The elimination of illiteracy and empowerment through education were used for the social advancement of slaves and free blacks. The first mosque in Dorp Street had originally been a warehouse, and was later used as a school. The history of Islam at the Cape would have been very different had it not been for the emphasis on education and the institutionalisation of Islam by means of the mosque–madrassah complex. The scale of this educational project is impressive even by today's standards. Accounts confirm that by the first quarter of the nineteenth century, well over 500 free black and slave scholars attended the school founded by Tuang Guru.

Slavery and manumission: the role of literacy

Tuang Guru not only founded a school, but also wrote *kitabs* (textbooks on jurisprudence and related Islamic disciplines). Some of these *kitabs* have survived in the form of copies that were circulated and transcribed by his students and followers. These were in the lingua franca of the slaves, a Dutch-based dialect. Social necessity had produced a dialect which contained elements of slave mother-tongues, such as Javanese and Bouganese. Since the majority were not literate in the culture of the ruling classes, they wrote in a script familiar to them, Arabic. This produced the novel script of Arabic–Afrikaans, phonetic Afrikaans written in Arabic script. The first printed *kitab* in Arabic–Afrikaans, which appeared in 1856, preceded the first Afrikaans book printed in roman script by almost six years. It is only of late that historians of language have admitted the contribution of 'the words slaves made'[6] to the Afrikaans language.

The final emancipation of slaves in the Cape in 1834 is in part intricately related to the ceaseless struggle of enslaved Muslims to liberate themselves. While in one sense the Qur'an and medieval Islamic culture acknowledged the institution of slavery, in another sense the evolutionary ethos and spirit of Islam ensured its abhorrence. It is therefore not surprising to find that the well-known practice in Islamic law of *mukatabah*, a contract whereby slaves could purchase their freedom, was prevalent at the Cape. G. M. Theal cites a report which states that 'this has been more particularly the case with slaves of Mohammedan proprietors who, if their slaves profess the same faith, allow them to purchase their freedom at cost price, and for that purpose often permit them to work on their own account'.[7]

The Arabic word for a contract of manumission, or *mukatabah*, shares the root *k-t-b* with the word for 'writing', from which is derived *kitab*, 'book'. *Mukatabah* literally means 'mutual writing', but technically it is a written agreement between a master and slave whereby the latter paid the former a sum in return for his or her liberty. The contract itself partially manumits the slave to enable him or her to be free to earn income.

An irony associated with this semantic link lies in the desire of the colonial authorities that slaves become literate in order to become 'civilised'. Clearly, what they had in mind was European literacy and alphabetisation. What Tuang Guru's school initiated and promoted was Arabic alphabetisation and literacy in a hybrid language, Arabic–Afrikaans. In short, the slaves eschewed the cultural prison of the oppressive culture and secured their liberty through literary means. It is also interesting to observe how conceptual literacy and knowledge becomes the gateway to freedom. Through the process of empowerment – knowledge and literacy – the Cape slaves procured their inevitable liberation. To 'know' was not only to control, but to put slavery to death.[8]

Slavery and conversion

Emancipation was itself fraught with anomalies and ambiguities. The colonial authorities and slave-owners were caught in a double bind. On the one hand, slaves were viewed as a form of property; on the other, public opinion in

Europe increasingly regarded slavery as morally reprehensible. By the middle of the eighteenth century, the sale of Christian slaves was illegal. This led to Muslim slaves acquiring a premium, partly for their habits of sobriety, but more because there was no restriction on their resale. Strangely, the material context encouraged and favoured the conversion of slaves to Islam, a faith to which many free blacks turned, as it was more advantageous to own saleable Muslim slaves than unsaleable Christian slaves. However, because of colonial and missionary concerns about the spread of Islam, Christian masters were forbidden to allow their slaves to convert to Islam, an offence that carried the penalty of confiscation of the slaves and a 500 rixdollar fine. Simultaneously, the communal and religious ethos of Islam at the Cape discouraged free Muslims from owning Muslim slaves.

The growth of Islam can be attributed to several causes. Prominent among these were conversion, adoption, the purchase of slaves by free Muslims, and intermarriage. Because of its egalitarian spirit, Islam became an attractive option for the underclasses and dispossessed. At the same time, an Islamic identity differentiated them culturally from their masters. Easy assimilation into Islamic culture made conversion attractive compared with the strictures of the dominant and elitist Christian culture. Since slaves were excluded from the right to marry in the Christian church, easy access to Muslim marital rites further encouraged conversion. Conversion also took place as a result of the assimilation facilitated by the religious schools, madrassahs, founded by the Cape imams.

Islam certainly swelled numerically as a result of these social processes. If population estimates are anything to go by, then by the first quarter of the nineteenth century there were some 3 000 Muslims in Cape Town, and by the middle of the same century there were some 8 000. Islam attracted all shades of race and class at the Cape; however, adherents to this faith were erroneously called 'Malays'. In 1860, Lady Duff Gordon, an English visitor to the Cape, observed: 'Malay here seems equivalent to Mohammedan. They were originally Malays, but now they include every shade, from the blackest nigger to the most blooming English woman.'[9]

Strategies for autonomy

It appears that Tuang Guru's strategies for dealing with officialdom varied, depending on the context and the colonial power with whom he dealt. Against the Dutch powers who brought him to the Cape, his opposition was consistent and uncompromising. With the British, he seems to have adopted a more conciliatory attitude. In later life, he appears to have counselled subservience and prophesied deliverance. He is reported to have said: 'Be of good heart, my children, and serve your masters; for one day your liberty will be restored to you, and your descendants will live within a circle of *karamats* (shrines) safe from fire, famine, plague, earthquake and tidal waves.'[10]

Much of this statement was actuated by the pragmatic concern for survival as well as by religious millenarianism. For example, it was politically expedient for the British to honour a pledge made by the defeated Dutch Governor,

Janssens, of greater autonomy to the Muslims if they participated in the defence of the Cape against the British invasion in 1795. The result was that during the period of British rule following the occupation of the Cape, Muslims were able to negotiate terms allowing them to build a mosque and have a separate burial place. This suggests British awareness of Muslim resistance at the Cape and a subsequent bid to neutralise it by tolerating limited religious autonomy. Likewise, in an effort to generate support for the short-lived Batavian Republic between 1803 and 1806, the Dutch allowed greater freedom of worship to Catholics and other religions like Islam, as well as Chinese religions. The effect of this at the Cape was noticeable, especially among the Muslims, who from then on, steadily but gradually, organised themselves in order to acquire greater communal autonomy.

Islam and the church

The last quarter of the nineteenth century witnessed an unprecedented proliferation of Muslim institutions at the Cape. The increased public visibility of Islam can be attributed to a decline in legislative restrictions on the public expression of non-Christian religions, to a large extent as a result of persistent Muslim effort to transcend the disadvantages of displacement, colonisation and prejudice. Among the more challenging difficulties with which Muslims had to contend, some of which survive to this day, were official and social prejudice, combined with paternalism in matters of public policy.

Reflecting a pervasive European mentality during the past four centuries, white colonial authorities and settlers at the Cape unfailingly viewed Islam as the 'Other'. In Euro-Christian terms, Islam was a heresy and the very antithesis of Christendom. Muslims at the Cape were the object of sustained proselytising efforts. The low success rate in converting free Muslims and slaves to Christianity, and their gradual but noticeable upward social mobility, evoked the scorn of colonial settlers and of churchmen. John Centlivres Chase, a prominent colonist and civil servant at the Cape, encapsulates this attitude:

> In numerous cases the emancipated slave deserted the Christian faith, in which he had been instructed on the estate of his former proprietor for the dull, cold creed of Mohammedanism, everywhere a detestable heresy, but in this colony in particular, bereaving its votaries of the few virtues, which save that and all other false truth from execration.[11]

Demonising imagery like this fed the colonial bias against Islam. Muslims were seen as good slaves and skilful artisans, but were unpredictable and quick to 'run amok', a favourite phrase of derogation. The attempt was made to associate hostile Crusader imagery with Islam in Southern Africa. Islam had the immense capacity to cause 'mischief' among the 'simple and credulous negroes still halting between Christ and Islam', observed one anonymous writer.[12]

Paradoxically, the white colonists also admired Muslims for their sober habits, and for their exotic beauty, as Lady Duff Gordon suggests: 'They wear a very pretty dress, and all have a great air of independence and self-respect; and the real Malays are very handsome.'[13] Deriding the Dutch, the same observer also reveals the attitude of the colonists towards the Muslims: 'They [the Dutch] hate the Malays, who were their slaves, and whose "insolent prosperity" annoys them ... The English ... curse the emancipation, long to flog the niggers, and hate the Malays, who work harder and don't drink, and who are the only masons [and] tailors.'[14]

An extract from a report in 1826 put it this way:

> The exclusion of the free blacks and Malays from the right of acquiring property has partly arisen from an aversion to their religious creed, and partly from the spirit of jealousy and discouragement with which the Dutch East India Company regarded the efforts of any of these individuals that might tend to withdraw them from a state of servile dependence. If the first of these feelings arose from serious and conscientious objections to the propagation of the Mohammedan faith it has met with great disappointment, for the number of the coloured inhabitants professing that faith has continued to increase in spite of their exclusion from the rights and privileges of the burghers.[15]

These statements describe the Muslim–settler relationship as being tense, and indicate a desire to subject the Muslim underclasses to settler hegemony. The organised church, and particularly the missionaries, played a leading role in this regard. As is evident from the statements of missionaries, travellers and officials, concerted efforts were made to convert Muslims, to the extent of utilising state power and legislation to make this possible. Against such odds it cannot be denied that the achievements of Islam occurred in spite of colonialism.

RELIGIOUS DIVERSITY AND THE GROWTH OF ACTIVISM

It was predictable that the death of a charismatic figure like Tuang Guru would create a leadership vacuum. As with the experience of charismatic leadership in other instances, fragmentation and division in the Muslim community at the Cape should be viewed as part of a process of resocialisation, of the redistribution of power and prestige. Not long after his death, Tuang Guru's followers found several issues on which to differ, especially the question of succession. The struggle over religious leadership positions such as *qadi*, or chief imam, was one of the key issues. Davids reports that in the short period between 1866 and 1900, over twenty cases reached the Cape Supreme Court for resolution of disputes over mosque leadership.

Religious practices

Given the repressive socio-political climate at the Cape, early Islam was very much an underground faith. Slaves and free black converts practised their religious rituals far from the eyes of the settlers. The charismatic leaders, mainly Sufi shaykhs (mentors) who arrived at the Cape at various intervals, did make an impact on the community. The earliest and most prominent practitioner of *tasawwuf,* or Islamic mysticism, was Shaykh Yusuf. The traditions and rituals which survived their death sustained Islam over the centuries.

From historical sources it can be deduced that the Muslim saints who were exiled to the Cape did have contact with their co-religionists, most of whom were slaves. Traces of mystical practices that prevailed at the time can still be detected in contemporary Muslim religion.

One of the earliest practices was that of *dhikr,* during which the Divine names are repeated liturgically. This became a standard practice on Thursday evenings, the start of the Muslim Friday. This nocturnal gathering appears to have been held in lieu of the compulsory Friday midday congregational prayer. The prohibition on the public practice of Islam prevented slaves from holding open Friday prayers. Furthermore, in terms of Islamic law, slaves were not obliged to attend Friday prayer.

Many of the hymns and songs in praise of the Prophet have survived orally, and provide evidence that they were Sufi-inspired, particularly by the Qadiriyyah order.[16] It is also known that Shaykh Yusuf was an initiate of the Khalwatiyyah Sufi order and Tuang Sayyid of the Alawiyyah order.[17]

It is not known to what extent *tasawwuf* became a widespread practice, or to what extent lay persons became initiates of the Sufi orders. While some historians claim that elaborate Sufi networks existed, others tend to discount these claims as exaggerated. It is indisputable that some of the early leaders were Sufi initiates. It is known that Sufism as well as Sufi intellectual thought was perhaps the single most important factor in the Islamisation of Southeast Asia. But the socio-political conditions at the Cape may have prevented these formalised networks from taking root. Therefore, some very specific Sufi rituals and hymnology may have survived, but there is little, if any, evidence of traditional Sufi networks (*turuq*).

What these rituals suggest is that folk, or 'low', Islam and folk mysticism were practised at first, rather than the 'high' Islam of scripturalism and puritanism. The difference between 'high' and 'low', or universal and local, Islam is not a sectarian schism, but rather a gradual continuum, not superficially perceptible.[18] Despite the ambiguity between the two forms, there remains a distinction, yet there is no recognised boundary. So practitioners of the two styles of Islam can at times coexist amicably, as was the case in early Islam; at other times they coexist violently, as is evident in twentieth-century Islam.

A characteristic feature of 'low' Islam is the cult of saints. Because there were no living Sufi shaykhs at the Cape, spiritual pilgrimages and visits to the shrines of saints (*karamats*; literally, supernatural events) became a compelling component of popular religion. What may also be unique to the Cape is that many people considered themselves initiates of deceased shaykhs whom they had never met in life, a practice which is perhaps rare, if not unknown, in popular *tasawwuf*.

This 'shrine cult' should not be underestimated as a source of religious inspiration in the history of early Islam. Combined with other practices of folk mysticism such as ecstatic supererogatory rituals and mystical exercises, it provided an escape from the misery of exile, slavery and social disadvantage. The Cape Peninsula is dotted with shrine sites. *Karamats* can be found as far apart as Faure, where Shaykh Yusuf was originally buried; Constantia, where Sayyid Mahmud and Sayyid 'Abd al-Rahman were buried in the seventeenth century; the slopes of Table Mountain near Camps Bay where Sayyid Nur al-Mubin lies buried; and on Signal Hill, where lies Tuang Sayyid. Adil Bradlow has identified 27 shrines in the Peninsula alone.

'Low' Islam thrives on magic, ecstasy and saint cults. The influence of the pre-Islamic cultures of Southeast Asia on Islam in that region is now well documented. Similar effects are clearly traceable in the folk mysticism of Cape Islam. The most prominent example is the practice of *ratib*, also called '*khalifa* display'. It is a ritual in which the participants, under a hypnotic trance induced by chants in Arabic, strike themselves with swords or pierce their flesh with skewers, without bleeding. While this has impressed audiences, Muslim and non-Muslim alike, it has also caused considerable disagreement amongst the Muslim community and consternation among city officials. Some of the imams, under the influence of 'high' Islam, have refused to acknowledge it as an Islamic practice and thus eschew it, while others favour it. On one occasion in the nineteenth century, a *ratib* ceremony became boisterous enough to rouse the alarm of the white citizenry of Cape Town, and the practice became the subject of a government inquiry. In the end it was restricted to certain days of the year and to special occasions.

Other popular practices, such as the use of talismans and amulets (*azimat*), the communal celebration of the Prophet Muhammad's birthday (*milad* or *mawlud*), and occasional collective prayers to bless the dead, are also widespread at the Cape. While some puritan strains of Islam may renounce these practices, Islamic orthodoxy at the Cape has incorporated them in an established tradition.

Indian influences: traders and missionaries

The arrival of the SS *Truro* in 1860 brought indentured South Indian labourers to work on the sugar-cane fields of Natal. While the majority of them were Hindu, some 7–10 per cent of them were Muslims. A second group of immigrants that arrived in Natal were the so-called 'passenger Indians', who paid for their passage to Africa. They settled in Natal, Transvaal and the Cape. Later this group was to form the commercial bourgeoisie among the Indian community.

Two factors clearly contributed to the establishment and spread of Islam in

Natal and Transvaal: the influential Sufi missionaries, and the *'ulama,* or jurist–theologians. The latter were essentially teachers and mosque leaders. The network of mosques spread rapidly with the movement of Muslim traders into rural Natal and Transvaal. Within two decades after their arrival, the first mosques were established in Natal and the Transvaal, where Islam grew swiftly, given favourable economic and social factors, compared with the restrictive conditions it faced in the Cape. The first mosque in Natal was built by Indian Muslim businessmen in Grey Street in 1884, while the mosque in the Pretoria city centre dates back to about 1887.

The saints of Durban: Badsha Pir and Sufi Sahib

Sufi missionaries, the first among them being Badsha Pir and, later, Sufi Sahib, also laid the foundations of Islam in Natal. Ahmad (1820–94), popularly known as Badsha Pir ('King Saint'), is believed to have been a Malayalam, who arrived with the third batch of indentured labourers from South India in the early 1860s. His prestige was boosted by the fact that he was alleged to have been a descendant of the family of the Prophet, and therefore bore the title of *sayyid.*

A study of some of the religious practices attributed to him suggests that he followed a brand of intoxicating Sufism. This was possibly why he was called *majzub,* 'the one intoxicated with divine ecstasy'.[19] He claimed affiliation to the well-known Qadiriyyah Sufi order. Legend and social memory portray him as a person who had acquired the power to perform miracles. He had an extraordinary reputation among both his followers and the colonial authorities. It is difficult, however, to separate legend from fact in accounts of charismatic figures, precisely because the legends appear in the form of hyperbole.

For most of the three decades he spent in South Africa he was an itinerant preacher. Badsha Pir appears to have been the source of religious inspiration for many of the early Muslim Indian contract workers. He is buried at the Brook Street cemetery in Durban.

Sufi Sahib (1858–1910), as he is popularly known, assumed the mantle of spiritual leadership from Badsha Pir. His proper name was Shah Ghulam Muhammad, but his piety so impressed his spiritual mentor in Hyderabad, Khawaja Habib Ali Shah, that he lovingly named him 'Sufi'. This epithet stuck and he became popularly known as Sufi Sahib ('Sufi Master'). He had a traditional Islamic education but later in life gravitated towards mysticism.

He arrived in Durban around 1896 on the orders of his spiritual mentor to work among the Indian Muslim workers in South Africa. He found them straying from traditional Islamic practices and set about the work of spiritual reform. He was also responsible for establishing several mosques in Natal, the Cape and Lesotho, as well as networks of Islamic propagation.

The 'ulama

From their very inception in classical Islam, the *'ulama* (literally, 'the learned', or jurist–theologians) played an important role in shaping the character of Islam. Although Islam does not have any clearly defined priesthood, the '*ulama* seem to play this role in effect. To a large extent the '*ulama* are proponents of 'high' or scriptural Islam. Historically, the term was used to describe both academic lawyers who occupy professorial positions in traditional institutions of learning, and clergymen who play a role in pastoral care. In contemporary Islam, the latter is more commonly meant.

The earliest Muslim savants at the Cape were trained '*ulama*, like Shaykh Yusuf and Tuang Guru. While they were both educated in the East, Tuang Guru is known to have trained some lay priests – imams – during his years at the Cape. Once the Cape Muslims had made contact with the Islamic heartland for the annual pilgrimage (*hajj*), as early as 1799, it is likely that some of them studied there as '*ulama*. However, it was only in the early twentieth century that trained '*ulama* exerted any real influence in South Africa.

Very little is known of the structures and practices of the '*ulama* save court records and other official sources, which reflect the nature of disputes over mosques in the Cape between rival imams, and the issues affecting their communities. The establishment of the first mosque suggests that the '*ulama* played a central role in educating the community, in both conceptual and religious terms. That the '*ulama* did have some structure by which they interacted with the community is borne out by the Colebrooke and Bigge Commission report of 1825, in which the imams interviewed described how they dealt with religious offenders and how they discouraged the practice of polygamy and slavery. One of the imams admitted that offenders were flogged, while the other denied it. From this it is difficult to determine whether a religious judiciary (*qada*) existed with the power to enforce sanctions.

Shortly after the arrival of the first Indian Muslims in Natal came Abubakr Effendi (*c.* 1835–80), a scholar of Kurdish origins, who made a dramatic impact on Cape Islam from 1863 onwards. P. E. de Roubaix, a prominent colonist, known for his Muslim sympathies, was largely responsible for Effendi's appearance at the Cape. After De Roubaix had been appointed Consul of the Ottoman Sultan at the Cape, he requested through his British contacts that a scholar be sent to resolve the unending religious disputes among Cape Muslims.

Ironically, Effendi's arrival was itself marked by controversy. Firstly, his language difficulties inhibited communication with the Cape Muslims. Secondly, he was a staunch follower of the Hanafi legal school, which was at variance with the local practices of the majority, all followers of the Shafi'i school. His legal chauvinism as a Hanafi gave offence to the community and fomented dissent, especially when the courts considered his opinion decisive in inter-Muslim litigation.

Despite his controversial nature, he soon had an influential following and established a school for women. He eventually mastered the Cape 'Malay' lingua franca, Arabic–Afrikaans, and wrote a treatise on religious ritual called 'The Elucidation of the Religion' (*Bayan al-Din*), which was published in Turkey.

In terms of Islamic law, the Cape was and remains an area in which the Shafi'i school prevails, because Islam in the region stems from Southeast Asia where the Shafi'i school is predominant. This is one of the four prominent Sunni legal schools dating back to the ninth century. It is a traditionalist school. Traditionalism in this case means that the concrete precedents of the past become the models of exemplary religious behaviour, and of ethical and juristic morality. Rational interpretation of the prophetic practices is eschewed, and choices suggested literally by tradition are favoured.

Although the legal schools do not, strictly speaking, have any doctrinal implications, inter-school conflict has in the past produced fanatical rivalry. One such event was the fierce Hanafi–Shafi'i dispute at the Cape associated with the arrival of Effendi in the late nineteenth century.

Resistance at the turn of the century

Towards the last quarter of the nineteenth century there were several instances of collective Muslim resistance against white colonial authority. The confrontation between two communities, Muslim and Christian, emphasises the religious dimension of politics. For instance, Muslims refused to be vaccinated during the 1882 smallpox epidemic in Cape Town. This was a statement of protest against racial prejudice and social grievances. Ostensibly, the reason for refusal was a religious one: Muslim leaders explained that disease was an affliction imposed by the will of God; accordingly, mortals could not interfere with divine predestination. Although disguised in religious language, such statements as that of a Muslim leader who declared that his religion was above the law conveyed a political message. Clearly the Muslims rejected what they saw as the opportunism of the white authorities, who were only concerned about poor sanitary conditions among the non-white community when white health was at peril. In ordinary circumstances the authorities ignored the abject living conditions which directly affected the Muslims in the city.

Again, in 1886 during the cemetery riots, Muslims resorted to civil disobedience in protest against the Public Health Act of 1883, which closed all cemeteries within the city. After failing to persuade the colonial authorities through deputations and representations to open the cemeteries, on the eve of the enforcement of the proclamation some three thousand defiant Muslims buried one of their dead in a prohibited cemetery. This led to the imposition of martial law for three days.

One of the figures who emerged during the cemetery riots was Abdul Burns, an educated cab driver. He became a fierce advocate of civil rights for Muslims, an eloquent and impressive figure in the politics of the city. His approach was initially reformist and constitutionalist, a stance that was widely acclaimed in the local white liberal press. When this approach failed, he resorted to more radical means. This earned him the opprobrium of his liberal admirers. For his role in the cemetery riots, he was fined and sentenced to two months' hard labour.

One of Burns's close associates was the enigmatic Ahmad Effendi, son of the famous Abubakr Effendi. The younger Effendi was the first non-white person ever to contest an election to parliament, in 1894. As he had a reasonable chance of winning, Cecil John Rhodes and the Afrikaner Bond conspired to keep him out by supporting legislation that abolished the cumulative vote in Cape Town. Voters, with four votes each, could no longer cast them in favour of one candidate. Under the abolished system, the effective Malay vote could have brought Effendi to office. Effendi's mistake had been to announce his candidature for nomination while the 1893 term of parliament was still in session; this gave his opponents time to introduce the legislation that was to thwart his prospects.

THE TWENTIETH CENTURY

From 1902 to Nationalist rule

By the end of the Anglo-Boer War in 1902, there were substantial centres of Muslim religious and political expression in the Cape, Transvaal and Natal. In the Cape, several Muslim organisations arose, each with different political objectives.

In about 1903, the short-lived South African Moslem Association was formed. Its demise was due to lack of support from the Cape 'ulama, of whom it was critical. About the same time, the African Political Organisation, later the African People's Organisation (APO), captured the imagination of Cape Muslims because of the highly visible participation of one of their co-religionists, Dr Abdullah Abdurahman (1872–1940).

Where Ahmad Effendi's career had ended in failure to be elected to parliament, Dr Abdurahman's began. He was born in Wellington, into a family that only two generations before had purchased its freedom from slavery. His grandfather was a successful and prominent businessman, and educated his son in Cairo and Makkah. Abdullah's father, by contrast, sent his son to an exclusively white grammar school in Cape Town, and later to Glasgow to study medicine. On his return, the young Abdurahman practised as a doctor, but was passionately drawn to politics and education. It was due to his pioneering efforts that several Muslim mission schools were established. In addition, he was elected to the Cape Town City Council and later the Provincial Council, positions he held until his death.

One of the more prominent and influential organisations to emerge in the early part of the century was the Cape Malay Association (CMA), founded in 1923. Prominent in this body was the actor Arshad Gamiet, as well as 'ulama like Shaykh Ahmad Behardien and Imam Moegamat Sudley Awaldien. Although the CMA was essentially socio-religious in nature, some of its leaders were sympathetic to General J. B. M. Hertzog's appeal for 'coloured' and black support for the National Party. Later, Dr D. F. Malan was strongly supported by the CMA, and in return promised the Malays an 'enhanced status' similar to that of the 'coloureds', a pledge on which the Nationalists reneged when they took power in 1948.

By the 1930s the CMA was eclipsed by the younger and more radical intelligentsia, who espoused secular politics without any appeal to Islam. Among them was Dr Abdurahman's daughter, Zainunisa 'Cissy' Gool, and her husband, Dr Goolam Gool. The prominence of the young radicals, as well as the support given by the CMA for the discredited Coloured Affairs Department, sounded the death-knell of this once-popular cultural–religious organisation.

In Natal and Transvaal, early Muslim activism was conducted not under the aegis of Islam, but as part of the Indian civil rights campaign. Among the demands made during Gandhi's passive resistance campaigns in 1906 was a call that Muslim and Hindu marriages be legally recognised. While politics in this context was not overtly couched in religious language, religious issues were central to the individual and communal self-assertion of Indian Muslims.

One of the earliest religious organisations in the Transvaal was the Habibia Muslim Society, about which little is known. It is interesting to note that Muslim organisations were visible at an earlier period in the Boer Republic of the Transvaal than in the British Colony of Natal. Closely aligned to Mahatma Gandhi was the association known as the 'Pretoria Group', led by Moulana Mukhtar and Ahmad Muhammad Cachalia. Gandhi expressed great admiration for the loyalty and commitment of Cachalia.

The 'ulama in the twentieth century
If folk Islam reflects local knowledge and parochial religion, then the *'ulama* tradition is unmistakably the carrier of 'high' or universal Islam. In the practices of the *'ulama* this effect is discernible at two levels, juristic and theological. As Islam is nomocentric in its public character, it elevates the status of the law, as does rabbinic Judaism. In the Transvaal and Natal, the Muslims of Indian origin followed the legal doctrines of the eighth-century Hanafi school. To be precise, it is a version of the Hanafi school as interpreted by *'ulama* of the Indian seminary of Deoband, founded in 1867 near Delhi, and its satellite colleges in India, Pakistan and South Africa. In its Arab mutation, the Hanafi school is considered one of the more liberal and rational legal schools. Thus, during the Ottoman Empire, the Hanafi school was the pioneer of legal reform to meet the demands of modernity. However, on the Indian subcontinent the pervasiveness of *hadith* (prophetic tradition) studies since the sixteenth century has compelled legal scholarship to adopt more traditionalist approaches.

Neo-Sufism is also another feature of Indian 'high' Islam. Both conservative traditionalism and neo-Sufism are finding entry into South African Islam by way of the *'ulama* bodies of Transvaal and Natal, which are the purveyors of the Deoband school. They are similarly rigid in their commitment to the Hanafi school. Creative and independent thinking in religious law is hardly promoted among the *'ulama*, and imitation (*taqlid*) of the Hanafi school is generally viewed as imperative.

The other mainstream Sunni legal schools, like the Maliki, Shafi'i and Hanbali, are variants of the traditionalist (*hadith*) movement, in which fideism rather than rationalism prevails. In the Transvaal, followers of the Shafi'i school, which traces its ideological roots to regions south of Bombay, are also to be found. At least two mosques in the greater Johannesburg area follow the Shafi'i code.

In the Cape, the traditionalist Shafi'i school remains dominant, but at two mosques the Hanafi school is recognised. By definition the Cape ought to be conservative, given its Shafi'i majority, yet legal dogmatism is on the wane here. One reason for this change in attitude is that most of the Cape *'ulama* were trained in the Middle East, in places like Egypt, Saudi Arabia, Lebanon and Jordan, where legal eclecticism (*talfiq*) is encouraged and legal dogmatism abjured.

The difference between the Shafi'i and Hanafi *'ulama* is not entirely due to the influence of the ideas of 'high' Islam. The regional cultures in which Islam finds itself also have an impact. The Muslims of Malay origin have managed to develop a unique culture over nearly 300 years of coexistence with diverse communities. A synthesis of Southeast Asian Islam and elements of Afrikaner and indigenous cultures has most likely had an effect. This has given Cape Islam its visible cultural flexibility and adaptability. Indian Muslims, on the other hand, are comparatively recent immigrants, given their presence here for just over a hundred years. They therefore have resisted acculturation and emphasise a cultural particularism which fosters rigidity and conservatism. In their legal and ethical vision, both the Shafi'i and Hanafi *'ulama* are perhaps equally conservative and resistant to innovative jurisprudence.

Associations, tendencies and schisms

The Jamiats: the Deoband tradition

At first neither the indentured labourers in Natal nor the merchants in Transvaal had any *'ulama* to provide education or religious leadership. Basic religious functions were fulfilled by the labourers and merchants themselves. Only after 1880 did the authorities permit religious teachers and imams to enter the country, for special purposes only. These communities thus managed subsequently to employ *'ulama* and some school teachers from India, and so ensured the formation of religious education structures.

The Indian Muslim merchants, as a class, formed a stable and strong alliance with the *'ulama* over the decades. This alliance led to the establishment of a new association of *'ulama*, the Jamiat al-'Ulama in Transvaal in 1922. Although that attempt was short-lived, an organisation by the same name was revived in 1935 by Mufti Ebrahim Sanjalvi (d. 1983). This took place with the assistance of the affluent Mia family, several of whose members were themselves *'ulama*, together with Mufti Sanjalvi, who founded the Jamiat al-'Ulama of Transvaal (the Association of Transvaal *'Ulama*), in 1935. The attempt to organise religious leaders into a guild or association was part of a modernising strain evident in the Muslim world from the eighteenth century onwards. This association clearly derived its impulse from tendencies prevalent among the counterparts of the *'ulama* in India. Modernisation in this context meant adopting modern administrative and organisational skills, while resisting the cultural and intellectual aspects of modernity.

In Natal, the Sufi-based form of Islam with its popular religious practices was more resilient to encroachment by the *'ulama*, although it was not totally impregnable. As the *'ulama* became a significant presence only after 1880, the conflict between 'high' and 'folk' Islam did not occur till well into the twentieth century. The first attempt to organise the *'ulama* in Natal took place in 1955 with the formation of the Jamiat al-'Ulama Natal (Association of Natal *'Ulama*).

Islam in Natal was clearly marked by class interests. On the one hand there was a large group of Muslims from a working-class background who were, in terms of ethnicity and language, very different from the merchant-class Muslims. The latter hailed primarily from the Indian state of Gujarat, while the former were from the Deccan and South India, speaking Urdu and other South Indian languages. This was further expressed as differences in religious outlook, to be discussed below.

Popular Islam

The religious proclivities within each group were determined by the religious tendencies prevalent in the regions in India where the groups originated. In the same way that different strains of Islam, scriptural and popular, could coexist amicably, they could also be found within the same class. Among the merchant class one could easily find orthodox puritans, as well those more inclined to charismatic rituals and ecstatic practices. In other words, class divisions and cultic practices do not always coincide.

Until the middle of the twentieth century, certain practices among Indian Muslims, like the public celebration of the Prophet Muhammad's birthday and veneration of saints (*urs*), which today may be deemed an aspect of folk Islam, were prevalent among all sectors. Given the historical class and ethnic elements within Islam in Natal, these religio-ethnic divisions took on a stronger ideological character in the second half of the twentieth century. Fragmentation and schism were precipitated by forces originating in India, where formerly peaceful relationships between puritanical scripturalist and charismatic folk tendencies erupted in conflict.

Tabligh Jama'ah

In South Africa one such force in the 1960s was the introduction of a movement originating in India, the Tabligh Jama'ah (Evangelical Association). This movement was founded in about 1919 by Mawlana Muhammad Ilyas (1885–1944), a member of the Indian *'ulama*, and aimed at reviving the foundational practices among Muslims. This movement has gained worldwide influence. Recruits do evangelical work on a voluntary basis, travelling inside their home countries and abroad, and recruiting new members to continue the cycle of evangelical work. These itinerant lay preachers use the mosques as spiritual retreats and as a base for their work. Seven fundamental teachings underpin their ideology: an understanding of the article of faith (that there is no God other the Allah and that Muhammad is his Messenger); prayer five times a day (*salah*); learning (*'ilm*) and remembering God (*dhikr*); service and honour of fellow Muslims; sincerity of intention; avoiding idleness; and doing evangelical work, *da'wah* (calling unto the way of God).

Most of the people associated with this movement tend to align themselves with the religious thinking of the Deoband seminary in India. Arabs, for instance, who identify with the movement follow conservative and scripturalist tendencies. The Tabligh Jama'ah was soon viewed as a wing of the Deoband seminary, which aimed at ending folk and popular Islam. Hence, Deoband began to receive opposition from other orthodox quarters, an antagonism which has only worsened over time.

The Barelwi tradition

One of the theological, and possibly political, opponents of Deoband was Mawlana Ahmad Riza Khan of Barelwi (1856–1921). Like the Deoband 'ulama, he was also concerned about the law, but in contrast was detached from political activity. With the aid of legal scholarship he justified the inter-cession of saints, and the role of social customs in Islam. While these debates are centuries old in Islamic theology, they coalesced at a critical moment in Indian politics, adding to the complexity of the issues.

This rift in Indian Islam ultimately spread to South Africa. The Barelwi movement accepts the celebration of the Prophet's birthday and defends the theological validity of veneration of saints and the doctrine of prophetic pres-ence among believers. The Deoband movement opposes this and adopts a more puritan approach. The opposition between the Deoband movement and the Barelwi movement is often acrimonious, leading to heated public debates and even fatal violence at times.

The Sunni Jamiat al-'Ulama of South Africa, supportive of the Barelwi cause, was formed in 1978. The Sunni Jamiat al-'Ulama has a visible presence in Natal, and an office in the Cape and some representation in Transvaal. This structure formalises the schisms within orthodox Islam in South Africa. (The term 'Sunni' as appropriated by the Barelwi movement is part of a polemic stemming from their claim that they are more committed to the pro-phetic practice (*sunnah*) than their opponents. Used in this context, it should not be confused with one term of the major schism in Islam between the Sunni and Shi'ah.)

The Muslim Judicial Council

In the oldest centre of Islam in Southern Africa, the Cape, the first formal 'ulama body to be formed was the Muslim Judicial Council (MJC), in 1945. The MJC stems from the Moslem Progressive Society, established in 1942, which primarily focused on issues dealing with social relief and welfare. One of its objectives, however, was to 'urge the religious leaders to elect a judicial coun-cil to which all religious matters could be referred to for solution'. It is evident that some turmoil in Islamic affairs in the Cape precipitated the emergence of the MJC. Prior to its formation, disputes were settled by the *bechara* method, a type of informal conference which antagonists would attend together with their followers. A viewpoint would be accepted or rejected according to the response it evoked from those in attendance. Professionals with secular education in the Progressive Society clearly found these dispute resolution mechanisms unsatis-factory and thus urged the 'ulama to establish a body along modern lines.

It was such professionals who drafted the founding documents of the MJC and its constitution in the form of a ten-point programme. This defined the goals of the MJC as uniting Muslims; promoting education by setting up a Muslim college where students would receive religious and secular education; issuing religious decrees that would be binding and final; and securing legal recognition by government of marriages by Muslim rites (and other transactions according to Muslim law). The MJC also had broad political goals of forging unity 'in the interest of all non-Europeans' in order to combat all 'oppressive forces' that would hamper their progress.

In its formative years the MJC adopted a non-political stance, although some members did espouse political views, such as Shaykh Hanief Booley and the late Imam Abdullah Haron. It was Imam Haron's death in detention in 1969 that set the scene for a more politically aggressive Muslim stance a decade later.

The Islamic Council of South Africa

A more ambitious project in the form of the Islamic Council of South Africa (ICSA) was launched in 1975. ICSA was to become an umbrella body that would speak officially on behalf of all Muslims in South Africa. It would have both a religious judiciary and a programme of action. The leadership represented both the *'ulama* and professionals. ICSA also attempted to include the traditionalist and adaptationist strands of Islam in one embrace. Youth groups, *'ulama* organisations, professional associations and other socio-religious groups all joined this body.

However, differences among the affiliates and problems related to foreign funding soon ensured that the larger project was abandoned. Although ICSA still exists, it does so with very little effect since religious leadership remains in the hands of its affiliates.

The Ahmadiyyah

During the late 1960s another tendency deriving from the Indian subcontinent surfaced in South Africa. This was the Ahmadiyyah movement, an individualist assertion based on charismatic leadership, which was founded by Mirza Ghulam Ahmad of Qadiyan (1839–1908). He claimed special revelation from God and regarded himself as a prophet and messiah. In South Africa most of the Ahmadis consider themselves within the bounds of the Islamic tradition, but the majority of Muslims reject them as heretics.

Circles, books and revolution

The 1950s witnessed the rise of national independence movements in Africa, the Middle East and Southeast Asia. At that time influential Third World personalities, like the Egyptian premier Gamal 'Abdul Nasser and Ahmad Sukarno of Indonesia, were role models for politically aware South African Muslim youth. Drawing inspiration from pan-Africanism and pan-Arabism, and the association of the pan-Arabian with pan-Islamism, a youth formation known as the Muslim Youth Movement was founded in District Six, Cape Town, in 1957. A year later, the Claremont Muslim Association

(CMA) was founded by followers of Imam Haron. These movements addressed political questions concerned with human rights and democracy, and social issues affecting the poor and the aged.

Inspiration for these groups can be traced to the Salafiyyah writers, such as the famous pan-Islamic reformer, Jamal al-Din al-Afghani, the Egyptian reformer, Shaykh Muhammad 'Abduh, and Shaykh Rashid Rida, his Syrian disciple. At the same time the youth were also concerned about the quality of leadership which the clergy (*'ulama*) offered. They called for a more effective style of preaching in the mosques, and agitated for more socially relevant sermons. Perhaps the greatest impact of these movements lay in the publication of newsletters and pamphlets. As a result of the death of Imam Haron and the repressive policies of the apartheid era, the youth organisations gradually became inactive.

The mid-1950s was a watershed phase in the broader pattern of modern Islamic expression in South Africa. In various centres of the country there was vocal disenchantment with the *'ulama* and their leadership. An index of this dissatisfaction was the mushrooming of small study groups and associations in the Vaal Triangle, Natal and the Cape.

These organisations, consisting of a younger generation of Muslims such as the youth groups in the Cape, encouraged lay persons to study the Qur'an on their own by reading English translations. There was a strong emphasis on reading accessible Islamic literature in a bid to reduce, if not break, the customary dependence on the clergy. While this rather protestant activity did not evoke vehement opposition from the *'ulama*, relations between the two were certainly strained from time to time. In the Cape at least, these youth groups became the purveyors of a modernising tendency, rather than being modernist. In other words, they adopted technology and contemporary know-how in the service of faith, rather than embracing the knowledge and intellectual legacy of modernity.

The group that did indeed provoke the hostility of the *'ulama* was the Arabic Study Circle, established in 1950 in Durban. Consisting mainly of young Muslim businessmen and professionals who were thoroughly disenchanted with the conservative discourse of the *'ulama*, the Circle set out to gain direct access to the Qur'an. The rationale of this approach was that because the Qur'an is in Arabic, proficiency in the language is necessary. If this were achieved, it would end the dependence of lay persons on the clergy. Ambitious as it may have been, the Arabic Study Circle did to some extent promote modernisation, given its opposition to the hidebound tradition of the *'ulama*. The clergy certainly viewed them with suspicion and condemned their activities in strong language as 'misguided'. Despite these misgivings, it was the Study Circle's efforts to promote the study of Islam at a tertiary level that led to the establishment of Arabic and Islamic studies at schools and at the University of Durban–Westville.

The Muslim Youth Movement of South Africa (MYMSA), not to be confused with the MYM of Cape Town, was established in 1970 in Natal. It continued the processes developed by the Arabic Study Circle of modernisation, self-empowerment in matters of religion, and independence from the *'ulama*. The silence of Muslim political discourse in the 1960s and especially after the death of Imam Haron had created a leadership vacuum among Muslim youth. It was at this juncture that MYMSA emerged as a national movement. It started out primarily as a religio-cultural body with a muted political agenda. Drawing largely from the middle class, the MYMSA was unmistakably influenced by the ideologues of the Muslim Brotherhood of Egypt and the Jamat Islami of Pakistan. The intellectual diet of this youth movement consisted of writings by people such as Hassan al-Banna (1906–49), founder of the Brotherhood; Sayyid Qutb (1906–66), a journalist and militant ideologue of the same group, who was executed by Nasser's government; and Abu al-A'la Mawdudi (1903–79), founder of the Jamat Islami of Pakistan. Idealism clearly marked this phase of the MYMSA.

In its early phase, MYMSA operated along the lines of similar organisations elsewhere. The most enduring feature of this movement was the emphasis on self-education in matters of religion by way of small study circles. In these weekly circles members were encouraged to read and reflect on the Qur'an in translated form, master the works of the ideologues, and familiarise themselves with the history of Islam. Members saw such training as a fortification against the Westernising influences of society, on one hand, and the anachronistic interpretations of the conservative *'ulama* on the other. The ultimate goal was to prepare for the inauguration of an Islamic state.

Together with the Muslim Students' Association (MSA), which later worked closely with MYMSA, the Muslim Youth Movement had a significant influence on Muslim youth for more than a decade. Within a short time MYMSA had set up an impressive array of social organisations on a national scale. These include a major welfare body, the South African National Zakaat Fund (SANZAF); the Islamic Medical Association, which serves as a guild for Muslim doctors and provides health services to disadvantaged communities; a number of training and orientation schools for converts to Islam in townships; and an active disaster and relief agency, the Islamic Relief Agency (ISRA).

The youth groups, especially the MYMSA, found it difficult, however, to make the transition from a religio-cultural ethos to a socio-cultural one. They lacked a contextual Islamic idiom through which they could articulate their political concerns, especially during the tumultuous 1970s and the Soweto uprising in 1976. The Islamic revolution in Iran in 1979 provided a vital impetus for global Islamic political discourse. For those Muslim communities far away from the Muslim heartland, like South Africa, it had special significance. For the first time, Muslims found a point of reference for their religious and moral struggle, which coincided with the revolutionary zeal prevalent at the time among liberation movements in South Africa. However, it was not MYMSA so much as the Qiblah Mass Movement and, to a lesser extent, the Muslim Students' Association, which embraced the charged rhetoric and fervour of the Iranian revolution.

Founded in 1980, Qiblah immediately identified itself with Islamic Iran, and especially its main architect, Ayatollah Khomeini. Qiblah's main ideo-

logues were longstanding supporters of the Pan Africanist Congress and Black
Consciousness tradition. Its key rallying point was the unity of Muslims and
the desire to transform South Africa towards Islamic ideals. It supported the
armed struggle by actively seconding some of its members to this task, as part
of an effort of *jihad*, or religiously sanctioned armed resistance. This tendency
can be described as an idealist one, which constantly offers radical critiques of
Muslim society and South African society at large.

Marches, rallies and funerals

The advent of the tricameral constitution in 1984 and widespread repression during P. W. Botha's presidency provoked spontaneous political opposition. One focus of opposition was the ANC-backed United Democratic Front
(UDF), which successfully lobbied the religious sector, Muslims included.

A dispute within the ranks of MYMSA over the issue of political alliances
with the UDF gave rise to a breakaway group, which formed the pro-UDF
Call of Islam (COI) in 1984. The COI articulated a form of Islam which fitted
well with the vision and goals of the UDF, in the same way that Qiblah promoted the PAC agenda. COI emphasised the centrality of the leadership of
the clergy and consistently dragged its reluctant partners, the MJC, into political issues.

By the mid-1980s, MYMSA had entered a revisionist phase together with
the MSA, and in conjunction with other groups began to develop a contextual
expression of Islam with a strong focus on South African political realities. At
the same time, the MJC was unique among the *'ulama* groups in siding with
the liberation movement; some of its key officials were also members of the
COI. Together these groups developed a hermeneutic code of Islam opposed
to oppression (*zulm*), of God siding with the oppressed (*mustad'afin*), and of
justice (*adl*) and equity (*qist*) being the goals which Muslims should strive to
achieve as part of the ongoing struggle, *jihad*.

While some Muslim organisations may have privately accepted the tricameral dispensation by tacitly supporting members of parliament who were
Muslim, few publicly did so. Among the northern *'ulama* groups, only the
Jamiat al-'Ulama of Natal and the Sunni Jamiat al-'Ulama issued statements
opposing the tricameral constitution. By the early 1980s the divide between
the politically conservative *'ulama* organisations and the progressive socio-
cultural and political bodies was marked.

The Nationalist government's reforms provoked popular political upheaval.
In various parts of the country, stone-throwing youths fought street battles
with security forces. The progressive Muslim movements were in the forefront
of this popular resistance, striking formal and strategic alliances with political
formations spanning a range of political tendencies. While some Muslim
groups espoused Black Consciousness, others favoured the PAC, and yet
others were aligned with the Charterists.

It was the killing fields of apartheid that succeeded in uniting historically
and culturally divided communities. During the period 1984–9, the main features of civil rights activities were protest marches, political rallies and funeral

services of victims of political brutality. At these funerals, a new inter-faith ecumenism of Muslims, Christians, Jews, Hindus and secularists surfaced, establishing unprecedented common moral foundations from which to oppose the apartheid system. The Islamic organisations at the forefront of this new ecumenism were the COI, the MSA, the MJC, MYMSA and Qiblah. At mass meetings and funerals, Islamic symbols were highly visible in Muslim areas. Youths donning Palestinian headgear (*kaffiyehs*), frenzied with revolutionary zeal, raised the war-cry of 'One solution – Islamic revolution'. Conservative *'ulama* groups for their part denounced alliances with 'infidels' and the free association of sexes in political activities, dubbing these un-Islamic practices of the worst kind. For progressive Islamic elements, the moral demand to oppose apartheid superseded the narrow theological interpretations of the clergy.

This historic moment generated innovative discourses on religious pluralism, liberation, gender discrimination, and environmental destruction which were unprecedented in modern Muslim history. This phase also saw a decline in Islamic particularism and greater emphasis on Islamic humanism and universalism. At the conservative end of the ideological spectrum it provoked a reactionary response, resistance to the contextual expression of Islam. It would be true to say that the destruction of the old society spawned the elements of a new vision for South Africa.

During the months of turmoil, the progressives achieved a marginal dominance, while the national context aided their highly politicised agenda. But that was temporary. State attempts to mollify Muslim anger by means of recognition of Muslim marriages and divorces, and opportunities for international trade with Muslim countries (part of a major campaign of sanctions-busting), allowed the conservatives to regain the initiative. The intense struggle of the 1980s may have sensitised the *'ulama* to some of the needs of the youth, but it hardly effected any transformation in their religious and cultural thinking.

The period of transition

The De Klerk reforms in the 1990s and the unbanning of the liberation movements raised the prospect that South Africa would head towards full democracy. In the wake of the national debate on negotiations with the apartheid regime, a historic Muslim National Conference was convened which included the bulk of Muslim organisations. After two days of lengthy deliberations, the conference resolved that Muslims were not unanimous in their support for negotiations – some supported the strategy and others opposed it. The same conference highlighted the fact that Muslims are not a homogeneous and undifferentiated group, as is assumed by both insiders and outsiders.

In modern South Africa, Muslims have made great strides in their visibility in public life, despite their limited numbers (an estimated half a million). In the fields of medicine, building, small business, music, art, drama, politics and law, Muslims have maintained a significant profile. The first 'black' person to be permanently appointed a Supreme Court judge in the annals of South African judicial history was a Muslim. Whereas earlier generations of Muslims were either artisans (Malay Muslims) or small shopkeepers (Indian Muslims), the new generation are increasingly entering professional careers, such as nursing, social work, teaching, medicine and law.

Conversion and growth

During the oppressive years of apartheid it was *jihad*, understood as 'struggle' against an oppressive regime, that made Islam attractive to many black people in South Africa. For the black underclasses whose wretched experience of life was ostensibly sanctioned by Christianity, Islam was an attractive alternative. Since the 1950s, several Muslim organisations have undertaken missionary work (*da'wah*) among African communities, with a growing rate of conversion. These two factors, politics and missionary work, have given rise to several Muslim communities in African townships throughout the country.

Islam is today one of the fastest-growing religions in the world. The question remains whether the religious demography of the country will change as a new society emerges in South Africa. Islam shares the African continent along with two other traditions, African religion and Christianity: three religions vying for Africa's soul.

Islam in a post-apartheid South Africa

As South Africa slowly but painfully turns its back on the apartheid era, Muslims face a new and challenging future. For the first time in history, all South Africans participate in a democratic political dispensation. The new openness, pluralism and multi-culturalism make new demands of adaptation and adjustment on all communities, including religious ones.

Exposure to the international community, and new relations with other Muslim communities, will most probably generate new patterns of social identity among South African Muslims. Cultural and social contact will inevitably introduce new tendencies of thought, which may have significant consequences.

Simultaneously, pressing domestic issues of reconstruction and nation-building will make demands for adaptation. In the past, Muslims felt alienated by the structures of colonialism and apartheid. For the first time the new dispensation considers them an integral part of society. For the first time South African society faces the real prospect of a multi-culturalism in which all cultures and value systems will be considered full participants in society. The challenge lies in how Muslims will formulate and exercise their right to be treated the same as all other citizens and at the same time insist on their right to be different.[20]

NOTES

I would like to thank my colleague Dr Abdulkader Tayob for his suggestions and advice on this article. The errors and mistakes remain mine. I would also like to acknowledge the University of Cape Town for their research grant.

1. Robin Hallett, *Africa to 1875: A Modern History*. Ann Arbor: The University of Michigan Press, 1970, p. 17.

2. There is also a suggestion that they may be falashas of Jewish descent; see G. C. Oosthuizen, 'Hebraic–Judaistic Tenets in the African Independent Churches and Religious Movements in South Africa', in David A. Shank (ed.), *African Independent Churches*. Elkhart, Indiana: Mennonite Board of Missions, 1991. For further reading see Ephraim Mandivenga, 'The History and Re-conversion of the Varemba of Zimbabwe', *Journal of Religion in Africa*, 19, 2 (1989), pp. 98–124.

3. The Khalwatiyyah has some obscure roots in thirteenth century Turkey and Persia. It is alleged that it gained the named *khalwatiyyah*, meaning 'the retreating one', due to the frequent spiritual retreats undertaken by its founder, Muhammad Nur al-Balisi. Others say the founder was 'Umar al-Khalwati, who was born in Lahij, Jilan, and who died in Tabriz in 800/1397 (see *Encyclopedia of Islam*, vol. 6. Leiden: E. J. Brill, 1978, pp. 991–93).

4. For further details see G. M. Theal, *History of South Africa*, vol. 3. London: Sonnenschein, 1911, pp. 261–63.

5. Theal says: 'They [free blacks] consist of persons, who during the existence of the Dutch East India Company, were sent from Batavia or the other dependencies, either as convicts or in attendance upon their masters, or as manumitted slaves, and many of them consist of Malays and Natives of Malabar, who were not in a state of servitude.' See *Records of the Cape Colony*, vol. 28. London: Clowes, 1897–1905, p. 66.

6. Achmat Davids, 'The Words the Slaves Made'. Unpublished paper.

7. Theal, *Records of the Cape Colony*, vol. 32, p. 140.

9. Michel Serres, 'Hermes: Literature, Science and Philosophy', in J. V. Harari and D. F. Bell (eds.), *Knowledge in the Classical Age*, p. 28.

9. Lady Duff Gordon, *Letters from the Cape*. London: Humphrey Milford, 1921, p. 81.

10. I. D. du Plessis and C. A. Luckhoff, *The Malay Quarter and Its People*. Cape Town: Balkema, 1963, p. 33.

11. John Centlivres Chase, *The Cape of Good Hope and the Eastern Province of Algoa Bay*. London: Pelham Richardson, 1843, p. 235.

12. 'The Cape Malays', *Cape Monthly Magazine* (10 July 1861), p. 358.

13. Lady Duff Gordon, *Letters from the Cape*, p. 31.

14. *Ibid*, p. 40.

15. Theal, *Records of Cape Colony*, vol. 28, p. 38.

16. The Qadiriyyah was founded by the reputable Sufi Shaykh 'Abd al-Qadir ibn Abi Salih Jangidost (1079–1165) who was born in Jilan, Iran, and is therefore called al-Jilani. This order is perhaps one of the most popular Sufi orders and is widespread, with a stronghold on the Indo-Pak subcontinent.

17. The 'Alawiyyah order was founded by Muhammd ibn Ali (1178–1255) of the Ba Alawi tribe in southern Arabia.

18. Ernest Gellner, *Postmodernism, Reason and Religion*. London: Routledge, 1992, p. 10.

19. See 'Islam' in J. W. de Gruchy and M. Prozesky, *A Southern African Guide to World Religions*, Cape Town: David Philip, 1991, p. 230.

20. Albie Sachs, *Protecting Human Rights in a New South Africa.* Cape Town, Oxford University Press, 1990, p. 44.

SELECT BIBLIOGRAPHY

Bradlow, Frank R. and Margaret Cairns, *The Early Cape Muslims.* Cape Town: A. A. Balkema, 1978

Bradlow, Muhammad Adil, 'Imperialism, State Formation and the Establishment of a Muslim Community at the Cape of Good Hope, 1770–1840: A Study in Urban Resistance'. MA thesis, University of Cape Town, 1988

Dangor, Suleman Essop, *A Critical Biography of Shaykh Yusuf.* Durban: Centre for Research in Islamic Studies, University of Durban-Westville, 1983

Davids, Achmat, *Mosques of the Bo-Kaap.* Cape Town: South African Institute of Arabic and Islamic Research, 1980

Du Plessis, I.D., *The Cape Malays.* Cape Town: Maskew Miller, 1947

9

The Jewish Community in South Africa

JOCELYN HELLIG

Any examination of the history of the Jews of South Africa must consider not only the special nature of the broader South African society but the particular characteristics of the Jewish experience itself. Diaspora Jews (Jews of the dispersion), wherever they reside, are always in a vulnerable situation. For almost two thousand years, from 70 CE until the re-establishment of the State of Israel in 1948, Jews have lived as a relatively powerless minority in a variety of host countries. Their well-being, or lack of it, has been in direct proportion to the positive or negative attitudes of their host governments. Jews have been accepted as equals or subjected to various forms of discriminatory legislation. Deprived of significant political power, the primary behavioural mode of Jewish communities has been one of conciliation. In addition, anti-Semitism is a ubiquitous feature of Jewish experience. Thus, Jewish communities tend to respond to the world around them in a manner which seeks to minimise overt negative action against them.

Some of the earlier recorded histories of the Jews in South Africa tend both to give more weight to the contribution of successful Jews, such as mining magnates, and to emphasise the homogeneity of the community. The current tendency is to demystify the South African Jewish past. In reconstructing the history of early Johannesburg, for example, with its burgeoning economy and influx of varied fortune-hunters, scholars have attempted to examine the contribution of the lower classes in all communities. This applies equally to the Jewish community. When it is looked at from this perspective, a more balanced picture emerges than has hitherto been presented.[1] In the scramble to make a living, there was a considerable amount of insensitivity to and exploitation of one group by another. Jews were but one set of participants in the ruthless economic interaction of early Johannesburg, the black labour force having been exploited by all groups that were in a position to do so.

The Jewish community of South Africa resembles most other New World Jewish communities. However, it is unique in the sense that Jews are part of the white privileged class in a country in which one criterion, namely race, has been the primary determinant of people's lives. This was bound to shape the distinctive nature of the South African Jewish community. In a country which always promoted ethnicity, the Jews, like other ethnic groups, were encouraged to maintain their separate identity. There has never been a melting-pot dynamic in South Africa. The very converse prevails. Jews have been able to maintain one of the most basic features of orthodoxy, namely separateness.

There has been, as Gideon Shimoni pointed out, no inclusive South African identity – no sense of nationality equivalent to that provided by the concept of being 'British' or 'American'. South African society has been segmented primarily into racial groups and, secondarily, among the white group, into English- and Afrikaans-speakers. The white sector is thus culturally dualistic. This helped to preserve Jewish identity; there was thus more leeway for the retention of Jewish religious identity, and for the expression of its national element through Zionism.[2]

Although Jews were exempt from the discrimination suffered by people of colour, and although they enjoyed full civil rights in the parliamentary democracy limited to whites, the Jewish community has been subjected to more discriminatory legislation than any other white group in the country.

A small community, numbering about 100 000 people, the Jews constitute 0.3 per cent of the entire South African population, and 2 per cent of the white population. Jews have tended to acculturate to the English-speaking sector of the white group and are a highly urbanised community. More than half reside in the vicinity of Johannesburg, while about a quarter live in Cape Town. Most of the rest can be found in some of the other major cities, such as Durban and Pretoria. They are predominantly active in commerce and the professions, often successfully so. Their numbers have diminished over the past two decades primarily as a result of emigration. This loss has been partly compensated for by a fairly large but indeterminate number of Israeli immigrants.[3]

The South African Jewish community is often lauded as the most organised diaspora community in the world. This can be attributed to its smallness, to its compact concentration in two major centres, and to its relatively homogeneous Anglo-Litvak (English and Lithuanian) origins. The two major bodies which govern the general relations of the community with its surrounding world are the South African Jewish Board of Deputies and the South African Zionist Federation. The former deals with the overall protection and well-being of the community, guarding its civil and religious rights, and acting as its official representative on all matters of importance. The South African Zionist Federation deals with matters relating to Israel.

It has always been difficult to gauge the political leanings of Jews in South Africa because the Jewish community is not monolithic and there is no such thing as a 'Jewish vote'. Although, historically, Jews have tended to adopt centrist policies and were ardent supporters of J. C. Smuts's United Party, it is not possible to ascertain a normative pattern of Jewish attitudes. There was, for example, evidence of a distinct socialist leaning among the Yiddish-speaking immigrants from Eastern Europe, expressed as opposition to discrimination based on skin colour. However, many others felt that blacks were their inferiors.

Having experienced severe anti-Jewish legislation during the 1930s at the instigation of the National Party – such as the Immigration Quota Act of 1930, which severely limited Jewish immigration into South Africa from Eastern Europe, and the Aliens Act of 1937, which effectively halted Jewish immigration from Germany[4] – Jews were deeply apprehensive when the National Party came to power in 1948. Their fears turned out to be unfounded in that successive Nationalist governments showed no official anti-Semitism in their policies and maintained a consistently cordial relationship with Israel after its re-establishment in 1948. Jews have given consistent support to what is today the Democratic Party. They did, however, become more visibly associated with the National Party in the 1980s, a feature that increased after the then State President, F. W. de Klerk, initiated a negotiated political settlement in February 1990. Because National Party policies were racially based, this visible association of even a minority of Jews with the governing party was a source of great discomfort for the Jewish community. It was criticised by more liberal Jews as alien to the ethical and prophetic spirit of Judaism. Many based their criticism on the argument that the Jews' experience of suffering and persecution, particularly during the Holocaust, should steer them away from any policies based on race.

Jews, as individuals, have always been in the forefront of the struggle for social justice, a factor which has been widely appreciated by black leaders and which caused a great deal of suspicion in right-wing circles. For example, in the Treason trial of the late 1950s, 23 of those on trial were white, and more than half of these were Jews, while the advocate who led the defence, Israel Maisels, was also a Jew. Helen Suzman's name became a symbol of opposition at parliamentary level to the apartheid system, and was so for decades: 'Single-handedly, relentlessly, and with superb analytic prowess, she assailed the apartheid system from the floor of Parliament, where she also had to endure an occasional anti-Semitic taunt.'[5] In addition to political action, Jewish individuals have been active in the amelioration of poor living conditions among blacks. A noteworthy example is Arthur Chaskalson, who left a hugely successful legal practice in 1979 to found and direct the Legal Resources Centre. This provided essential legal services for thousands of victims of the apartheid system. Another example of a Jew who assisted the victims of apartheid was Franz Auerbach. He concentrated on the huge discrepancy between white and black education, establishing the Funda Centre teacher-enrichment programme in Soweto.[6] Some synagogues, both orthodox and progressive, have instituted social action programmes to assist the underprivileged black population, notably the Oxford Synagogue in Johannesburg. It would be false, however, to regard all members of the Jewish community as being thus involved.

Religiously, the Jewish community has tended to be conservative in practice, exhibiting a strong attachment to tradition, an attachment which has been tempered by pragmatism. While it is impossible to ascertain exact numbers, about 85 per cent of the South African Jewish population belonging to a congregation is affiliated to orthodox Judaism, while about 10–15 per cent is affiliated to reform (progressive) temples. There are constant developments in the religious expression of the community. Some Jews are being lost to Judaism through intermarriage or conversion, neither of which has assumed alarming proportions in South Africa, but – more important – on the other side of the religious spectrum, there is a lively resurgence of orthodoxy, accompanied by the emergence of new sub-communities that may be termed 'ultra-orthodox' or, more accurately, *haredi*.[7] There are also interesting developments emanating from the progressive movement.

The religious expression of South African Jews has been determined largely by its Anglo-Litvak legacy. The Anglo-Jewish aspect is most obvious in the order of service of the major synagogues and in the organisation of the community, while Lithuanian influence can be observed in the commitment to tradition and in the overwhelmingly pro-Zionist stance of South African Jews. The only exception to this pro-Zionist stance may be observed among some of the *haredi* groupings who believe that the State of Israel should have been inaugurated by messianic rather than by secular means. However, rather than anti-Zionist, their attitude should more accurately be called 'non-Zionist'.[8]

Judaism

'Hear O Israel, the Lord our God, the Lord is one' (Deut. 6:4). Uttered daily by devout Jews, these words summarise the central conviction of Judaism. They affirm monotheism, the belief that there is one God who created the universe, who cares for his creation, and who therefore reveals his will to humanity. Working in and through history, God chose the Jewish people from among all the nations to bring about his purpose for the world. Jews believe that God will ultimately bring about a consummation of history. The Jewish view of history is therefore linear.

Judaism has three major foci – the Torah, the people and the land. Rooted in history, Jewish self-consciousness goes back to the promises made by God to Abraham that he would be the father of a great nation, that he would be taken to a land which God would show him, and that through him all the families of the earth would be blessed. The pivotal revelatory event of Judaism is the subsequent Exodus from Egypt in which God chose a particular people, redeemed them from bondage in Egypt, and led them to their promised land, Israel. They were chosen not for special privilege but for special obligation. This entailed obedience to the covenant (Torah) that God entered into with them. Loyalty to this covenant entailed an obligation to observe the *mitzvot* (commandments) of the Torah, both ritual and ethical, the latter being inseparable from social justice. Observance of the obligations of the Torah would merit 'life and length of days' in the land which God had given them, while infidelity would result in exile from that land. God, through giving them the Torah and the free choice to obey or ignore its precepts, had set before the Jews 'life and death, blessing and curse' (Exod. 30:19). They were, however, enjoined to choose life: 'For I have no pleasure in the death of anyone, says the Lord God; so turn, and live' (Ezek. 18:32).

Seeking repentance and return (*teshuvah*) to the obligations of Torah rather than punishment, God sent the prophets to warn the people of impending doom if they refused to change their ways. In 586 BCE they were exiled to Babylon. During the exilic and subsequent restoration period, a new method of teaching the Torah was developed. This was the oral Torah, an explication of and commentary on the written Torah. A second major exile took place in 70 CE. This was a catastrophe for the Jewish people in that it inaugurated a two-thousand-year period of existence as a diaspora. It transformed the Jews from a people with their own land and power to make their own political decisions into a powerless, landless people, destined to wander over the face of the earth.

Stripped of national identity and bereft of their holy shrine in Jerusalem, Jews found their main focus in observance of the Torah. The oral Torah (subsequently written down as the Talmud) became the vehicle through which the Torah was interpreted, understood and lived. Using the Torah as their basis, the rabbis evolved an intricate legal system (*halakhah*), which governed every aspect of life and which was designed not so much to procure salvation as to hallow the mundane act.

By following the laws, *halakhot,* the Jew's entire life is subjected to holy discipline. Whether eating, dressing or mating, the Jew utters the appropriate blessing, which, by fostering a constant sense of gratitude for God's bounty and promoting awareness of human creatureliness, raises every small act to holiness. Some laws, such as the dietary laws (*kashrut*), and observance of the sabbath, both promote discipline and enforce a degree of separateness from other religions, thereby lessening the temptation to assimilate.

The bleak centuries in exile fuelled the messianic expectation. Faithfulness to the Torah would, it was believed, lead ultimately to a messianic redemption and a return to the land of Israel. Being both particular and universal, the Jewish messianic idea asserts that there will first be a national redemption by which God will restore the scattered Jewish people to their land, and only thereafter will the entire world be redeemed, and peace and justice reign on earth.

The Enlightenment, a European movement that arose in the late seventeenth century, had as its major thrust the elevation of reason to supremacy. This resulted in scientific progress and a corresponding decline in the authority and credibility of religion. A broad humanism pervaded the thought of European intellectuals, which was to bring about a change, known as the Emancipation, in the status of Jews. The long-established separation of Jews from non-Jewish society broke down. This had the effect of catapulting Jews into the mainstream of modern life and releasing them from their previous pariah status. Jews, in the meantime, had experienced their own emancipation, known as the Haskalah.[9] Centred on the work of Moses Mendelssohn (1729–86), it enlightened Jews, familiarised them with the world of European civilisation, and rationalised and modernised Jewish life.[10] Significant changes occurred in Judaism itself, an important one being the questioning of the authority of the oral Torah. It was out of this development that the reform, or progressive, movement of Judaism arose, its central trend being the rejection of the binding authority of the *halakhah*. Political emancipation and the development of nationalism also influenced the growth of Zionism.

In Judaism, ethnicity and religious calling are inextricable. Ideally they should be held in tension. Jews are a religious community who are separate from the rest of society, but who live in the world, participating in every sphere of activity. One of the problems one encounters when studying communities of the Jewish diaspora is that religious calling and ethnicity are often confused, not only by gentiles, but by Jews themselves.

South Africa presents peculiar problems in that by the nature of their commitment to a particular religious way of life, Jews are bound by an ethical imperative which demands that they observe the highest level of social justice, showing concern for the oppressed. This has placed extreme pressure on South African Jews, who, living between conflicting streams, have not easily been able to respond in like manner to other national minorities in the country. They are subjected to often unattainable demands and then judged by the harshest of standards. To compare their actions and reactions to those of other groupings is tempting, but often spurious. Jews are a minority both ethnically and religiously. Other minority groups, such as the Greek or Portuguese communities, belong to the majority religion, Christianity, and are minorities only ethnically.

No modern study of Jews can be undertaken in isolation from the two most formative events in twentieth-century Jewish experience, the Holocaust and the re-establishment of the State of Israel. The former, which can be interpreted as the culmination of powerlessness for the Jewish diaspora, has left ineradicable scars on Jewish self-consciousness. The return to Israel has normalised Jewish existence in that, by having been returned to power, Jews can now exercise it, and are active participants in history rather than merely its objects. A bulwark against impotence and marginality, the existence of an independent Jewish homeland is essential for the ongoing survival of the Jewish people.

White exploration and settlement: 1652–1902

There has been a Jewish presence in South Africa since the beginnings of white settlement in the country. When the Dutch East India Company established a permanent settlement at the Cape in 1652, it recruited employees from Protestant countries throughout Europe. In fact, for the greater part of the seventeenth century, regular attendance at Reformed services was enforced. Because the Dutch East India Company would only employ Protestant Christians, the handful of Jews who first settled in the country tended to convert to Christianity. The earliest records of a Jewish presence go back to 1669, seventeen years after settlement, and are to be found in church registers. Two young Jews, Samuel Jacobson, aged 20, and David Heijlbron, aged 22, converted to Christianity, and were baptised on Christmas Day of that year.[11] It was only with the religious tolerance introduced by the Batavian Republic in 1804 and continued by the British that practising Jews began to settle in South Africa.

The early Jewish settlers came from England, Germany and Holland, several arriving with the 1820 British Settlers.[12] While many Jews were economically successful, some made important contributions to the economy of the country. During the mid-nineteenth century, for example, the Mosenthal brothers founded trading centres for mohair and merino fleece in the Eastern Cape and were responsible for establishing the basis of South Africa's wool industry, while Daniel de Pass pioneered sugar-planting in Natal and Jonas Bergtheil formed the Natal Cotton Company.

Since Judaism is a religion which demands communal institutions such as the synagogue, Judaism could not flourish in the absence of congregational facilities. The early settlers had no focal point for their religious expression and they tended to assimilate and disappear. Life as a religious community achieved secure expression only in 1841 with the establishment of the first synagogue, the Tikvat Israel (Hope of Israel), in Cape Town. This was followed in successive years by the formation of other synagogues.

Because the Cape was at that time a British colony, the earliest rabbis were English-speaking orthodox rabbis from Britain. This was important with regard to the development of the service which was based on the model of the Great Synagogue of London. It probably played an important role in the preservation of Jewish orthodoxy in South Africa. Unlike America, where the orthodox rabbis were Yiddish-speaking, early South African rabbis were native English-speakers; there has never been a need for the laity to move towards alternative movements within Judaism on the grounds of an inability to communicate.

The Jewish community in the mid-nineteenth century was homogeneous and was regarded as assimilable within society at large. This was to change with the industrial revolution resulting from the discoveries of diamonds in 1867 and gold in 1886, which affected South African society as a whole. With the flood of fortune-hunters who flocked to the Transvaal came a large number of East European Jews. Social movement, disruption and alienation were characteristic of the period. Underlying it all was the exploitation of black labour, which was to influence the future of South Africa so decisively.

The gold-rush years happened to coincide with severe persecution of and discriminatory legislation against Jews in Eastern Europe, and hence with a massive movement of European Jews to the Western world. Tales of fabulous opportunity attracted many of these immigrants to South Africa, particularly from the Russian-controlled province of Lithuania; South Africa was second only to America as a destination for immigrants. There was no suggestion of the sweatshop image that filtered through from correspondence from immigrants to America. The South African economy offered particular scope to the non-wage-earners from pre-industrial Lithuania. While Jews from countries in central Europe such as Germany and Poland streamed to America, where they found employment as factory hands in the garment workshops of New York, Jewish pedlars, craftsmen and shopkeepers from Lithuania were more suited to conditions in South Africa.[13] So many came to South Africa that it was referred to as a Lithuanian colony.

In the early years of East European Jewish settlement, Jews could be found in various parts of the country. They tended to settle in boom towns such as Oudtshoorn when the ostrich feather industry was at its height, or Kimberley when the diamond-mining industry was burgeoning, and to leave when the boom was over. Many became pedlars (*smouse*) who supplied the rural Afrikaner community with commodities to which they did not have ready access.

The influx of East European Jews into the country irreversibly changed the Jewish community in religious, social and economic terms. This went hand in hand with a change in the perception of Jews by outsiders. There were obvious cultural differences between the existing Jewish community and the East European Jews. The latter were Yiddish-speaking, and their dress, mannerisms, speech and general way of life did not easily merge with their societal surroundings. They transformed a relatively homogeneous community into what Milton Shain calls a 'motley combination of cultures bound by a common religious heritage.'[14]

The attitude of the local population was ambivalent. Accounts of the cordial relationships set up between the rural Afrikaner community and the Jewish *smouse* abound. The Bible-loving Afrikaners saw the Jews as 'the people of the Book'. Identifying Israel, the promised land of the Jews, with South Africa as their own promised land, they saw in the wanderings and homelessness of the Jews an analogue of their own travails. However, there was also a great deal of animosity expressed against the Jews both in the rural and urban areas.

The Jewish community itself was not entirely hospitable to the arrival of these immigrants in large numbers. Religiously, and in other areas, there was division between the two sets of Jews. While the East Europeans regarded the Anglo-German Jews as ignorant and heathenish, the latter regarded the new arrivals as crude and unmannerly.[15] Because the Lithuanian Jews – or 'Russian' Jews as they were called in official documents – who settled in Cape Town initially felt an antagonism both towards and from the Anglo-German Jews, they refused to join existing synagogues. Soon after their arrival, they established their own synagogues and *landsmanschaft* organisations where they could express their own cultural patterns.[16]

Oudtshoorn, which had such a vibrant Jewish community during the boom years that it was called 'the Jerusalem of South Africa', provides a good example of this type of development. The religious activity there is indicative of some of the tensions which prevailed between the Anglo-Jewish sector and the East European Jews, and also reveals something of their differing perceptions of what constituted authentic Jewish orthodoxy. The Queen's Street synagogue was established in 1888. Only eight years later, in 1896, the St John Street synagogue was established because the former was regarded as 'too anglicised' by some of the newcomers. The new synagogue catered for the 'more orthodox' section of the community. The Queen's Street synagogue became known as the *Englishe shul*, while the new synagogue was known as the *Greene shul* (*greene* meaning a greenhorn or newcomer).

From the perspective of Jewish religious development, the influence of the Litvaks was overwhelmingly positive. They imbued South African Jewish religious life with a particular form of talmudic piety and a love of tradition, introducing a strong Mitnaged tradition.[17] While synagogue worship and institutions were Anglo-Jewish in form, the new immigrants infused them with a new ethos. As Gustav Saron put it, 'it was a case of filling the Anglo-Jewish bottles with Litvak spirit.'[18] Intense love of and desire to return to Zion were a pervasive feature of Lithuanian piety, one that would inform all aspects of South African Jewish religious life.

The poverty of a large number of Litvaks was also to influence the religious expression of South African Jewry. Although economic necessity often forced them to transgress *halakhic* observance, particularly sabbath observance, they did not expect the synagogue or orthodoxy to change in order to accommodate them. Deeply attached to Lithuanian piety, they made every attempt to remain faithful to Jewish tradition and struck a pragmatic balance between the strictures of orthodox practice and the need to transgress some observances. This pragmatism was to grow into the phenomenon of the 'unobservant orthodox', a term that describes a wide sector of the Jewish community who are drawn to traditional Jewish values and are affiliated to orthodox synagogues, but who do not necessarily live a fully committed Torah-governed lifestyle. The existence of a large body of unobservant orthodox Jews is the key to understanding the dynamics of South African Jewry.

While some East European Jews became exceptionally wealthy, a notable example being Sammy Marks, most made a living in whatever way they could, a great many of them finding occupation in the subsidiary services spawned by the mining industry. Many were prominent as concession-store and canteen owners for black mine-workers.[19] As part of the disruption and social movement caused by the gold rush, some Jews were caught up in the illicit liquor trade. Some were exploiters, while others, who were so poor that they welcomed any opportunity to make a living, were themselves exploited. Activities such as these, in addition to the foreign language, appearance and customs of the East European Jews, led to vicious anti-Jewish prejudice.[20]

The 'poor white' problem dominated the last decade of the nineteenth century and the East European Jews formed an easily identifiable scapegoat for widespread white unemployment. While white immigration was viewed positively as advantageous to the black–white ratio in South Africa, and while there was, in fact, a shortage of white labour, there was also a fear that increased immigration, particularly of Polish and Russian Jews, would aggravate the problem because able-bodied whites would be displaced by the 'paupers' or 'Semitic scum' of Europe.[21] As penniless and largely unskilled workers, they were viewed with suspicion by the gentile community. This was exacerbated by the fact that Jews were middlemen rather than manual labourers. Perceived as 'unassimilable', they were pejoratively named 'Peruvians'[22] and were deemed undesirable. Anti-Semitic propaganda portrayed Jews as a threat. They were depicted either as fat, over-fed, exploitative capitalists, or as poverty-stricken, ugly, smelly and dirty. The resultant contradiction was easily solved by implying that the wealth had been acquired illicitly while the poverty was not real but feigned.[23]

The Immigration Restriction Act of 1902 was ostensibly aimed at curtailing the influx of Asians to South Africa, but it was quite clearly aimed at Jews as well.[24] It was not accidental that the primary requirement of the new immigration law was that immigrants should be able to write their disembarkation application in the characters of a European language, which immediately ruled out Yiddish, whose characters are Hebrew.

It was in the face of discriminatory immigration legislation and the general animus expressed against Jews that the need arose for a secular body to represent their cause. Despite opposition by some religious leaders, notably Rabbi Alfred Philipp Bender of Cape Town, who believed that the religious leadership should take up the cudgels for the Jewish community, the Cape Jewish Board of Deputies was established in 1904, while the Transvaal Board was formed in 1903. These were based on the Anglo-Jewish model and amalgamated in 1912, after Union, to form the South African Jewish Board of Deputies. The function of the Board, then as now, was to protect the civil and religious rights of Jews within the wider South African environment. One of the first acts of the Cape Board of Deputies was to obtain the recognition of Yiddish as a European language.

The South African Zionist Federation, the other main governing body of the South African Jewish community, had been formed in 1898. A product of Zionist feeling among Lithuanian immigrants, it originally functioned not only to promote Zionist ideals, but to represent the cause of Jews in confronting anti-Semitism, and as a philanthropic organisation. Because it was already defending the rights of Jews, it offered considerable resistance to the formation of the South African Jewish Board of Deputies. Today, while tensions between the two governing bodies have not disappeared, their separate functions have been more specifically defined, and the Federation assumes responsibility for all matters that pertain to the South African Jewish community's relationship with Israel.

Although Jews, along with all *uitlanders*, suffered several restrictions under Kruger's Transvaal Republic, these were not inspired by anti-Semitism but by the fundamentally Protestant base of the Boer Republic.[25] Jews, then as now, were never monolithic in their attitudes. During the Anglo-Boer War, although most Jews sided with the British, there was considerable sympathy for the Boer cause: Jews fought on both sides.

Rabbi Dr Joseph Hertz of Johannesburg, who later was to become Chief Rabbi of the British Empire, was an ardent champion of the cause of both Jews and Catholics in the fight against inequality. He was in fact expelled from the Transvaal Republic during the war because of his outspoken support of the *uitlander* cause.[26] The war broke out while modifications to the prohibitory laws were being debated and implemented in the Volksraad. When it ended in 1902, there was no longer an independent Boer Republic in South Africa.

White domination and the quest for liberation: 1902–1990

A striking feature of the early twentieth century was the blindness shown by one racial group to the indignities imposed on another. While the South

African Jewish Board of Deputies concerned itself only with the rights of Jews with regard to the Acts restricting immigration, fighting not against the principle behind the Acts but for the recognition of Yiddish as a European language, Gandhi showed a similar blindness with regard to Africans. Even though he sympathised with the even lower status endured by Africans than by Indians, he did not initiate a common non-white front but concentrated his efforts on the plight of the Indians alone.[27] As Gideon Shimoni points out, this phenomenon of mutual blindness is only comprehensible within the context of the caste-divided pluralism of South African society.[28]

Although the Jewish communal stance showed a detachment from the fate of non-whites, Jews as individuals have responded to the indignities suffered by those around them. In fact, Jewish individuals predominate among the few whites who fought for the cause of underprivileged groups. Significantly, Gandhi's closest white friends and advisers were Jews. Notable examples were Henry Polak from England and Hermann Kallenbach from Lithuania. Polak was brought into Gandhi's *Satyagraha* struggle as a Jew 'who had tried to remember that Judaism is a matter not only of belief but also of action'.[29] Having come to South Africa and learnt about the difficulties facing Indians in this country, he drew parallels between their plight and the age-old Jewish problem. He was ashamed at Jewish failure to champion the Indian cause, although there is no evidence that Gandhi expected Jews to make common cause with Indians.[30]

The 1930s proved to be difficult years for the South African Jewish community. Jewish immigration once again became a scapegoat of poor white animosities. The urbanisation of a large number of impoverished Afrikaners and their competition with blacks in areas of unskilled labour were projected onto the so-called Jewish problem. This resulted in restrictive legislation with regard to Jewish immigration from Europe in the form of the Quota Act of 1930 and the Aliens Act of 1937. Although there was little opposition to these restrictive laws from any quarter, it was the National Party that spearheaded them. Various South African Nazi-style movements of the 1930s also had a clear Afrikaner base.

In religious terms, the 1930s was also decisive. Significant religious movements developed within South African Judaism, and religious life became increasingly organised. Although Johannesburg was gradually becoming the centre of Jewish life, Cape Town remained an important focus. Because Cape Town was the mother city and was so far from Johannesburg, the two cities remained, for many decades, fairly independent centres of Jewish organisational activity.

Originally, the Chief Rabbi of Great Britain was regarded as the spiritual head of the South African Jewish community. His decisions were respected and his authority was real. In 1915 South African Jewry appointed Rabbi J. L. Landau as Chief Rabbi of the (Johannesburg) United Hebrew Congregation. It was only later, when many of the country's synagogues were affiliated under the (Transvaal) Federation of Synagogues in 1933, that Rabbi Landau became Chief Rabbi of this grouping. It took some time for the role of the

Chief Rabbi to be clearly defined. While today it still remains a prestigious position, it does not possess the power of its British counterpart, and its authority is being eroded by the emergence and splintering-off of a variety of *haredi* sub-groups. In South Africa it has generally been the incumbent himself who determines the importance of the office through his ability and personal qualities.

The Federation of Synagogues, formed in Johannesburg in 1933, soon incorporated the majority of orthodox synagogues in the Transvaal, Orange Free State and Natal. It governed orthodox Jewish life for these provinces, supplying essential services for outlying country synagogues. It maintained an internationally recognised Beth Din (rabbinic court), whose *dayanim* (judges) were appointed by the Federation. The main functions of the Beth Din are the supervision of *kashrut* (dietary laws), the granting of *gittin* (bills of divorce), the performance of conversions, and the settling of disputes. Until very recently, the Cape synagogues were affiliated to the Cape United Council of Orthodox Hebrew Congregations, which had its own Beth Din. In 1986 the two major organisational bodies for orthodoxy were amalgamated into the Union of Orthodox Synagogues of South Africa, which performs all the functions previously undertaken by the Cape and Transvaal governing organisations. The Union continues to maintain two internationally recognised Batei Din, one in Cape Town and the other in Johannesburg.

Reform, or progressive, Judaism was established in South Africa in 1933. Its coordinating body is the South African Union for Progressive Judaism, located in Johannesburg. Started by a handful of dedicated people of German-Jewish origin (the movement having originated in Germany), and cemented by the subsequent arrival in Johannesburg of Rabbi M. C. Weiler, it was to bear his imprint and become a phenomenon unique in the world. His scholarship, pro-Zionism, oratory and organisational ability all combined to mould its character.[31]

A notable characteristic of the South African Jewish progressive movement is that it has never been anti-Zionist. It was the first reform movement in the world to establish a pro-Zionist party, Artzeinu, and its youth movement, Maginim, has always had a pro-Zionist ideology, promoting *aliyah* (settlement in Israel). At the time of the inception of reform Judaism in South Africa, the reform movement elsewhere in the world was opposed to the concept of Israel as a Jewish homeland. Believing in the potentiality for goodness in humankind, it felt that with education, anti-Semitism would cease. It saw no reason why Jews could not be equal citizens in the countries of their habitation, melding comfortably with the surrounding population. This view was radically changed with disclosure of the horrors of the Nazi death camps. It was then quite clear that, no matter how like others Jews became, they were always subject to the possibility of anti-Semitism, which, in extreme forms, can result in annihilation of the Jewish people. Thus, after the Holocaust, the world-wide progressive movement adopted a pro-Zionist policy.

Progressive Judaism in South Africa initially met with 'bitter hostility from those who resented the intrusion of an apparently schismatic movement, as well as timidity on the part of those who sympathised with the Progressive point of view'.[32] The difference between progressive and orthodox Judaism is that progressive Judaism does not accept the binding nature of the *halakhah* in the oral Torah, while for orthodoxy it was revealed to Moses on Mount Sinai with the written Torah. Because of this seminal difference, orthodox Judaism . sees reform teaching as heretical, 'idolatrous' and 'assimilationist', while reform Judaism perceives orthodoxy's stance as 'fanatical', 'obscurantist' and 'medieval'.[33] Reforms introduced by the reform movement in Germany and later in America were sometimes so radical that there was little to differentiate the Jew from the surrounding society. South African reform Judaism has always been conservative in practice. Progressive rabbis prefer, for example, that divorced couples obtain an orthodox *get* (bill of divorce) in order to avoid complications involving the future status of the husband and wife.[34]

Observers often gain the mistaken impression that reform Judaism in South Africa is no different from conservative Judaism in America. Conservative Judaism regards the *halakhah* as binding but permits greater flexibility with regard to its interpretation than does orthodoxy. South African reform, like reform everywhere else, emphasises the ongoing nature of revelation, seeing Judaism as dynamic and growing. Judaism, it believes, continues to be adapted by legitimate exponents for its time and circumstances throughout the ages. This process, once passive, has now become reactivated. It views many of the historic developments in Judaism as reforms that were introduced throughout the ages in order to make the religion meaningful for Jews in their particular historical situation. Thus, progressive Judaism sees itself as being as old as Judaism itself.[35]

The 1930s also saw the emergence in Yeoville, Johannesburg, of a small, separatist and very orthodox community made up of a group of immigrants from Frankfurt am Main. This is known as the Adas Yeshurun[36] congregation. As part of its perception of orthodoxy, it has run its own *hashgashah* (supervision) for kosher meat, milk and other products. For many years it had the only *mikve* (ritual bath) available to Johannesburg Jews. Until recently, it did not run its own Jewish day schools but sent its children to ordinary government schools and amplified this with an intensive Jewish education through its *heder* (extramural Hebrew class) system in the afternoons.

The 1940s saw active changes in the Jewish community, both religious and in the wider context. The year 1948 proved to be a watershed: the National Party came to power and the State of Israel came into existence. The Jewish press in 1948 showed two major foci of attention: fears about the possible victory of the hitherto anti-Semitic National Party, and deep concern for the fledgling State of Israel. Both of these assumed particular importance in the light of the fact that the Second World War had only recently ended. With the annihilation of six million Jews, a Jewish homeland was imperative, while the anti-Semitic stance of the National Party was deeply threatening.

An editorial in the *South African Jewish Times* (7 May 1948) suggested that a change in the Nationalist policy towards Jews would be welcomed. This might gain the Nationalists support from 'those Jews who uphold their social programme'. It, however, urged allegiance 'only to such political groups as are ready to act democratically, not only on the question of the Jew but in every field of socio-economic endeavour. For a civilisation in which the people as a whole can participate in the vast economic and cultural resources that are at hand, is the best guarantee against the emergence of the anti-Semite as a significant social force.'

Jews were shocked by General Smuts's defeat. He had gained considerable support from the Jewish community not only for his centrist policies, but because he had supported the Balfour Declaration of 1917, in which the British government viewed with favour the establishment of a Jewish home-land in Palestine. A week after Israel had been declared an independent Jewish homeland, and less than a week before polling day in the Union of South Africa, the editorial in the *South African Jewish Times* (21 May 1948) urged support for Smuts, the 'doughty protagonist' of the Jewish state. Significantly, the same issue carried an article on general press reactions to the Jewish state, pointing out that the Afrikaans press had, on the whole, welcomed it, while the English newspapers, with the exception of the *Rand Daily Mail*, had expressed open hostility.

Chief Rabbi Louis I. Rabinowitz, an ardent Zionist who came to South Africa from England in 1945, played an important part in establishing the character of South African Judaism. At the same time as the establishment of Israel in 1948, he introduced the Sephardic pronunciation of Hebrew into the liturgy.[37] This continues in the major synagogues throughout the country. The *haredi* groupings have, however, returned to the previous Ashkenazi pronun-ciation, seeing it as more faithful to tradition.

The Chief Rabbi also instituted kosher catering for all Jewish functions in South Africa. From small beginnings, in which a part of a hotel kitchen would be made kosher for a wedding or other Jewish celebration, the situation pre-vails today in which the catering for all Jewish functions has to be kosher if there is to be any participation by the orthodox rabbinate. Kosher catering is easily available in all major cities in South Africa and is utilised by almost all orthodox Jews, even if they do not follow a fully observant lifestyle.

Chief Rabbi Rabinowitz interpreted his task in terms of the widest applica-tion of social justice, denouncing apartheid as alien to the authentic voice of prophetic Judaism. Prior to his settling in Israel in 1960, his sermons became increasingly outspoken and he lashed out vehemently at the cowardice of his community:

> Have Jewish ethics ever descended to a more shameful nadir?... I have practically abandoned all hope of effecting any change in this matter. The power of fear and the possibility of our security being affected is too strong... Do not think that I am proud of my record in this matter, that I do not squirm inwardly at the thought that on many occasions I have been infected with that same fear and that same cowardice and have failed to rise to the level which my calling demands of me. But when ... a blatant, glaring injustice occurs,

and it is one in which there is a hope that my intervention may possibly have a salutary effect, then no power in the world can prevent me giving expression to what I conscientiously believe to be the authentic voice of prophetic Judaism.[38]

The senior rabbi of the progressive movement, Rabbi Weiler, also displayed his condemnation of apartheid by joining Christian clerics in protests against its more outrageous manifestations, a policy continued by his successor, Rabbi Arthur Saul Super.[39]

The year 1948 also saw the establishment of the King David School, the first Jewish day school in South Africa. Since Judaism is a way of life, the traditions must be transmitted from generation to generation and learned at an early age. While this is achieved in the home among religious families, with increased secularisation the school has had to play a larger role. The emergence of Jewish day schools gave important impetus to the transmission of Judaism. The emphasis of King David School has been 'national–traditional', which implies a Jewish education that promotes Zionism, along with an excellent secular education. Over the years, various schools of this nature were established in the major centres of South Africa. The 1950s saw the emergence of the more traditional Yeshiva College. While being similar in orientation to the schools already mentioned, it devotes far more time to study of the Torah and Talmud. The more recent emergence of the *haredi* sub-groups has resulted in the establishment of their own schools, which cater for their particular religious ideologies; they are non-Zionist in orientation.

It is noteworthy that the majority of Jews in South Africa can be labelled 'unobservant orthodox'. Officially, orthodoxy is based on Torah Judaism, which involves the meticulous observance of Jewish ritual. The majority of Jews who are affiliated to orthodoxy are drawn to tradition, attend synagogue and observe the major festivals and rites of passage. They feel no discomfort in driving to synagogue on the holy days and choosing to neglect a great many of the ritual observances. Some keep kosher homes, but do not mind eating non-kosher food out of the home. Others may be more or less observant. It is the presence of these Jews in substantial numbers that gives South African Judaism its special character. The flexibility of South African orthodoxy as it is understood by the average congregant, although it markedly strains the true definition of orthodoxy, may account for the minor impact of reform Judaism in South Africa.[40]

The mainstream orthodox rabbinate does not encourage this unobservant orthodoxy but does not condemn it either. Being so intrinsic a part of the South African Jewish way of life, it is accepted in the hope that, ultimately, religious observance will increase. The charge is often made against orthodoxy that the only difference between it and reform Judaism is that reform Jews are not 'hypocrites'. The orthodox rabbinate counters this by pointing out that since orthodox Judaism holds firm to the validity of the *halakhah* in the oral Torah, there is at least an ideal which, it claims, is conspicuously absent from reform observance.

The current religious situation in South African Judaism is anything but static. It appears to be moving in the general direction of increased observance, evidenced by both the proliferation of *haredi* groups and the establishment of two conservative congregations in Johannesburg.

There is great variety in the forms of religious expression. The main body of orthodox Jews represents the Mitnaged tradition. The Hasidic tradition is represented by the influential Lubavitch movement. There have been a few Sephardic Jews in South Africa for several decades but in recent years there has been a resurgence of the movement with the entry into the country of Sephardic Jews from Zimbabwe and Zaire. There is a particularly lively congregation in Cape Town and a smaller one in Johannesburg.

The South African progressive movement appears presently to be in a state of decline. The decision in 1991 by the Imanu-Shalom congregation, led by Rabbi Ady Assabi, to suspend its membership of the South African Union for Progressive Judaism was aimed primarily at fostering a vital new religious ideology and implementation of a concomitant lifestyle. The move, which culminated in the emergence of the independent Shalom Congregation in 1994, sought on the one hand to free the congregation of the rigidity of reform Judaism as it was seen to have ossified within the South African context and thus make room for real reforms, and on the other hand to dissociate the congregation from the label 'reform' and the American radicalism the term may evoke. Although part of the congregation, the Temple Emmanuel, has reverted to progressive Judaism, this split threatens the survival of the progressive movement, which is suffering a crisis in rabbinic leadership. There are only seven progressive rabbis in South Africa: two in Johannesburg, three in Cape Town and two in Durban.[41] If the progressive movement is to survive as a distinct entity, there is an urgent need to attract new rabbis from abroad to lead its lay members, whose numbers have remained fairly stable.

Despite the apparent resemblance of South African progressive Judaism to American conservatism, or perhaps because of it, there has, until recently, not been an official conservative congregation in South Africa, although it is often asserted that Rabbi Ben Isaacson's former congregation in Houghton, the Har'el congregation, was close to becoming one. During 1991, a conservative congregation, the Ohev Shalom, was established in Johannesburg under the spiritual leadership of Rabbi Nissim Wernick. In 1992, the Imanu-Shalom congregation became affiliated to the World Council of Conservative/Masorti Synagogues, thus becoming the first congregation in South Africa – and, indeed, on the continent of Africa – to be officially affiliated to the world conservative movement.

The first important split in orthodoxy took place in 1969. The Adas Yeshurun congregation, which places great emphasis on Torah study, gave rise to a *kollel*.[42] Intended originally to provide a small group of married men with the opportunity to devote their entire day to the study of Torah, the *kollel* now has a very different connotation in the South African context. It denotes an entire, fast-growing community of *haredi* Jewish families, with their own schools, adult education programmes and synagogues. Today there are two *kollel* communities, the one having split off from the other. The main aim of the movement is to counter assimilation of Jews by promoting Torah learning and Torah living. It places great emphasis on the *baal teshuvah* (penitent), and has drawn many unobservant Jews into its ranks. Its members exhibit a return to East European tradition, worshipping in a *shtiebl* (small, intimate house-*shul*) rather than in a large formal synagogue, and using the Ashkenazi pronunciation of Hebrew in religious services. The *kollel* espouses a strong Mitnaged tradition.

The Hasidic Lubavitch Foundation was established in the early 1970s in Johannesburg. This was an extension of the religious empire of Rebbe Menachem Mendel Shneerson, the late Lubavitcher Rebbe who, located in Brooklyn, New York, aimed to achieve a Jewish empire on which 'the sun never sets'. Employing an active outreach programme, the movement seeks to revitalise authentic Jewish life for all Jews. Like its counterparts the world over, it employs high-profile methods in the performance of the *mitzvot*, such as the lighting of giant *menorah* during the festival of Hanukah at major shopping centres. It attempts, thereby, to spread the message of *ahavat Yisrael* (the love of all Jews) as widely as possible. It holds that every action, word or thought that is in tune with the Torah is important. Each one of these expresses a person's bond with his Creator and kindles one more light to help dispel the darkness in the world. If one Jew, performing *mitzvot*, can produce light, all Jews united can kindle a flame that will banish darkness permanently and usher in the messianic era. The movement has been remarkably successful in involving alienated young Jews and those who have turned to drugs and other social ills.[43]

Although there is a tendency for Jews to cluster in certain residential areas which are close to Jewish amenities, the *haredi* communities have given certain suburbs a markedly Jewish appearance. They live in areas where there are extensive facilities for orthodox Jewish life, such as synagogues and religious schools, and shops which sell exclusively kosher foodstuffs. Yeoville, Johannesburg, has become one such area. There is overt identification with Judaism in dress and lifestyle. On the sabbath, for example, one may observe families walking to or from several informal house-*shuls*, the men wearing their prayer shawls openly. On any day of the week, one can observe black-coated men with side-locks, wearing *tzitzit* (ritual fringes), going about their daily affairs. One can also observe modestly dressed women, with wigs or kerchiefs covering their hair, often accompanied by a number of young children, as true orthodoxy expects the fulfilment of the commandment to 'be fruitful and multiply'.

Lying somewhere between the ultra-orthodox and the unobservant orthodox there is a fair percentage of pious, practising orthodox Jews who observe Judaism assiduously but somewhat more moderately. Showing fewer overt signs of their religiousness, the only outward sign of Jewishness in the case of men being the wearing of a *yarmulke* (skull-cap), they pursue a productive secular life and tend to be more outward-looking than the *haredi* groups. These could perhaps be termed 'neo-orthodox' and have stemmed largely from the religious youth movement, the Bnei Akiva,[44] which gave rise ultimately to the Yeshiva College.

It has been argued that the unobservant orthodox stance of South African Jewry, had it developed unchecked, would have led eventually to assimilation. Apart from the entry of the Adas Yeshurun community during the thirties, the first meaningful check on the laxity of observance was the development of the Bnei Akiva youth movement, which consolidated itself in the 1950s. A religiously observant and pro-Zionist group, it revitalised Jewish life. The institutions which have developed from it are moderate within the spectrum of orthodox practice in South Africa.

The observance of orthodox Judaism goes hand in hand with intensive study of the Torah. With the general revival of orthodoxy, there has been a proliferation of small 'holistic' orthodox communities, particularly in Johannesburg. These provide facilities for study of the Torah and worship, the hallmark of which is worship in a small informal *shtiebl* rather than in a large formal synagogue. In keeping with this emphasis on Torah study and Torah lifestyle, they also form vibrant social centres at which young Jews can attend a variety of adult education programmes and participate meaningfully in the life of the community. There are several such groups, and others are still forming; a noteworthy example is the Ohr Somayach (Joyous Light) congregation in Glenhazel, Johannesburg. As a local branch of an international movement, it emphasises outreach programmes for young adults and forms a centre for the active expression of Jewish religious life. Young people flock in their hundreds to the lectures, on a variety of topics relating to Jewish life, given by its 'charismatic' rabbis.

These groups demand more stringent supervision of *shechitah* (ritual slaughter) and *kashrut* than that offered by the Beth Din. Although the Beth Din supervises the manufacture of a large variety of foodstuffs, these groups demand yet higher standards. Foodstuffs appropriate to their needs are labelled *mahadrin*, which denotes 'yet higher' standards of *kashrut*. This term has become the peculiarly South African equivalent of the more globally used term *glatt kosher*.[45] While the observance of these groups is meritorious, the challenge they represent to established authority is real. These sub-groups, regarding themselves as truly orthodox, stretch the definition of 'orthodoxy' from the right, just as the existence of the non-observant orthodox does so from the left.

With the inception of the various religious streams, inter-group relations have tended to be strained. This has always been so in regard to orthodox–reform relations. Whereas the rank and file of the orthodox and reform seek cooperation in the pursuit of communal interests, the rabbinate remains implacably hostile. For orthodoxy, reform is regarded as heretical, while for reform, orthodoxy is regarded as archaic and obscurantist. This hostility is more obvious in Johannesburg than in other major centres. The *haredi* groupings display a more low-key rivalry. The rank and file of orthodoxy are ambivalent about these groups. On the one hand, they are impressed by the revival of true orthodox practice and by the outreach to previously distanced

Jews. They are, however, often critical of their stringency, resentful of the air of exclusivity which they project, and confused by their dietary requirements and the petty discord which exists among them. There is no doubt, however, that the proliferation of the various groups is a positive feature in South African Jewish life, and a mark of vibrant growth.

This proliferation, if it continues to challenge established authority, may lead ultimately to a new form of religious organisation in which there is greater autonomy for individual congregations or groupings. The greater freedom evident in the country at large, with the establishment of a new democratic South Africa, will result in the breakdown of old structures generally. This may be reflected in Jewish religious and lay organisation.

The Jews of South Africa have made an immense contribution to the development of the country and, as individuals, played an indispensable part in the struggle against apartheid. Although the Jewish communal stance tended to be somewhat timid, this must be understood in the light of the centrality of anti-Semitism to the National Party's policies before it came to power in 1948. The subsequent reversal of this policy served to intimidate Jews whose visibility and minority status have led them, at times, to become the scapegoat for a variety of society's ills. The openness and transparency that are evident in the Government of National Unity, as well as the ANC's revulsion towards any form of racism (including anti-Semitism), have resulted in a Jewish communal stance that enthusiastically embraces the new democratic spirit in South Africa. Encouraged by President Mandela's assurances at the 39th Congress of the South African Jewish Board of Deputies in 1993 that an ANC-led government could never 'indulge in or connive at anti-Semitism' and that it would address the fears of the Jewish community as a minority within a white minority, Jewish communal leaders are anxious to help in the rebuilding of South Africa. In accord with the outward-looking attitude of the current Chief Rabbi, Cyril Harris, they wish to guide the community towards sharing its considerable skills with the underprivileged masses of South Africa.

NOTES

I wish to acknowledge the information given to me by Rabbi A. H. Tanzer of the Yeshiva College, Rabbi M. Standfield of the Temple Israel, and Rabbi A. Assabi of the Shalom Independent Congregation.

1. For this type of approach to the history of communities in South Africa, see Charles van Onselen, *Studies in the Social and Economic History of the Witwatersrand 1886–1914*, vol. 1: *New Babylon*. Johannesburg: Ravan Press, 1982; and Bozzoli Belinda (ed.), *Class, Community and Conflict*. Johannesburg: Ravan Press, 1987.

2. Gideon Shimoni, 'South African Jews and the Apartheid Crisis', in David Singer and Ruth R. Seldin (eds.), *American Jewish Year Book, 1988*. Philadelphia: The Jewish Publication Society, 1988 (cited hereafter as *Year Book*), p. 6.

3. It has been estimated that in 1987 there were at least 6 000 Israeli Jews living in South Africa. See A. Dubb and S. Della Pergola, 'South African Jewry: A Sociodemographic Profile', in *Year Book*, p. 75.

4. For a brief description of these restrictive acts, see Steven Cohen, 'The Histori-

cal Background', in Marcus Arkin, *South African Jewry: A Contemporary Survey*. Cape Town: Oxford University Press, 1984, pp. 3–10.

5. Shimoni, *Year Book 1988*, p. 19.

6. For details on these and similar efforts, see *ibid.*, pp. 21ff.

7. The term 'ultra-orthodox' may not be accepted by those Jews whom it is intended to describe in that they regard their religious expression as truly orthodox, anything less falling short of orthodoxy. *Haredi*, denoting 'God-fearing Jews', is a more neutral and universally accepted term.

8. For a more detailed analysis of the nature of South African Judaism, see Jocelyn Hellig, 'The Religious Expression', in Arkin, *SA Jewry*, pp. 95–116, as well as J. Hellig, 'South African Judaism: An Expression of Conservative Traditionalism', *Judaism*, 35, 2 (1986), pp. 233–42.

9. *Haskalah* derives from the word *sechel*, 'reason' or 'intelligence'.

10. For more detail, see Bernard Martin, *A History of Judaism*, vol. 2. New York: Basic Books, pp. 189–231.

11. See Louis Herrman, 'Cape Jewry before 1870,' in G. Saron and L. Hotz (eds.), *The Jews in South Africa: A History*. Cape Town: Oxford University Press, 1955, pp. 1ff.

12. *Ibid.*

13. See Antony Arkin, 'Economic activities' in Arkin, *SA Jewry*, pp. 57–78.

14. Milton Shain, *Jewry and Cape Society*. Cape Town: Historical Publications Society, 1983, p. 3.

15. Gustav Saron, 'The Making of South African Jewry: An Essay in Historical Interpretation' in L. Feldberg (ed.), *South African Jewry 1965*. Johannesburg: Fieldhill, 1968, pp. 19f.

16. *Ibid.* See also L. A. Herrman, *A History of the Jews of South Africa*. London: Gollancz, 1935, pp. 262ff.

17. The Mitnagdim are defined in opposition to the Hasidim, who emerged in the eighteenth century. The word *mitnaged* refers to a non-Hasidic tradition.

18. Saron, 'The Making of South African Jewry', p. 17.

19. See Louis Hotz, 'Contributions to Economic Development' in Saron and Hotz, *Jews in South Africa*, pp. 348–369.

20. See Van Onselen, *New Babylon*, for an analysis of this economic involvement.

21. Shain, *Jewry and Cape Society*, chapter 3.

22. The origin of this term is not certain but is thought to have resulted from the acronym formed from 'Polish and Russian' Jews.

23. Shain, *Jewry and Cape Society*, p. 47.

· 24. While Gustav Saron suggested that the exclusion of Jews was unforeseen, Milton Shain claims that it was part of the basic intention of the Act. See Saron and Hotz, *Jews in South Africa*, p. 95 and Shain, *Jewry and Cape Society*, pp. 25–7.

25. Gideon Shimoni, *Jews and Zionism: The South African Experience, 1910–1967*. Cape Town: Oxford University Press, 1980, pp. 61–4.

26. *Ibid.* See chapter 3 for more details on this subject.

27. *Ibid.*, p. 82.

28. *Ibid.*

29. Shimoni, *Jews and Zionism*, p. 82.

30. *Ibid.*

31. See Hellig in Arkin, *SA Jewry*, p. 104.

32. Words of the Hon. Lily H. Montagu on the resignation of Rabbi Weiler from his Johannesburg post prior to his settlement in Israel, in *The Jewish Herald*, 1 February 1957, cited in my chapter in Arkin, *SA Jewry*, p. 110.

33. *Ibid.*, p. 110.

34. *Ibid.*, p. 105.

35. *Ibid.*

36. *Yeshurun* is a poetical appellation of the people Israel meaning 'the beloved upright'. *Adas* is a congregation. The term Adas Yeshurun therefore means 'Congregation of the beloved upright of Israel.'

37. The term 'Sephardi' applies to Jews from the West, predominantly Spain and North Africa, while the term 'Ashkenazi' applies to Jews from Eastern Europe. The two groups have differing customs as well as a different way of pronouncing Hebrew. Modern Hebrew, as spoken in Israel, uses Sephardi pronunciation, while the liturgy in Eastern Europe made use of the Ashkenazi pronunciation.

38. Cited from Rabbi Rabinowitz's 1959 Yom Kippur sermon by Shimoni, *Year Book*, pp. 33f.

39. *Ibid.*

40. See Hellig in Arkin, *SA Jewry*, pp. 102ff.

41. There are eleven temples in existence in South Africa: three in Johannesburg, two in Cape Town, and one each in Springs, Bloemfontein, Durban, East London, Port Elizabeth and Pretoria. Because there are more temples than rabbis, lay leaders run the daily and weekly services, and visiting rabbis, often from abroad, officiate on the High Holy Days of Rosh Hashanah and Yom Kippur.

42. A *kollel* is a small yeshivah of about a dozen men that promotes and makes facilities for full-time Torah study. Because the highest virtue in Judaism is the study of Torah, full-time study is encouraged among highly observant communities. In the modern world, this is not easy as economic accommodations have to be made if a number of men are to be released from normal employment.

43. See Hellig in Arkin, *SA Jewry*, pp. 108f.

44. The Bnei Akiva (Children of Akiva) is an international Jewish youth movement and has branches in the main centres of South Africa. It is named after one of the most influential rabbis in Jewish history, Rabbi Akiva ben Joseph (*c.* 50–135 CE), who was actively associated with the Bar Kochba rebellion (132–5 CE) and who was tortured and put to death as a result. The movement promotes a love of Zion and an orthodox lifestyle.

45. *Mahadrin* is a Talmudic term that derives from the word *hiddur*. *Hiddur mitzvah* means giving special attention to the performance of the *mitzvot*. *Glatt* is the Yiddish word for 'smooth'. *Glatt kosher* therefore indicates 'smoothly' or 'unambiguously' kosher.

SELECT BIBLIOGRAPHY

Arkin, Marcus (ed.), *South African Jewry: A Contemporary Survey*. Cape Town: Oxford University Press, 1984

Bozzoli, Belinda (ed.), *Class, Community and Conflict*. Johannesburg: Ravan Press, 1987

Dubb, A. A. and S. Della Pergola, 'South African Jewry: A Sociodemographic Profile', in David Singer and Ruth R. Seldin (eds.), *American Jewish Year Book, 1988*. Philadelphia: The Jewish Publication Society, 1988

Hellig, Jocelyn, 'The Religious Expression', in Marcus Arkin (ed.), *South African Jewry: A Contemporary Survey*. Cape Town: Oxford University Press, 1984

Hellig, Jocelyn, 'South African Judaism: An Expression of Conservative Traditionalism'. *Judaism*, 35, 2 (1986), pp. 233–42

Hellig, Jocelyn, 'The Religious Expression of South African Jewry'. *Religion in Southern Africa*, 18, 2 (1987), pp. 3–17

Hellig, Jocelyn, 'Anti-Semitism in South Africa Today'. *Jewish Affairs*, 44, 2 (1989), pp. 37–43

Herrman, Louis, *A History of the Jews in South Africa*. London: Gollancz, 1935

Hoffmann, Tzippi and Alan Fischer, *The Jews of South Africa: What Future?* Johannesburg: Southern Book Publishers, 1988

Krut, Riva, 'The Making of a South African Jewish Community in Johannesburg, 1886–1914', in Belinda Bozzoli (ed.), *Class, Community and Conflict*. Johannesburg: Ravan Press, 1987

Saron, Gustav, 'The Making of South African Jewry: An Essay in Historical Interpretation', in L. Feldberg (ed.), *South African Jewry 1965*. Johannesburg: Fieldhill, 1968

Saron, Gustav and Louis Hotz (eds.), *The Jews in South Africa: A History*. Cape Town: Oxford University Press, 1955

Schwarz, Harry, 'South African Jewry Today'. *Research Report no. 10*. London: Institute of Jewish Affairs, October 1986

Shain, Milton, *Jewry and Cape Society*. Cape Town: Historical Publications Society, 1983

Shimoni, Gideon, *Jews and Zionism: The South African Experience, 1910–1967*. Cape Town: Oxford University Press, 1980

Shimoni, Gideon, 'South African Jews and the Apartheid Crisis', in David Singer and Ruth R. Seldin (eds.), *American Jewish Year Book, 1988*. Philadelphia: The Jewish Publication Society, 1988

Van Onselen, Charles, *Studies in the Social and Economic History of the Witwatersrand 1886–1914*. vol. 1, *New Babylon*. Johannesburg: Ravan Press, 1982

10

Hinduism in South Africa

PATRICK MAXWELL, ALLEYN DIESEL &
THILLAY NAIDOO

Hinduism is one of the oldest religions in the world, having been in existence
for at least 4 000 years (some would claim even longer). It includes various
streams of belief and practice, some of which have their roots in ancient traditions in India that predated the so-called Aryan[1] invasions of about 1500
BCE. In subsequent centuries, a great variety of cultural, philosophical and
religious elements has been incorporated into the broad Hindu tradition.

The ancient term 'Hindu' comes from the name of the North Indian river,
the Indus, and was used by foreigners to refer to the inhabitants of India, who
lived beyond this river. The word 'Hinduism' is much more recent, and is not
often used by Hindus themselves, who usually sum up their tradition by using
the term *Sanathana Dharma* (the Eternal Way). This expression is particularly
appropriate, as the Hindu tradition has no specific historical founder.

In the past, Hinduism was confined to the Indian motherland, but since the
nineteenth century there have been increasing numbers of Hindus living elsewhere in the world, for example in Southeast Asia, Bali, Mauritius, South
Africa, Britain and the United States. The South African Hindu community is
the second largest outside of India and Sri Lanka, with the Malaysian community being the largest.

Expatriate Hindus try to follow their ancient traditions faithfully, although
inevitably certain modifications and adaptations creep into the practice of
their religion, mainly because of influences from their new environments.

There are at present about 987 000 Indians in South Africa, of whom
approximately 520 000 are Hindus. Religious affiliation in the local Indian
community can be approximately represented as follows:[2] 62 per cent Hindu;
19 per cent Muslim; 13 per cent Christian; and 6 per cent belonging to other
religious or philosophical persuasions, or to none. Indians make up 99 per
cent of South African Hindus, but there are a handful of Hindus who belong
to other racial groups.

Since the arrival of Hindu Indians in South Africa in 1860, Hinduism has
spread to all the provinces of South Africa, but in terms of both influence and

numbers, Natal has remained the bastion of Hinduism – over 80 per cent of the country's Hindus live in Natal. Hindus constitute 35 per cent of the population of Durban and 18 per cent of the population of Pietermaritzburg.

Many observers have commented on the tensions and difficulties that have affected the South African Hindu community, due largely to the sociopolitical upheavals of apartheid. Between 1961 and 1970, substantial numbers of Durban and Pietermaritzburg Indians were uprooted and resettled in new areas, especially Chatsworth and Northdale. Most of these new areas were far from their workplaces and their traditional places of worship. The resulting disorientation has been exploited by Christian evangelists, especially Pentecostals, who have long been active in the Indian community. A significant number of Hindus, especially from the Tamil and Telugu communities, have converted to Christianity.[3] More than half the Indian Christians in South Africa are Pentecostals of one sort or another.[4] Despite these setbacks, the various Hindu communities have reorganised themselves in their new areas, built new temples and ashrams, and continued their religious customs.[5]

Any discussion of Hinduism involves the problem of words that have a number of alternative spellings, particularly names of temples and deities. Spelling has been standardised to a large extent, but two notable examples of variant spellings that remain are Shiva/Siva and Mariamman/Mariammen/Marriamen.

THE EARLY HISTORY OF HINDUISM IN SOUTH AFRICA

In 1857 because of a dearth of labour in the sugar industry, the Natal government made arrangements for the importation of indentured labourers from India. Nearly 350 Indian immigrants disembarked from the SS *Truro* when it arrived in Durban on 16 November 1860. About 90 per cent of these were Hindus, from the Tamil- and Telugu-speaking communities from the southern Indian state of Madras (now Tamil Nadu). A few days later, the SS *Belvedere* arrived from Calcutta with mostly Hindi-speaking people from the states of Bihar and Uttar Pradesh in northern India on board. Many of these indentured labourers were of lower-caste origin, although most complements appear to have included a few Brahmans and other higher-caste Hindus. About ten years later, the 'free' or 'passenger' Indians, who held British travel documents, started arriving. This group included many Muslims and Gujarati-speaking merchants from the Bombay area and Gujarat.[6]

Indentured labourers continued to arrive in South Africa at regular intervals. Altogether, approximately 150 000 indentured Indians came to Natal in the period between 1860 and 1911, when Indian immigration came to an end.

It is not possible to construct a continuous history of Hindu religion and life in South Africa before 1902 (as distinct from Indian political history in general), as not much information is available. What follows is a selection of some of the more interesting episodes and events during this early period.

In spite of their miserable working conditions on the sugar estates of the Natal north and south coasts, the Hindu Indians showed their commitment to their traditions by continuing their customary worship and soon built small shrines and temples to their chosen deities. After their indentures came to an end, many Indians took up market gardening, the hawking of fruit and vegetables, and other occupations in the various towns of the Natal Colony, at first in Durban and then further afield. This movement of Indians away from the coast was accelerated by the fact that many were employed by the Natal Government Railways, which was extending the rail service further inland.

Indians appear to have arrived in Pietermaritzburg from about 1863, and settled initially in the lower Church Street and Longmarket Street areas. From here they moved north into the rest of Natal, and in the late 1870s into the Transvaal. The Natal south coast has the distinction of possessing the two oldest existing temples in South Africa, namely the Equefa Perumalsami Temple, near Umzinto (1864), and the Umzinto Beri-Beri Farm Temple (1874).[7]

There are four main streams in South African Hinduism, namely Sanathanism, Arya Samaj, neo-Vedanta, and Hare Krishna. Before 1902, South African Hinduism was almost exclusively Sanathanist in character, emphasising the practical and ritual dimensions of the religion rather than the doctrinal aspects. It is certain that firewalking, an extremely popular traditional festival which has flourished for centuries in India, was first practised in South Africa before the turn of the century.

The Indian languages spoken by Hindus who came to the country can be classified either as Dravidian (e.g. Tamil and Telugu) or as Indo-Aryan (e.g. Hindi and Gujarati). Although many Hindus today are no longer familiar with these languages, there is a growing concern to preserve them and teach them to young people. Hindu individuals and groups are often still classified according to their linguistic–cultural backgrounds, so that one can distinguish between Tamils, Telugus, Hindis and Gujaratis. Some minor differences regarding details of worship, ritual and social customs exist between these groups.[8] The linguistic groupings differ in size. Tamils make up 45 per cent of the South African Hindu population (originally from the Madras area in Tamil Nadu); Telugus make up 18 per cent (originally from Andhra Pradesh); Hindis make up 30 per cent (originally from Bihar and Uttar Pradesh); and Gujaratis 7 per cent.[9] The Gujarati community includes both Surtees (originally from Surat in India) and Kathiawadis (originally from Kathiawad in India). The Surtees significantly outnumber the Kathiawadis.

South Africa's most famous Gujarati Hindu was Mahatma Gandhi, who spent about twenty years of his life in this country. He arrived in South Africa in May 1893, and only a month later was embroiled in the country's political problems when he was evicted from a first-class train compartment at the Pietermaritzburg station. In 1894, the Natal Indian Congress was founded, and Gandhi became its first secretary.

STREAMS WITHIN SOUTH AFRICAN HINDUISM

As has already been explained, Hinduism in South Africa includes at least four main streams:
- Sanathanist Hinduism, i.e. traditional, ritualistic Hinduism;
- Arya Samaj, whose focus is on one almighty, formless Deity;
- neo-Vedanta, of which the most familiar examples are the Ramakrishna Centre and the Divine Life Society;
- Hare Krishna, the overwhelming majority of whose followers are affiliated to the International Society for Krishna Consciousness (ISKCON).

Arya Samaj, neo-Vedanta and Hare Krishna are often collectively known as neo-Hinduism (sometimes called reformed Hinduism). Disciples of the miracle-working God–man Sathya Sai Baba have become more numerous in South Africa in recent years. The following of Sai Baba belongs within neo-Vedanta, but in practice in South Africa it tends to straddle the Sanathanist (traditional) and neo-Vedanta groupings. South African Sanathanist religion has flourished since the earliest years of Hinduism in this country. Neo-Hinduism arrived in stages during the present century. The arrival of Arya Samaj teachers early this century brought new emphases to the local Hindu community, and neo-Vedanta became firmly established in South Africa in the 1940s and 1950s. The Hare Krishna movement arrived during the 1970s, and about this time interest in Sai Baba began to crystallise.

Although the four main streams of South African Hinduism have their own distinctive features, they do have certain things in common. What unites them all is, firstly, a belief in the interminable process of reincarnation, which is governed by *karma*, the universal and impersonal law of cause and effect. Reincarnation is the belief that the essential 'self' (soul) of each human being, which is immortal and indestructible, is repeatedly reborn in a variety of different life-forms. The basic conditions of each life (fortunate or unfortunate) are determined by one's overall orientation and conduct in previous lives.

A second common characteristic is the conviction that there is one ultimate Divine Reality, who is the spiritual goal of all life. This Divine Absolute is symbolised by the pervasive AUM (or OM) symbol. AUM is the ultimate sacred sound, which is basic to all Hindu life and worship. This symbol, in its Sanskrit or Tamil form, adorns most Hindu places of worship. The basic Hindu affirmation of one ultimate Reality should be emphasised in the light of the popular impression that Hinduism is essentially polytheistic. The firm belief in one ultimate Reality is summed up in the words of the Rig-Veda, one of the earliest scriptures of India: 'They call it Indra, Mitra, Varuna, Agni ... the Real is One, though sages give it various names' (Rig Veda 1.164.46).

Sometimes this one Reality is conceptualised in threefold form as the so-called Trimurti, consisting of Brahma the Creator, Vishnu the Preserver, and Shiva the Destroyer; but this somewhat stereotyped formulation has never been as widespread as is sometimes assumed. Brahma is seldom worshipped (even in India), and hardly any temples are dedicated specifically to him. No Brahma temples are to be found in South Africa.

Many Hindus concretise the ultimate Divine Reality as the Supreme God Vishnu, or the Supreme God Shiva, or the Supreme Goddess (Shakti).

A third common feature is the importance of *dharma* (duty and moral obligation); this includes such principles as telling the truth, living a pure life, exercising forgiveness, practising self-control, goodwill, generosity, and non-harmfulness to living beings. Fourthly, there is the perception that the only way to achieve final spiritual liberation (*moksha*) is to break free from the chain of reincarnations, and to experience a profound realisation of the Divine Reality. A fifth characteristic that is to be found in the main forms of Hinduism in South Africa is the acceptance of certain scriptures, notably the four Vedas, the *Ramayana,* and the *Bhagavadgita* (Song of the Lord), though it must be emphasised that some Hindus, especially the Sanathanists, are less scripturally oriented than others. Lastly, all South African Hindus, to a greater or lesser degree, observe a number of time-honoured religious festivals.[10]

Hindu social life: caste and family

Hindu social life in South Africa has many different dimensions, some of which have positive effects and others which have negative implications. These include the celebration of various festivals, the social upheavals caused by apartheid legislation, the gains made by Christian evangelists, and caste observance and family life. This section deals only with the areas of caste and family life. Both caste observance and the joint or extended family have become considerably eroded in South Africa owing to Westernisation and increased education.

Hindus have traditionally believed that there are four great social classes (*varnas*) into which society is divided: *brahmans* (many of whom are priests), *kshatriyas* (warriors), *vaishyas* (merchants and farmers), and *sudras* (labourers). This idea of class should be distinguished from the phenomenon of caste (*jati*); while there have been only four great classes, over the centuries in India more than two thousand castes developed, including goldsmiths, blacksmiths, musicians, carpenters, weavers, oil-pressers, potters, barbers and leatherworkers.

Indian castes were arranged hierarchically, with priests at the top and the 'untouchables' (who perform tasks such as handling excrement and dead animals) too low even to be included in the caste hierarchy. Although unfair discrimination based on caste and untouchability has been outlawed in India for the last forty years, it has not yet been eliminated. One of the most moving aspects of Mahatma Gandhi's life and work was his championing of the cause of untouchables, whom he referred to as *Harijans* (children of God).

Caste membership is hereditary in Hindu tradition, and determined by the following characteristics: endogamy (marriage can occur only within the group); commensality (one should not associate with, and certainly not eat with, those outside one's own group); and a common traditional occupation. Caste observances have been increasingly eroded in South Africa because of the pressures of Westernisation generally and because the observances are very difficult to maintain in the modern workplace.

Hinduism in all its main streams has always valued religion in the home. The home and the extended family have been an essential part of Hindu religious life. The extended family usually consists of at least two nuclear families extending over at least three generations.[11] It is through the family that most Hindus learn about and experience their religious practices and teachings. The performance of life-cycle rituals and the observance of certain festivals, for example Diwali (Festival of Lights), all have important links with the home.

Hinduism has always believed that ritual pollution and impurity are caused by contact with certain things and contexts (such as sweat, saliva, nail-parings, birth, death, eating, excretion, menstruation and sexual activity). Consequently, social and caste life have traditionally paid careful attention to the regulations controlling the avoidance of pollution and the maintenance of purity. It is mainly within the home context that the means of purification are carried out, such as bathing, putting on clean clothes, fasting, abstaining from sex, and reciting appropriate religious formulae. Vegetarianism is obviously one way of avoiding the pollution associated with contact with dead animals.

In many Hindu homes, one still encounters some sort of daily domestic worship (*sandhya*), which is traditionally performed in the morning and the evening. This is an obligatory duty, the purpose of which is purification of the self. Part of *sandhya* usually involves the lighting of a sacred oil lamp, representing the divine light-energy, and accompanying prayers.[12] This is believed to sustain the life and prosperity of the home. Most Hindu homes have some sort of religious shrine incorporating the holy lamp, but the shrine can vary from a special room to a few simple images or pictures of favourite deities. Kuper observed more than thirty years ago that in South African Hindu religion it is the mother and wife who carry out the main devotions.[13] This remains largely true today, despite the increasing secularisation and Westernisation of the Hindu community.

An important facet of domestic Hinduism has traditionally been the performance of the life-cycle rituals known as *samskaras,* which mark the various significant landmarks of a person's life: birth, marriage and death.

The extended family system has declined in South Africa,[14] partly because many of the houses built for Indians who have been resettled under the Group Areas Act are too small to accommodate large numbers of people.

Sanathanist Hinduism

The term 'Sanathanist' is derived from the Sanskrit expression *Sanathana Dharma* (Eternal Way). Whereas *all* Hindus would see themselves as followers of *Sanathana Dharma*, in the South African context the narrower term 'Sanathanist' is used in two main ways, either for traditional (ritualistic) Hindus from a Hindi-speaking background in particular, or for traditional Hindus generally, regardless of their linguistic background. Here the term 'Sanathanist' is used in the latter sense.

Sanathanists in this sense are Hindus whose religion is, firstly, focused on the practical and the ritual rather than the philosophical and the doctrinal; this is why it is difficult to give a clear characterisation of Sanathanist beliefs. Secondly, Sanathanists are less scripturally oriented than other Hindus, although they are familiar with some of the dramatic stories and legends which are found in Hindu tradition and in scriptures such as the *Ramayana* and the *Mahabharata,* as well as the Puranas. (The *Ramayana* and the *Mahabharata* are the two great epics of classical Hinduism.) Thirdly, Sanathanist religion observes certain time-honoured rituals, ceremonies and festivals which are not emphasised by other branches of Hinduism. Kavadi, Mariamman prayers and the Draupadi firewalking festival are good examples of Sanathanist festivals.

The South African Sanathanist tradition incorporates the so-called Brahmanical[15] (Vishnu, Shiva, and Shakti or Goddess) traditions, as well as the indigenous Indian folk traditions, but most South African Hindus would be unaware of, or uninterested in, this rather technical distinction. Sanathanist worshippers in the Vishnu tradition are known as Vaishnavites, those in the Shiva tradition as Shaivites, and those in the Shakti (Goddess) tradition as Shaktas.

'To worshippers of Vishnu or Shiva or the Goddess, their chosen God is not merely a partial aspect of deity. A Vishnu-worshipper would regard Vishnu as the great all-encompassing God who himself creates, preserves and destroys; and similarly for worshippers of Shiva or Shakti. Most Hindus in fact worship such an *ishta-devata,* a "chosen deity".'[16]

Although ultimately all Hindus, including Sanathanists, accept one supreme Reality, it is true that Sanathanist worship, on the surface, often operates with a plurality of divine manifestations. The main divine manifestations of Sanathanist religious life (including the great deities themselves, their female companions or consorts, their offspring and so on) can be described in the following way. The Vaishnavite tradition includes the great God Vishnu himself, who is also known as Narayan (Narainsamy), Perumal (Emperumal) and Jagannath (Juggernathi); Vishnu's consort Lakshmi (Laxmi), who symbolises good fortune and prosperity; Vishnu's incarnations, of which there are traditionally ten, the two most important and popular being Rama, the hero of the *Ramayana* epic, and Krishna, the main figure of the *Bhagavadgita;* Rama's faithful devotee, Hanuman, whom Hindus usually conceptualise as the monkey god; and, lastly, Krishna's consort Radha.

In the Shaivite tradition the main divine manifestations are, firstly, the great God Shiva (Siva) himself, who is a mysterious and paradoxical deity. On the one hand he is represented by the *lingam* (a sacred pillar with connotations of fertility),[17] yet on the other he is portrayed as the great ascetic yogi. In his form as Nataraja (Cosmic Dancer), Shiva dances out the creation and destruction of the universe. Secondly, there is Shiva's consort, Parvati, also known as Uma, Durga or Kali. (In the Shakti tradition, Shiva's consort has been elevated to the status of a great Goddess in her own right). Thirdly, there is Shiva's son Subrahmanya (Soobramoniar), whose Tamil name is Muruga. He is the patron of the popular Kavadi festival. Fourthly, there is Shiva's son Ganesha, the elephant-headed deity, who removes obstacles.

We now look at the main manifestations of the divine in a further facet of

Sanathanist religion, the Goddess tradition. Among world religions Hinduism is virtually unique in its worship of a goddess as supreme being. Goddess worship plays an important part in South African Hindu religious life. This worship was brought from India, where there is a fairly clear distinction between the Brahmanical Shakti and indigenous folk Goddess traditions. In South Africa, Hindu Goddess worship has tended to fuse these two traditions so that it is conducted with little awareness of this distinction.

For most Hindus, both female and male divine energies are necessary to sustain the universe, and particularly in the Goddess and Shaivite traditions it is the female who is regarded as the dynamism that empowers the more passive and contemplative male (Shiva). Shakti, meaning 'power' or 'energy', is therefore an appropriate name for the Goddess. Goddess devotees regard her as not only the animating power of existence, but also as the Supreme Deity, the one who, out of her limitless energy, generated Vishnu, Shiva, the lesser divinities, and the universe itself.

The Goddess is believed to manifest herself in a wide variety of forms, both benign (such as Lakshmi and Sarasvati) and fierce (such as Durga, Kali and Mariamman). Some devotees would be more aware of the ultimate divine unity underlying these various forms than would others. The Goddess's various forms represent both the life-giving, preserving forces of nature, and the destructive forces of disease, decay and death. Her most important South African manifestations are Mariamman, Draupadi, Durga, Kali, Genga (Gengaiamman), Parvati, Lakshmi and Sarasvati. The Tamil word *amman* means 'mother' and 'respected woman', and appears often in the names of the fierce folk goddesses of South India. These goddesses are usually found in South Africa in temples dedicated specifically to Mariamman. There is an interesting fluidity about some of these names, especially with regard to Kali, Draupadi and Mariamman.

Mariamman, originally the South Indian village goddess Mari(y)amma(n), is a fearsome goddess, believed to be the cause and cure of smallpox and other infectious diseases. She is also the divine patron of rain. Draupadi, the goddess of firewalking, is often closely associated with Mariamman. Durga, one of the most ancient goddess manifestations, is famous for her mythological slaying of the evil demon Mahisha. Kali is the fierce goddess of death and destruction, who is sometimes also worshipped as the protective Mother. Parvati is traditionally the consort of Shiva. Lakshmi, traditionally the consort of Vishnu, is the goddess of good fortune and prosperity. Sarasvati, nominally the consort of Brahma, is goddess of learning and the arts. Gengaiamman is the water goddess of the Ganges River.

In her fierce mode, the Goddess is believed to be able to help her worshippers to realise the truth that destruction and death are, in fact, essential for continuity and new life. Because she evokes in them feelings of awe and dread, her worshippers feel a strong obligation to propitiate her, although paradoxically she can also be the focus of tender devotion. At times various propitiatory rituals such as blood sacrifice and firewalking are practised in order to maintain or restore the health and well-being of individuals and the community.

Although many Sanathanists specifically identify themselves as Vaishna-vites or Shaivites or Shakti worshippers, there are some who choose not to confine themselves to any one of these religious subtraditions.[18]

Sanathanist temples

There are dozens of unique and colourful traditional Hindu temples in South Africa,[19] the majority of which are in southern Natal. Some of the most interesting features of these Sanathanist temples are the images (*murtis*) and sculptures of the various divine manifestations, which are found both inside and outside.

Architecturally, Hindu temples in South Africa can generally be categorised as either North Indian or South Indian. However, the two styles are not as distinct in this country as they are in India. The architecture of some South African temples has been enriched with certain Islamic and colonial features.

North Indian temples in this country are usually square in plan, with a dome (*sikhara*) above the shrine-room in which the main deity is housed. This is surrounded by a verandah to allow devotees to walk round the shrine-room. The Seacow Lake Vishnu Temple, Durban, and the Durban Hindu Temple in Somtseu Road are two very good examples of this style.

South Indian temples in this country are basically rectangular in shape, with the main sanctuary at the far end. This sanctuary houses the deity to whom the temple is dedicated. A dome is built over the main sanctuary. The hall-like space in front of the main sanctuary is called the *mandapa*. In front of these temples there is usually a flagpole (*kodi maram*), which stands on a pedestal representing the sacrificial altar. Next to this stands the vehicle (*vahana*) on which the main deity rides, for example Nandi the bull for Shiva, the peacock for Subrahmanya or Muruga, the rat for Ganesha, and the lion or tiger for the Goddess. Two good examples of South Indian architecture are the Narainsamy Temple, Newlands, near Durban, and the Emperumal[20] Temple, Verulam (which was relocated from Canelands during 1985).

The dominant focus of a temple can be Vaishnavite, or Shaivite, or Goddess-oriented. Vaishnavite temples can be built in either the North Indian or South Indian styles. Vishnu (Perumal) or Krishna are the deities to whom North Indian Vaishnavite temples are dedicated. Hanuman and Rama are almost always present in Vaishnavite temples.

Shaivite temples are usually built in the South Indian style, and are dedicated either to Shiva or to his son Subrahmanya (Muruga), who occupies the central sanctuary, while Ganesha (Shiva's other son) always occupies the sanctuary to the right of the main deity (the observer's left). Because Ganesha is the remover of obstacles, worshippers are expected to approach him first, before approaching the main deity. Shiva *lingams,* which symbolise fertility, infinity or luminosity, are prominent in all Shaivite temples.

North Indian temples are almost always Vaishnavite in orientation, and have traditionally catered for Hindi-speaking and Gujarati communities, while South Indian temples are usually broadly Shaivite in orientation, and have traditionally catered for the Tamil and Telugu communities. Most Hindu temples in South Africa belong to the Tamil community because of their overall numerical strength, and most Tamil temples are dedicated to Shiva or Shiva–Subrahmanya, or to Mariamman.

In South Africa, the distinction between the Vaishnavite and Shaivite traditions has never been watertight. Although the main deity to whom the temple is dedicated is always found in the main sanctuary, images (*murtis*) of gods from other Hindu traditions are invariably found somewhere in the temple building. For example, Vaishnavite divine manifestations such as Vishnu, Krishna, Rama and Hanuman are present in a great number of temples which belong to the Shaivite tradition; whereas Shiva's *lingam* and Ganesha are often found in temples dedicated to a Vaishnavite deity. Reasons for this mixing of traditions include the poverty of the early communities, who could not afford the luxury of separate temple buildings for each tradition, and the close proximity in which Indians of different backgrounds were settled.

Many interesting and distinctive South African temples are dedicated to the worship of the Divine Mother (the Goddess), most of these belonging firmly within the South Indian Shaivite tradition. Most Goddess temples are in fact located on the same sites as Shiva temples, and the vast majority of the Goddess temples are dedicated to the ferocious and sinister aspects of the Goddess, particularly Mariamman. There are at least sixteen Mariamman temples in Natal alone. Two of the largest and best-known in South Africa are the Pretoria Mariamman Temple and the privately owned Isipingo Rail Mariamman Temple on the Natal south coast. Hardly any Goddess temples are dedicated specifically to the light and gentle divine manifestations, for example Sarasvati or Lakshmi. The images and pictures in Goddess temples represent the various aspects or manifestations of the Supreme Goddess, for example Mariamman, Kali, Durga, Genga, Sarasvati, Lakshmi and Draupadi.

Some of the older and most popular South African Sanathanist temples are the Umgeni Road Temple complex in Durban (the largest in South Africa), Siva Soobramoniar and Marriamen temples in Pietermaritzburg, Isipingo Rail Mariamman Temple, Pretoria Mariamman Temple, and Johannesburg Melrose Siva Subramaniar Temple.

Kistappa Reddy, an immigrant from South India, was one of the most competent and prolific of the early temple builders. Although he had no formal architectural training, he was responsible for some of the most attractive temples in Natal in the South Indian style: Emperumal Temple, Verulam; Ganesha Temple, Mount Edgecombe; Narainsamy Temple, Newlands; and the domes of the Siva Soobramoniar and Marriamen temples in Pietermaritzburg.

Sanathanist temple puja

Hindu *puja* (meaning devotional and ritual worship) can involve anything from private worship in the home or at a temple, to the popular practice of congregational hymn-singing, known as *kirtana*. More narrowly, *puja* usually involves worship of and ritual service to a deity and its visible image in an atmosphere of devotion. The relationship between the deity and the image is interpreted differently; to some Hindus, the image of stone or metal is the representative personal form of the deity, and may itself even be referred to as a 'deity'; to others, the image is no more than a symbolic reminder of the deity. A Hindu who performs *puja* hopes to receive *darshan* (good spiritual vibrations) from the relevant deity, as well as other blessings or favours. *Puja* in Hinduism is not limited to the Sanathanist community; it is an integral part of Hare Krishna worship, and is also often practised in some form by neo-Vedantists.

Only Sanathanist *puja* performed at a temple is dealt with here. In contrast to neo-Hindu groups, who use their temples and ashrams for regular congregational worship, Sanathanist temples are used mostly for purposes of individual and private worship, by the priest or the devotees. It is usually only at festival times that large numbers of people come together for worship at the Sanathanist temples.

With regard to temple *puja,* one can distinguish between regular (ideally daily) *puja* performed by the temple priest, and occasional or optional *puja,* whereby individuals visit the temple to carry out *puja* with the assistance of the priest. Regular *puja* involves the priest giving service to the deity. For example, he invites the god, who is treated like a royal guest, to be present; he greets, washes, anoints and dresses the image of the god, and presents offerings, and so forth. Occasional *puja* involves individuals or small groups of devotees visiting the temple and its deity for some specific religious purpose, such as to ask the god for a material or spiritual blessing, to offer thanks for healing or good fortune, or to fulfil a vow that was made earlier. The worshipper brings offerings of fruit, coconuts, milk and incense to the temple, usually on a small tray; these offerings are accepted by the priest on behalf of the deity, and camphor may be burnt. The priest then conveys a blessing, often using the ash (from the camphor or incense) to mark the foreheads of the devotees. The consecrated food (*prasad*), which is believed to be both physically and spiritually beneficial, is later eaten or given away. As part of occasional or festival *puja,* worshippers often walk round the temple three times in a clockwise direction,[21] as an act of devotion. Festival worship combines features of both regular and occasional *puja.* The Kavadi and firewalking festivals are excellent examples of festivals that incorporate such *puja.*

Fire offerings (of *samagree,*[22] grains, *ghee,* petals) can form part of *puja.* These offerings are called *havan* (or *homa*). *Havan* today is a modification of a very ancient Vedic fire ceremony, which historically predates the now familiar image-veneration of Hinduism.

Hindus often take their recently purchased motor vehicles to temples to have them blessed. An offering is made 'in order to invoke God's blessing for a long and trouble-free service'.[23]

Katha and jhanda

Red (or yellow) triangular flags, flying from bamboo poles, are a familiar sight in the gardens of many Hindu homes in Natal. This popular custom is part of a household or, more rarely, temple ceremony known as *katha* and *jhanda,* which is performed by many Sanathanists, traditionally people from a

Hindi-speaking background, though today Hindus from other linguistic backgrounds also participate. Relatives and friends are invited to these occasions.
This ceremony, conducted by a Hindu priest, involves the erection in the
garden of the flag (the *jhanda* aspect) and the telling of a sacred story (the
katha aspect). The central theme of the story is the triumph of good over evil.
Katha and *jhanda* may be performed in order to fulfil a specific religious vow,
or it may be simply an expression of thanksgiving. The flag usually has on it
the AUM symbol on one side and a picture of Hanuman on the other.[24] It is in
Hanuman's honour that the flag is raised during the *katha* and *jhanda* ceremony. The flag is often red, because this is Hanuman's colour. The bamboo
plant was probably chosen for the flagpole because it is a reminder of Hanuman, the monkey god.[25]

This ceremony is apparently a transplantation of a very minor Indian village custom which has become popular in South Africa in its present form.[26]
Kuppusami suggests that the South African version of the ceremony might
have developed as a home-based ritual before most of the present temples in
this country were built.[27]

Astrology

Sanathanist Hindus are likely to pay more attention to astrology than are
the adherents of other streams of South African Hinduism.[28] Many Sanathanist temples have special shrines dedicated to the *navagraha,* the 'nine
planets'. The *navagraha* images, made of black stone, represent both the nine
planets themselves and the deities associated with them. They are the Sun
(*Surya*), the Moon (*Chandra*), Mercury, Venus, Mars, Jupiter, Saturn, *Rahu*
(the astrological dragon's head), and *Ketu* (the astrological dragon's tail).
Appropriate rituals are performed by the priest and the worshippers; these
involve walking round the images in the hope of attracting the favour of the
planetary deities.

Hindu festivals

Hindu festivals are very numerous and colourful, and are celebrated by all
streams of Hinduism. The dates of the various Hindu festivals are determined
by reference to a twelve-month lunar calendar. Western dates of the various
festivals vary slightly from year to year. Some of the most widely observed festivals are Krishna Asthmee (Krishna's birthday), Diwali or Deepavali (Festival
of Lights), Ram Naumee (Rama's birthday), and Maha-Shivarathri (Night of
Shiva).

Kavadi, the Mariamman festival, and Draupadi (the firewalking festival),
are the most dramatic and colourful of all the Hindu festivals. They are practised mostly by the Sanathanist community. Kavadi and firewalking in particular are attended by very large numbers of people. These three festivals are the
most notable examples of ceremonies during which the state of trance features
prominently. Trances are believed to be the result of possession by a deity; by
these means devotees gain the right to act as healers or oracles. To demonstrate their devotion, some people have hooks stuck into their flesh, from

which fruit or flowers are suspended, and skewers through their tongues and cheeks. They seem to feel no pain, and there is no evidence of bleeding or swelling. These acts may be performed out of gratitude for some past blessing, in the nature of a penance, or in connection with a vow.

The three festivals are associated with the taking of vows (*vrata*), which play an important part in all traditional Hindu worship.[29] People can take vows on their own or another person's behalf. For example, if illness, misfortune, unemployment or barrenness is averted or overcome, or success is achieved in some enterprise, the person promises to walk across a firepit a specified number of times, or perform some other appropriate action. Serious consequences are believed to follow the breaking of a vow.

The festivals for the fierce goddesses, Mariamman and firewalking involve the carrying of *garagams*. A *garagam* is believed to be a manifestation of the Goddess, and consists of a clay or brass pot filled with sanctified water, with a coconut placed over the mouth of the pot. A conical bamboo frame is constructed over this and covered with marigolds and vines, with a lime placed on the top. Some devotees carry these tall, heavy structures on their heads.

The preparation for each of the festivals lasts for several days (13 days in the case of Kavadi, 10 days in the case of Mariamman, and 10–18 days for firewalking), and begins with an evening flag-hoisting ceremony attended by prospective festival participants and other worshippers. During the preparation period, participants must lead disciplined lives, involving fasting, prayer and sexual abstinence.

Kavadi

Kavadi is celebrated in many South African Sanathanist temples on two occasions each year – Thaipoosam Kavadi, in the Tamil month of *Thai* (January/February); and Chitraparvam Kavadi, in the Tamil month of *Chitray* (April/May).

Kavadi is held in honour of the god Muruga (Subrahmanya), the son of Shiva, who is believed to have great power to heal and to dispel misfortune. The name Kavadi comes from the decorated frames (*kavadis*) carried by the worshippers as a kind of penitential burden, usually in fulfilment of a particular vow; they do this in symbolic remembrance of certain events in South Indian religious mythology. An ancient myth tells how Idumban (Itampan) was commissioned to carry two mountains, which he accomplished by hanging them from each end of a pole borne across his shoulders. After setting down his burden, he found that the mountains had become fixed to the ground and could not again be lifted. Idumban angered the youthful owner of the mountains, who now appeared and killed him after a fight. The youth then restored Idumban to life, revealing himself as the god Muruga. Idumban, convinced of Muruga's divine power, vowed to serve the god forever. Idumban asked that whenever worshippers bear *kavadi* for Muruga, they may be blessed as he had been blessed. Muruga's *vel* (spear) plays a very visible part in the rituals of the Kavadi festival, as it is believed to enshrine his power.

Self-inflicted pain, usually in a trance state, is believed to be another sign of devotion to Muruga among those Hindus who 'carry *kavadi*' today. Because of this, some participants have their tongues and cheeks pierced with little *vels* (sometimes needles), and may also have rows of hooks inserted across their chests and backs.

The *kavadi* frame used today is made of two wooden end-pieces joined by a short pole, above which are semicircular strips of wood, bamboo or wire. The devotee carries the frame in one hand, balanced on the shoulder. The end-pieces are sometimes elaborately carved, and the frame is usually decorated with flowers, fruit and peacock feathers (the peacock being the vehicle of Muruga). There are small hooks near each end from which to hang brass receptacles containing milk.

The popularity of the worship of Muruga and of the Kavadi festival among South Indians in Natal is evidenced by the fact that a large number of temples are dedicated to him in the name of Subrahmanya.

The Mariamman festival

The annual Mariamman 'Porridge' festival is celebrated for ten days, usually during the Tamil month of *Adi* (July/August), which is specially associated with the Goddess Mariamman. She is a powerful and irascible South Indian folk goddess whose worship was brought to South Africa by the early Tamil-speaking settlers; many of them came from the Madras area, where she is still worshipped today. She is believed to be both the cause and the cure of small-pox and other infectious diseases. Her name Mari-amma (*amma* meaning mother, and *mari* meaning rain in Tamil and death or pestilence in Sanskrit) sums up the ambiguity and complexity of her life-giving and death-bestowing character.

Her anger needs to be appeased by offerings of 'cooling' foods such as porridge, milk, coconut and pumpkin, which is done at this festival. It is also believed that when she strikes a victim with fever, her anger overheats them so that the patients require treatment with this type of cooling food.

Special porridge, *kulu*, made from fermented maize, sour milk and onions, is placed in buckets with syringa leaves tied around them. Both the porridge (which is fed to the patients) and the syringa leaves (which are placed in the sick room) are believed to have a cooling effect on the fever. The porridge is also eaten by devotees during the festival.[30]

Supplications are made to Mariamman to cool her anger and to persuade her to send the rains needed to cool and nourish the earth. Part of her traditional worship also includes blood sacrifice, which entails the beheading of an animal, usually a chicken or a goat, the spilling of its blood on the earth, and the offering of all this to the Goddess. The blood represents life and fertility, which is poured back into the earth, and it is also believed to have a propitiatory and revitalising effect on Mariamman.

All temples dedicated to Mariamman celebrate this festival, but only a few practise blood sacrifice (for example, the Isipingo Rail Mariamman Temple), as today this is disapproved of by many Hindus.

The largest and most popular Mariamman festival is held annually at the privately owned Isipingo Rail Mariamman Temple, on Good Friday and the week preceding it.[31] Thousands of pilgrims arrive. Some of them make vegetable offerings, while others choose to offer blood sacrifices. Hundreds of chickens and goats are sacrificed during this festival. Mariamman's healing powers are particularly celebrated at the Isipingo festival.

Firewalking
Firewalking takes place annually, usually during March, April or May, at four traditional temples in Natal. Recently, three newer Chatsworth temples have started practising this ceremony, evidence of its growing popularity.

Firewalking is celebrated in honour of the goddess Draupadi, who is the heroine of the ancient epic, the *Mahabharata.* Although she is not depicted as a goddess in this book, and the original (Sanskrit) version of it does not contain any record of her walking through fire, later South Indian traditions include several stories in which Draupadi walks on fire,[32] either to confirm her chastity or to purify herself of a number of attempts to defile her. Eventually, by about 1400 CE, she had attained the status of the fierce South Indian goddess of fire, who requires propitiation but can also bestow great blessings on her devotees.

Firewalking in South Africa appears originally to have been a predominantly Tamil celebration, brought here from India, although today it extends well beyond Tamil circles.

The decision to participate in the festival is closely associated with the taking of vows. To come unscathed through the firepit, approximately ten metres long, is seen as proof of great virtue. After participating for 10–18 days in the various rituals and dramas that recall the trials and austerities borne by Draupadi, the climax of the festival is reached when the devotees walk across the firepit. The image of Draupadi is placed at the far end of the pit, and she is believed to protect her faithful devotees as they cross, and to bless them and bestow new life and health on the whole community. Rebirth from fire is a common theme in Hinduism.

It would appear from the increasing number of people who attend the colourful trance festivals that they are growing in popularity rather than diminishing, in spite of various recent predictions that this type of ritualistic Hinduism is on the decline.[33]

Neo-Hindu (reformed Hindu) movements
Modern neo-Hinduism (reformed Hinduism) began in India in the second quarter of the nineteenth century. In contrast to Sanathanism, the neo-Hindu groups such as Arya Samaj, the neo-Vedanta organisations, and Hare Krishna have several features in common. In the first place they all hold regular communal religious services, often referred to as *satsang.* Sanathanist temples are seldom used for such purposes. Secondly, there is an emphasis on the value of reading and the availability of important scriptures and religious literature. Thirdly, they all have contemplative practices such as yoga or meditation. This emphasis on inner contemplation does not mean that traditional reli-

gious rituals such as *puja* are ignored by neo-Hindus. Fourthly, there is an avoidance of some of the traditional observances of Sanathanist Hinduism, for example trance festivals such as Kavadi and firewalking.

Arya Samaj

Arya Samaj Hindus are often called 'Vedic' Hindus because of their belief that the scriptures known as the four Vedas contain infallible and universal teachings, which were revealed by God in ancient times. More than a century ago, Swami Dayananda Sarasvati founded a reform movement in India called Arya Samaj (Society of the Righteous), to bring Hindus 'back to the Vedas' and to Vedic truth.

Over eighty years ago, Hinduism in South Africa was favoured by the visits of two important Arya Samaj figures. The first to arrive was Bhai Parmanand, who stayed for a few months during 1905. Under his guidance, the Hindu Young Men's Association was established in Natal in October of that year. Swami Shankaranand was the next important visitor, arriving in 1908. He encouraged mother-tongue education and the use of the sixteen *samskaras* (life-cycle rituals). He also stressed the importance of observing Hindu festivals such as Diwali, Ram Naumee and Krishna Asthmee. These three widely observed festivals, along with the popular Maha-Shivarathri, are emphasised by Arya Samajists today.

Arya Samajists believe in one formless, almighty, immutable God, who has created the universe out of pre-existing matter and now sustains it. Each person possesses an eternal soul, and can find fulfilment and peace through knowledge of the truth, through prayer, worship, meditation and morality. Although individual souls can never actually become God, they can progress spiritually and finally achieve full God-realisation.

Arya Samaj adherents are clearly distinguished from virtually all their fellow Hindus by their conviction that the eternal, formless God can never take on any form, whether human or non-human. It follows that God has no incarnations and cannot ever legitimately be represented by any image or idol. Arya Samaj *mandirs* therefore contain none of these representations, but the AUM symbol always adorns these places of worship.

Arya Samaj, more than any other Hindu group, emphasises the observance of the *havan* ceremony and the *samskaras*. The *havan* (*hawan*) ritual, a modified continuation of a very ancient Vedic fire ritual, has a special place in the religious life of Arya Samaj Hindus. This involves fire-offerings of grains, *ghee* or *samagree*, and is performed as part of every context of worship. It is believed that it purifies the air and helps to increase spirituality and universal harmony.

The *samskaras* are life-cycle rituals marking the various significant rites of passage in a person's life. These are carried out mostly at home, although the initiation and death rituals can be carried out at any Hindu holy place. Between 12 and 40 *samskaras* were listed in classical times. Today, the most important of these are the ceremonies marking birth; the naming of the child; the child's leaving the house for the first time; initiation, by which a boy becomes 'twice-born', and is entitled to study the Vedas and perform Vedic rituals; marriage, which is a bond between families and not merely between individuals; and lastly, funerals.

The Pietermaritzburg Veda Dharma Sabha, one of the most significant Arya Samaj organisations in South Africa, celebrated its eightieth anniversary in 1989. This involved a number of religious, cultural and other events, spread throughout the year. The Sabha was founded in 1909 by Swami Shankaranand. The Arya Yuvuk Sabha of Durban was established in 1912, and built the well-known Aryan Benevolent Home in 1921. This institution runs four homes that provide accommodation and care for children, disabled people and the elderly.

The Arya Pratinidhi Sabha, which is the national umbrella body of the Arya Samaj in South Africa, was formed in 1925. The Arya Samaj organisations already referred to are members of the Sabha. Its golden jubilee brochure, issued in 1975, describes some of the influences of Arya Samaj on South African Hinduism:

> There are many practices for which the Arya Samaj can take some, if not whole, credit. They are the popularisation of the word 'AUM' as a symbol of God, the use of 'namaste' as a form of greeting, the singing of 'Jay jagdish hare' as Arti, the commencement of meetings and functions with the recital of the Gayatri Mantra[34] and the chanting of Shanti Paath[35] at the termination thereof.

The offices of the Arya Pratinidhi Sabha are in Carlisle Street, Durban, and next door is a large Veda Mandir (Vedic temple) for the worship of the one true God. The Sabha includes three important subsidiary bodies, which were established by Pandit Nardev Vedalankar. They are the Vedic Purohit Mandal (concerned with Vedic priests and the performance of the 16 *samskaras*); the Veda Niketan, which issues publications and coordinates religious examinations; and the Hindi Shiksha Sangh, which encourages the use of the Hindi language and coordinates relevant examinations.

The Arya Samaj has encouraged the emancipation and education of women. It is interesting that in March 1989, six women from the Durban and Pietermaritzburg areas were ordained Vedic priests.

Neo-Vedanta

The local ashram, with its guru or spiritual teacher, is integral to the life of Hindu neo-Vedanta. The Ramakrishna Centre of South Africa and the Divine Life Society of South Africa are typical examples of neo-Vedanta in this country. Their basic teachings can be summarised very simply in the propositions: God is the Real; God can be realised in the depths of one's being, because each person is potentially divine; to realise God is the supreme goal of human existence; God can be realised by following one or other of several religious means and paths.

The Vedantic Hindus (as well as Hare Krishna devotees) often stress the importance of the guru in the life of a disciple. A Divine Life Society booklet, *Faith and Self-surrender,* contains a section about faith in the guru:

> Faith in one's Guru or spiritual preceptor is the most vital factor in spiritual life ... The Guru has attained union with God. Hence, his words are the words of God Himself ... God's grace flows to the disciple through the Guru ... The importance of obedience to the Guru and faith in his words and teachings cannot be overemphasized ... The disciple's spiritual progress is assured if his surrender and faith in his Guru are strong.[36]

Neo-Vedanta was consolidated in South Africa during the 1940s and 1950s, though Vedantic initiatives had been greatly encouraged in 1934 by the first visit to this country of a representative of the Ramakrishna Mission in India, Swami Adhyanand.

The Ramakrishna Centre of South Africa was founded in Durban in 1946 by D. Naidoo and others, although an informal group had been meeting since 1942. Mr Naidoo took monastic vows in India, and returned in 1953 as Swami Nischalananda. He was succeeded as the spiritual head of the Centre by Swami Shivapadananda, who died recently. The Centre's main ashram, which was opened in 1959, is at Avoca. The essential message of the Ramakrishna Centre of South Africa follows the teachings of Swami Vivekananda (1863–1902), the chief disciple of Sri Ramakrishna (1834–86), the celebrated nineteenth-century Indian mystic. The Centre therefore emphasises the divinity within every human being as the foundation of spirituality, human dignity, equality and service to others. The various living religions are regarded as different paths of spiritual progress which all lead to the goal of God-realisation. An annual inter-faith Quest Conference is held in South Africa to discuss and reaffirm the unity of religions. In Ramakrishna's words: 'Many are the names of God and infinite the forms through which He may be approached. In whatever name and form you worship Him, through that He will be realised by you.'

The Ramakrishna Centre celebrated its golden jubilee during 1992. Highlights of the Centre's worship are *satsang* and *ar(a)ti*. *Satsang*, which consists of communal prayers, songs, rituals, discourses, readings and meditation, is held at least once a week. *Arti* involves the ceremonial waving of lights before the image of a deity or holy person, and is held twice a day.[37]

Ramakrishna ashrams observe the major Hindu festivals, particularly Maha-Shivarathri, Ram Naumee, Krishna Asthmee and Navaratri, as well as giving a special place to the birthdays of Sri Ramakrishna, Sri Sarada Devi (the wife of Ramakrishna), and Swami Vivekananda. Because of the Centre's stress on the universalism of religions, the birthdays of Muhammad, Buddha and Jesus are also observed. Lay and monastic devotees of both sexes are active in the movement. The monastic devotees undergo a lengthy training period, and are recognisable by their yellow or white robes.

Prior to 1965, the ashram (and headquarters) at Avoca in Durban was the only Ramakrishna ashram complex in South Africa.[38] There are now six full ashrams, all of which are in Natal, and over twenty branches throughout the country. The ashrams are at Avoca, Asherville and Chatsworth in Durban, at

Northdale in Pietermaritzburg, and at Ladysmith and Newcastle. Most of the branches are in Natal, although there are some in the Transvaal (for example, at Lenasia) and in the Eastern Cape.

The main ashram in Avoca is the oldest existing ashram institution in South Africa. It includes a shrine-room, living-quarters for members of the ashram, the Jyoti Press (publisher of the journal *Jyoti*), a bookshop and a library. In the shrine-room there is a large statue of Ramakrishna, with Swami Vivekananda and Sri Sarada Devi on either side of him. The AUM symbol is prominently displayed.

The Sri Sarada Devi ashram in Asherville, Durban, was officially opened in 1984. This ashram, named after the wife of Ramakrishna, is interesting because it follows the pattern of ashrams of this type established by Vivekananda in India, which cater for the needs of women devotees.[39] In the late 1940s Swami Ghanananda, a visitor from the Ramakrishna Mission in India, started the Ramakrishna-Vivekananda Hindu Study Circle in Pietermaritzburg. This ashram has recently become a branch of the Ramakrishna Centre of South Africa.

The Ramakrishna Centre endeavours to preserve and transmit the rich Hindu heritage of music, dancing, drama and art. It is also involved in upgrading black education in various ways, and it performs extensive charitable work, especially in rural areas. Its school-feeding scheme attempts to alleviate malnutrition among black schoolchildren. The Centre also distributes food, clothing, blankets and self-help items in various areas of the country. Clinics for poor people are provided.

The Divine Life Society of South Africa has its spiritual basis in the life and teachings of Swami Sivananda (1887–1963). Sivananda founded the Divine Life Society in India in 1936, and continues to be the spiritual inspiration of the Society. Its main ashram is at Rishikesh, in northern India. In 1949 Brother V. Srinivasan (now Swami Sahajananda) started a branch of the Divine Life Society in South Africa. The headquarters, which include the main ashram and printing press, are in Mountbatten Drive, Reservoir Hills, Durban. The Society is somewhat smaller than the Ramakrishna movement, and is active mostly in Natal.

Sivananda's *Gospel of Divine Life* gives an excellent account of the spiritual emphases of the Society, which include a life of compassion and service, and the cultivation of inner enlightenment. Like the Ramakrishna Centre, the Divine Life Society aims at promoting spiritual knowledge by distributing literature, holding regular religious services (*satsang*), and providing yoga instruction. The Society stresses the basic unity and universality of religions, all of which are believed to lead towards the same ultimate divine goal. It also organises numerous educational and cultural programmes.

Divine Life ashrams have long displayed pictures and images of Sivananda and a variety of images of popular deities. Recently, the Society has decided that all its ashrams should follow a uniform policy and their shrines may only contain representations of Sivananda, Krishna, Sarasvati and Shiva. The order of services follows strict guidelines, which are observed by all Divine Life ashrams in South Africa. The Society observes most of the prominent South African Hindu festivals, and pays particular attention to Sivananda's birthday, which is remembered on the eighth day of each month.

The Society carries out a variety of charitable works in the community, including the building of schools for Africans, the provision of medical services, and the distribution of food and clothing to the needy. In addition to the main ashram at Reservoir Hills, there are others at Pietermaritzburg, Chatsworth, Merebank and Tongaat. Recently, an International Children's Cultural Centre has been built on the Natal north coast at La Mercy.

The Chinmaya Mission is a world-wide Vedanta organisation which was founded by Swami Chinmayananda, who has visited South Africa a number of times. In January 1979, the South African Chinmaya Mission was established by Brahmachari Sri Mahavir Chaitanya, now known as Nirmalananda, who had studied in India. A Chinmaya ashram exists in Chatsworth.

The Vedanta Mission (Mission for the Eternal Religion) was founded in 1965 by Guru H. G. Dewa, who is also its spiritual head. The Mission is now permanently based in Isipingo Hills, about twenty kilometres south of Durban. This ashram contains a shrine-room, a printing press, and a pre-primary school with about eighty children. The Vedanta Mission lays special emphasis on the *Bhagavadgita,* and believes that Sri Krishna is the Absolute Supreme Being, who comprehends and transcends every conceivable idea of God, but who can bestow his saving grace on those who commit themselves to him.

The Adi Shankara Ashram in Johannesburg, established during the 1970s by Swami Shankarananda (formerly of the Divine Life Society), follows Vedantic teaching in general and the orientation of the medieval philosopher Shankara in particular.

The Gita Mandir, in Raisethorpe, Pietermaritzburg, is one of the most impressive and attractive Hindu religious structures in South Africa. This is the home of an independent neo-Vedanta group, whose spiritual leader was Guru Rambaran (d. 1984). What distinguishes worshippers at the Gita Mandir from Sanathanist Hinduism is the conviction that certain Sanathanist beliefs and practices are unnecessary or spiritually misleading, for example the mediating role of traditional priests, the 'unedifying' mythology of the Puranas, and the many 'superstitions' and popular rituals that are important to most Sanathanists. The religious emphasis of the Gita Mandir is on the Vedanta dimension of Hinduism, with the *Bhagavadgita* and the *Ramayana* being the primary scriptures.

The Gita Mandir is a spectacular white building, standing on one of the high points in the suburb of Raisethorpe so that it can be seen from a considerable distance. Its structure has religious significance, symbolising devotees' spiritual journey, beginning at the lower levels of intellectual understanding, incorporating worship and basic meditation, and culminating in God-realisation.

On the lowest level of the temple is a library containing scriptures and religious books from a variety of living faiths. On the next floor (the ground floor) is a large hall for religious services, which is dominated by a colourful life-sized image of the divine incarnation Krishna in a rural setting. There is a smaller meditation room on the next level, which contains images of many deities and religious figures. The topmost level has a dome-shaped Temple of Silence, which is only for the use of advanced students of yoga, who strive to realise union with the Absolute. The major weekly service is held on Sundays in the main congregational hall. Worshippers from all religious traditions are welcome.

Saiva Sithantha Sungum

There is some uncertainty whether to classify the Saiva Sithantha Sungum of South Africa under Sanathanism or neo-Hinduism. Because it has some obvious affinities with neo-Hinduism, it is discussed here. The Saiva Sithantha Sungum was founded by Guru Swamigal in 1937, and has traditionally been Tamil-oriented. Its main South African centre is in Derby Street, Durban; branches exist elsewhere in South Africa, specifically in Pietermaritzburg and Johannesburg, each under the supervision of a guru. There are some historical continuities between the medieval Indian Saiva Siddhanta (a religious and philosophical tradition emphasising the incomparable and gracious God Shiva) and the present-day Saiva Sithantha Sungum. The Sungum today is probably best known for its characteristically neo-Vedantic emphasis on the basic unity and universality of all religions.

Sathya Sai Baba organisations

Sathya Sai Baba is a much-revered Indian figure who is regarded by his followers as the supreme God in human form. He was born at Puttaparthi in South India in 1926. His South African following has grown spectacularly in recent years, and his influence is particularly strong in Natal. South Africa has many local Sathya Sai Baba groups, which are affiliated to larger, regional organisations, which in turn belong to the Transvaal-based Central Council of South Africa. The religious and cultural life of these groups revolves around the person of Sai Baba – his divinity, teachings and miracles. His wonderworking power, which includes healings, and materialisations of ash, *lingams* and jewellery, is directly dependent on his divine nature. He is believed to be an incarnation of an earlier revered Sai Baba (Sai Baba of Shirdi), who died in India in 1918.

Sathya Sai Baba's teaching emphasises the 'fatherhood of God and the brotherhood of man', encouraging people to identify with the Divine. This goal of God-realisation is believed to be the basic message of all the world religions. Sai Baba's ashrams in India, at Puttaparthi and Whitefield (near Bangalore), are visited every year by vast numbers of pilgrims and devotees, many of them from South Africa.

A number of private homes of Sai Baba devotees in Natal have become places of pilgrimage because of various manifestations of his presence, such as ash miraculously materialising on religious shrines and on pictures and images of Sai Baba.

Hare Krishna movement

The Hare Krishna movement, known officially as the International Society for Krishna Consciousness (ISKCON), was founded in America in 1966 by Swami Bhaktivedanta Prabhupada (d. 1977). This movement has become firmly established in South Africa during the 1980s.

The magnificent Hare Krishna Temple in Chatsworth, near Durban, was opened in October 1985. Officially called the Shri-Shri Radha-Radhanath Temple of Understanding, it can be seen from a considerable distance, and forms a spectacular landmark in the area. It has three golden towers, reminiscent of the North Indian *nagara* style of architecture.

The main sanctuary in the temple contains colourful images of Krishna, Radha (who is Krishna's consort) and Chaitanya, the sixteenth-century Bengali Vaishnavite reformer.[40] Pictures depicting scenes from the childhood and youth of Krishna adorn the inside walls, and the colours and lights from the chandeliers are reflected in the highly polished marble floor. A number of services are held during the day, with the main service occurring in the early evening. After this, the usual custom of distributing *prasadam* (vegetarian food which has been dedicated to Krishna) to the congregation is observed. The temple complex also houses its community of devotees who propagate the ISKCON message and engage in various charitable works in the Durban–Chatsworth area, such as their 'Food for Life' scheme. There is a vegetarian restaurant and take-away on the lowest level of the temple, and a bookshop in the temple foyer.

Hare Krishna cannot be confined to either Sanathanist or neo-Vedantic frameworks, and is quite distinct from Arya Samaj. The religion of Hare Krishna consists of a unique blend of traditional, Puranic, philosophical, ritualistic and innovative devotional elements. A prominent feature of religious life is repeated chanting of the name of Krishna, the supreme God.

The central scriptures of Hare Krishna are the *Bhagavadgita* and the Bhagavata Purana. These emphasise the sovereign reality of Krishna, the eternal yet essentially personal God who can grant release from the cycle of reincarnation to all who approach him with devotion and obedience. It is considered essential for all devotees to submit to the spiritual guidance of a guru.

It is not an exaggeration to say that the Hare Krishna view of God is significantly different from the theology of the Arya Samaj. In contrast to the 'formless God' of the Arya Samaj, the Hare Krishna can truly be said to believe in a 'God of form', in at least three senses. Firstly, God manifests himself from time to time in the form of divine incarnations, for example Rama; secondly, God becomes concrete in the 'deities' in the Hare Krishna temples at certain ritually appropriate times; and thirdly, the original, eternal, inherent nature of God is characterised by form: God, in his ultimate essence, is the two-handed Krishna, the beautiful one who carries a flute and wears peacock feathers in his hair.

The Hare Krishna Temple in Durban has become famous for its numerous spectacular festivals, most of which are observed annually. One of the most important of these is Krishna's birthday (Krishnasthami or Krishna Jayanti), which celebrates 'the appearance of Lord Krishna in this world 5 000 years ago'. The largest and most spectacular of Hare Krishna festivals is Ratha Yatra, the five-day festival of chariots, in honour of Lord Jagannath (Vishnu), 'Lord of the Universe'. Amongst other festivals, the temple celebrates Ram Naumee, Diwali, Vyasapuja (the birthday of the founder Prabhupada), and Sri Laxmi Narasingha (the festival which celebrates God's incarnation in the form of a man–lion).

ISKCON is represented in a few other centres in South Africa, apart from Durban. Although no Hare Krishna temple exists in Pietermaritzburg, ISKCON established a chapter in the city during 1987.

In contrast to most other Hindu groups, who tend to have a tolerant attitude to a wide variety of religious paths, the vast majority of Hare Krishnas regard their teachings as distinctly superior to those of other Hindu movements, and see Hare Krishna as offering the only true approach to God.[41] With regard to the social class of Indian Hare Krishna adherents in Natal, Sooklal states: 'The Hare Krishna movement ... has greater support in areas like Phoenix and Chatsworth ... than in the more affluent areas like Reservoir Hills and Westville.'[42] Some 'Krishna' groups in South Africa are not officially affiliated to ISKCON, but none can compare in scale or importance to the ISKCON establishment.

Some Hindu scriptures

The *Bhagavadgita* and *Ramayana* are the most widely used Hindu scriptures in South Africa. Also well known are, firstly, the four Vedas (Rig-Veda, Sama-Veda, Yajur-Veda and Atharva-Veda), the very earliest scriptures of Hinduism. These are acknowledged by all Hindus, but are especially emphasised in Arya Samaj circles. Then there are the Upanishads, which are mainly philosophical and mystical texts, composed after the Vedas. Thirdly, we have the two great epics called the *Ramayana* and the *Mahabharata*. (The *Mahabharata* is also known as the Great Epic.) Fourth comes the *Bhagavadgita*, technically a very small part of the *Mahabharata*. The *Gita* is almost always published and studied as a separate entity. It is without doubt the most widely acknowledged of all the Hindu scriptures.

The *Laws of Manu* is the most well known of the *Dharma-shastras* (law books), and is the fifth of the scriptures with which South African Hindus are more or less familiar, while the *Vedanta Sutra* (also known as the *Brahma Sutra*), a commentary on the Upanishads, is sixth. After it we mention the Puranas, great storehouses of popular mythological, devotional and sometimes philosophical religion. Lastly, there are three Tamil scriptures that are important in the South African context: the *Tirukkural* (or *Kural*), the so-called Tamil Veda; the *Devaram* (or *Thevaram*); and the *Tiruvachakam*.

Neo-Hindus tend to know and use the scriptures more than the traditional communities do. The scriptural stories and sayings most familiar to Sanathanists are found in the epics, the *Bhagavadgita* and the Puranas. Arya Samaj lays greatest emphasis on the earliest sacred writings of India, namely the four Vedas. Vedantists have always regarded the so-called *Prasthana-traya*, or triple foundation (the Upanishads, the *Bhagavadgita* and the *Vedanta Sutra*) as their essential scriptural basis.

Conclusion

It is worth emphasising that the various categories and distinctions which are used in this chapter for purposes of study and understanding (such as Vaishnavism/Shaivism and Sanathanism/neo-Hinduism) are inevitably provisional and artificial. Hinduism is a holistic and organic living reality which, to some extent, transcends analysis and dissection.

Since their earliest days the South African Hindu communities have shown an ability to survive considerable privations and upheavals. If they continue to uphold their cultural and religious traditions with the same determination and adaptability as they have in the past, they have every prospect of flourishing in a society that will be subject to unparalleled changes in the coming years.

NOTES

1. These aggressive invaders, who referred to themselves as 'Arya' (meaning noble), were of Indo-European (Indo-Aryan) stock. Their language was an early form of Sanskrit, which is related to other Indo-European languages such as Greek. The famous Hindu scriptures known as the Vedas were developed by these people.

2. P. Brijlal, 'Demographic profile', in A. J. Arkin, K. P. Magyar and G. J. Pillay (eds.), *The Indian South Africans: A Contemporary Profile.* Durban: Owen Burgess, 1989, p. 35.

3. G. C. Oosthuizen and J. H. Hofmeyr, *A Socio-religious Survey of Chatsworth.* Durban: Institute for Social and Economic Research, University of Durban–Westville, 1979, p. 241.

4. G. J. Pillay, 'Ritualistic Hinduism and Popular Pentecostalism: Two World-views in Dynamic Relation', *Religion in Southern Africa*, 6, 1 (January 1985), p. 29.

5. The Christian increase among Hindus between 1961 and 1981 was almost as great as the increase between 1860 and 1960. (We are indebted to Professor G. C. Oosthuizen of Durban for this information.)

6. Further information about the areas of India from which the indentured labourers came, the circumstances under which they worked, and the differences between the indentured immigrants and the 'passenger' Indians can be found in Hilda Kuper's detailed study *Indian People in Natal.* Kuper's fieldwork was carried out among Hindis and Tamils in Merebank, Springfield and Newlands. Although this book was published as long ago as 1960, many of her accounts of Hindu life and religion are still accurate. No comparable study of South African Hinduism has since been written.

7. Paul Mikula, B. Kearney and R. Harber, *Traditional Hindu Temples in South Africa.* Durban: Hindu Temple Publications, 1982, pp. 98, 100.

8. Nelistra Singh, 'The Divine Life Society in South Africa: A Study of Religion in Action', *Nidan*, 1 (December 1989), p. 41.

9. This situation differs markedly from that in Britain, where Gujaratis make up a far higher proportion of the Hindu population.

10. The use of the term 'festivals' in this context includes joyful religious celebrations as well as solemn fasts.

11. R. Ramphal, 'Social Transition', in Arkin, *The Indian South Africans*, pp. 74–85.

12. G. J. Pillay et al., 'Religious Profile', in Arkin, *The Indian South Africans*, p. 154.

13. Hilda Kuper, *Indian People in Natal.* Pietermaritzburg: Natal University Press, 1960, p. 121.

14. Jan Hofmeyr, 'Directions in the Evolution of Hinduism in South Africa', *Journal of the University of Durban-Westville*, 3, 2 (1979), p. 132.

15. 'Brahmanical' in this context means 'in continuity with the Vedic tradition', which includes at least the four Vedas and the Upanishads.

16. Patrick Maxwell and Thillayvel Naidoo, 'The Religions of India', in John W. de Gruchy and Martin Prozesky (eds.), *A Southern African Guide to World Religions*, Cape Town: David Philip, 1991, p. 58.

17. Historians of Indian religion are widely agreed that the *lingam* has been an explicitly phallic symbol for well over 2 000 years. However, in our discussions with South African Hindus, this phallicism is either totally rejected or modified into an emphasis on fertility in general or something more abstract like infinity or luminosity.

18. Pillay, 'Religious Profile', p. 155.

19. Interesting information about Sanathanist temples in this country can be found in the profusely illustrated *Traditional Hindu Temples in South Africa*, by Paul Mikula, Brian Kearney and Rodney Harber.

20. Emperumal and Perumalsami are variants of Perumal, one of the South Indian names of the god Vishnu.

21. Clockwise is considered to be an auspicious direction, and anti-clockwise an inauspicious direction. As Hindus would put it, when circling a temple or shrine, one should always keep one's right shoulder towards the deity.

22. *Samagree* consists of dried bark, flowers and other substances that give off an aromatic fragrance when burnt.

23. C. Kuppusami, *Religions, Customs and Practices of South African Indians.* Durban: Sunray, 1983, p. 100.

24. Hanuman was featured on the flag flown from Arjuna's chariot at the great battle of Kurukshetra mentioned in chapter 1 of the *Bhagavadgita*.

25. Kuppusami, *Religions, Customs and Practices of South African Indians*, p. 73.

26. It is very difficult to substantiate this statement, which is based on the suggestions of some local Hindus.

27. Kuppusami, *Religions, Customs and Practices of South African Indians*, p. 73.

28. The Arya Samaj are often very critical of the astrological dimensions of traditional Hinduism.

29. Kuper, *Indian People in Natal*, pp. 199–200.

30. Alleyn Diesel, 'The Worship and Iconography of the Hindu Folk Goddesses in Natal', *Journal for the Study of Religion*, 5, 2 (September 1992), pp. 12–13.

31. This temple was built over the hole of a sacred cobra, as snakes are associated with the Earth Mother and are believed to guard the treasures of the earth.

32. Alf Hiltebeitel, *The Cult of Draupadi*, vol. 1. Chicago: The University Press, 1988, pp. 436 ff.

33. Kuper, *Indian People in Natal*, p. 215; Thillayvel Naidoo (ed.), *Challenge: The Papers and Resolutions of the Seventieth Anniversary Convention of the South African Hindu Maha Sabha.* Durban, 29–31 May 1982, pp. 1, 4.

34. The Arya Samaj version of the mantra reads as follows: 'O God, the Giver of life, Remover of pains and sorrows, Bestower of happiness, and Creator of the Universe, Thou art most luminous, pure and adorable. We meditate on Thee. May Thou inspire and guide our intellect in the right direction.' A more widely known version is:

'O Supreme Lord, Self-existent, All-intelligence, All-bliss, Creator of the Universe! O Inspirer of good thoughts and good deeds, May we be imbued with Thy grace and glory; Mayest Thou be the unerring Guide of our minds, and May we follow Thy lead unto Righteousness.'

35. 'O Supreme Lord, Thy celestial regions are full of peace and harmony; peace reigns on Thy earth and Thy waters. Thy herbs and trees are full of peace. All Thy forces of nature are full of peace and harmony. There is peace and perfection in Thy eternal knowledge; everything in the universe is peaceful, and peace pervades everywhere. O Lord, may that peace come to me!'

36. *Faith and Self-surrender.* Durban: Divine Life Society of South Africa, n.d., pp. 33, 35.

37. Anil Sooklal, *Children of Immortality: The Ramakrishna Movement with Special Emphasis on the South African Context.* Durban: Ramakrishna Centre of South Africa, 1990, pp. 220, 231.

38. *Ibid.,* p. 153.

39. *Ibid.,* p. 157.

40. The Hare Krishna movement gives a very important place to Chaitanya, who regarded Krishna as God himself, rather than as merely an incarnation of the God Vishnu. In Hare Krishna eyes, Lord Chaitanya was one of Krishna's most important incarnations on earth.

41. Anil Sooklal, *A Socio-Religious Study of the Hare Krishna Movement in South Africa.* Durban: Research Unit – New Religious Movements and Independent Churches, University of Zululand, 1986, pp. 82–84.

42. *Ibid.,* p. 50.

11

Chinese Religion in South Africa

ARTHUR SONG

Chinese immigrants to South Africa brought their religious beliefs with them from their homeland. These religious beliefs centred upon the veneration of their ancestors, the existence of spirits indwelling nature, and the consequent acceptance of the principle of *feng shui* or geomancy. Various deities belonging to the polytheistic Taoist hierarchy and Buddhist traditions were also introduced to the religious system. Certain aspects of traditional Chinese religious beliefs continue to be practised in South Africa despite the growing tendency amongst the Chinese to identify with Christianity. This chapter briefly describes the history, nature and practice of some Chinese religious rites in South Africa and offers a few observations.

The practice of Chinese religion does not necessitate the existence of temples, as each family can become a congregation. Every traditional Chinese home contains an altar or 'god-shelf' where the deities are worshipped and the ancestors venerated. This is the most important reason why the South African Chinese have not felt it necessary to build a centre of worship.

The cultic requirements for the practice of Chinese religion are few and simple. It is more than probable that early immigrants brought with them joss-sticks and other cultic items, and religious paraphernalia have been available from a number of specialist Chinese supply stores in Johannesburg for at least half a century. An example of the simplicity of the cultic requirements may be seen in the preparation of the spirit tablet in which the ancestral spirit is believed to reside. A piece of wood of appropriate dimensions is prepared with the name of the deceased or the term for the collective clan ancestors written on it. As a substitute, a strip of red paper with the same inscription may also be used. The deities are represented pictorially, in the form of figurines, or by inscribing their names on a strip of red paper.

The Chinese immigrants who arrived in South Africa during the early 1900s included families, bachelors and married men without their families. The bachelors usually returned to China to marry after earning sufficient money in South Africa. The married men hoped to support their families in

China. They were to return to China later to live in relative luxury or migrate with their families to South Africa.

Some of these immigrants brought their ancestor tablets with them; unfortunately, many died without realising their familial dreams. Their funeral ceremonies were held in small halls attached either to a club or to a cultural association of which they were members. As no traditional priests were available in South Africa, these ceremonies were conducted by a respectable member of the community who was familiar with the basic traditional and regional funeral customs. Ancestor tablets belonging to deceased community members without offspring were stored by their clubs or cultural associations and, after two or more decades, were disposed of by incineration.

The nature of Chinese religion

Chinese religion in this context may be broadly defined as a polytheistic and animistic belief system which includes the ancestors and a pantheon of deities, spirits and cultural heroes. The concept of sin, which is central to Judaism and Christianity, is absent from the vocabulary of traditional Chinese religion. The word *tsui* (guilt or crime) is used in Chinese religious terminology, and guilt feelings are dealt with by offerings and efforts at self-improvement. This approach suits the humanistic tendencies of the Chinese.

Those who practise the traditional religious rites tend to be polytheistic. It is common for families to observe ancestor rites and simultaneously to seek the help of certain spirit entities. The three most popular deities in South Africa are Guan Yin (the goddess of mercy), Guan Ti (the god of war) and Choi Sun (the god of wealth). Guan Yin was originally an Indian Bodhisattva named Avalokiteshvara, whom the Chinese transformed into her present female identity. Guan Ti's worshippers believe that their military hero was a general of great integrity and that he vowed to help, posthumously, all who seek his aid. Choi Sun's popularity as god of wealth is self-explanatory.

Chinese religion also involves an amalgam of the three ancient philosophies of Taoism, Confucianism and Buddhism. These have been radically changed in the course of time by commentators and the grafting on of superstition and folklore. The philosophies of Lao-tzu (Taoism), Gautama Siddhartha (Buddhism) and K'ung Fu-tzu (Confucius) are also traditionally called the *San-chiao* (Three Teachings). Taoism represents an esoteric approach to the relationship of man with nature, while Confucianism examines ethical behaviour and interpersonal relationships. Buddhism, imported to China from India, was sinicised and so helped the Chinese find a measure of spiritual fulfilment. The early Chinese did not consider these Three Teachings religions but rather bodies of teachings enabling them to live a balanced life. Over a period of time, the Three Teachings became greatly intertwined.

South African Chinese also do not consider Confucianism a religion. They interpret its teachings as a system of humanistic ethics, and the only link Confucianism has with cultic practices is its historical association with the offerings made to the ancestral spirits. This practice is interpreted by Confucians as an attempt to instil filial piety, a well-developed cultural and ethical appreciation of parents; in fact, some of these rituals are traditionally continued long after the decease of the honoured parents. However, many Chinese in Taiwan do offer a form of worship to Confucius on his birthday at a temple dedicated to him. Some interpret this service as the honouring of his memory as patron of the teaching profession and of the civil service.

The worship of deities is usually accompanied by the daily offering of joss-sticks to the ancestors. Some families use flickering, candle-shaped electric bulbs instead of the ritual candles. However, less importance seems to be attached to the worship of the deities than to the ancestor cult.

Many families display pictures or ceramic images of their favourite deities on a 'god-shelf'. In practice, South Africa's Chinese people do not venerate or worship Confucius or Lao-tzu, but images of the Buddha appear frequently alongside those of the god of war, the god of wealth and the goddess of mercy. It is usual for representations of these deities to be placed in close proximity to the ancestor tablets.

The practice of the ancestor cult

In a Chinese home where traditional religion is practised, the death of a parent requires the observation of certain rites. Death seldom occurs at home, as the sick are usually hospitalised and the elderly and infirm are usually cared for in an old age home. The traditional funerary rites are therefore practised at the funeral parlour and at the graveside.

Upon entering the funeral parlour, each mourner is given a small white packet containing a five-cent piece wrapped in white paper. White is the Chinese colour of mourning, and the white wrapping symbolically unites the mourner with the bereaved family in their sorrow. It is usual for the body to lie in state for about an hour while mourners approach the casket and bow three times to pay their final respects. Because no Taoist or Buddhist Chinese priests are available in South Africa, the ceremony is a silent one. It has become traditional to burn a large quantity of mock, or funeral, money in a brazier at the funeral parlour. It is believed that this transfers money to the netherworld for use by the deceased. As the mourners leave the funeral parlour, each is given another five-cent coin. This is wrapped in red paper, which is the colour of joy and happiness. The purpose of the red packet is to offset the bad luck which the mourners have brought upon themselves by attending the funeral.

Upon arrival at the cemetery, the immediate family will gather round the open grave. As soon as all the mourners are present, the casket is lowered without any further ceremony. It is imperative that the casket be positioned absolutely level and straight in the grave. If not, it is believed that the spirit of the deceased will not rest well. Once petals have been strewn on the casket by the family and other mourners, the grave is filled. Immediately after the grave-marker has been placed at the head of the grave, either the eldest son or a male relative will burn joss-sticks and more funeral money. A ceremonial red candle is lit, and, with the final bowing by the family to the deceased, the graveside rituals come to an end.

At the cemetery gates, each person is again given another red packet similar to the one received earlier. As money received at funeral ceremonies may transfer bad luck to other homes, the mourners will spend the coins on their way home. The ceremonial candle is taken by the son of the deceased or one of the male relatives to the house where the ancestor spirit tablet is to be erected. The purpose of the burning candle is to lead the spirit of the deceased back home lest it loses its way and becomes a wandering spirit. This act strengthens the rationale of concern upon which the practice of filial piety is based. The fragrant smoke of joss-sticks serves as food for the spirits, and joss-sticks are therefore offered daily. On special occasions, festive food is placed in front of the ancestor tablets, which traditionalists believe house the spirits of the ancestors. These tablets of thin, red-painted wood measure approximately 10 by 30 centimetres, and have the name of the deceased written in black. The written name guarantees the indwelling presence of the ancestor. Occasionally a general reference is made to all the family's ancestors on one tablet.

The purpose of the ancestor cult is to continue the practice of filial piety after the death of one's parents. The rites also seek the protection of the ancestors and their goodwill for the family. As the spirits of the departed are believed to influence the living, a family neglects them at their peril. The practitioner of the ancestor cult is nominally the eldest son, who attends to the rites at the small altar, or 'god-shelf'. In practice, it is usually the son's wife who attends to the lighting of the joss-sticks. On special occasions such as births, marriages, New Year festivities, and especially the anniversaries of the birth and death of the deceased, the family participates in the offering of special foods. Such ritual offerings, it is believed, engender a deep respect for the ancestors and cause their memory to be retained by subsequent generations. The cult is therefore not dependent on professional priests or the existence of temples, and because it is family-based, it has been successfully perpetuated for millennia.

Twice a year, at the beginning of the summer and the winter solstices, appropriate food is offered and seasonal paper clothes and funeral money are transferred to the netherworld by incineration. These offerings provide creature comforts for the ancestors in the spirit realm. These acts also demonstrate the family's continued filial piety. In turn, the living hope for reciprocal favours of wealth and success from their ancestors. When these favours are experienced, the Chinese speak of *feng shui*, or the favourable flow of 'wind and water'. This concept may also be described as a doctrine of mutuality which involves a metaphysical symbiosis, a process in which the spirits of the deceased are cared for by the living and the deceased ancestors in return ensure good fortune for the living.

The ceremony of inviting home the soul is still practised by traditional Chinese who can afford it. This ceremony involves the immediate members of the male clan of the deceased, and is conducted by a team of Buddhist and Taoist priests whose task it is to invite the soul back into its ancestral home in China. One of the main purposes of this ceremony is to maintain the unity of the family lineage and the continued support of the ancestral clan temple or hall.

Practitioners have different expectations of the ancestor cult, and many fail to understand fully the religious implications involved in what they consider to be 'acts of remembrance'. No contradiction is experienced when the local Chinese mix their ancestor cult with the worship of heroes or other spirits and deities. Spirit beings and deities are viewed as 'external' forces which are available to the Chinese to bolster their efforts against bad luck and other misfortunes in life. By contrast, the ancestors are considered as potent spirit beings who are keen to help their offspring.

Observations and conclusions

Traditional Chinese religion, as practised in South Africa, does not differ in essence from that practised elsewhere, except that it may have been watered down to some extent because of many social and religious factors. One of the common features which South African Chinese traditional religionists share with their overseas compatriots is their pragmatic approach to their religion: what can religion, the deities and the spirits do for people in this life? Chinese religion often gives the impression that the spirits and deities can be manipulated by the worshipper. This appears in the symbiotic relationship cultivated between the worshipper and the spirit entities. Offerings seem to serve several purposes: appeasement of the spirits and deities, forestalling retributive punishment, and reward for filial piety and good deeds.

South African Chinese who practise the cult of the ancestors interpret the rites as a demonstration of their continued respect and concern for the welfare of their parents. They believe that they should show their piety while their parents are alive and continue to do so even after their death.

The observance of Chinese ritual practices is declining amongst the local Chinese. Significant inroads are being made by various Christian churches into the community, to the extent that many traditional beliefs are being rejected by most of the Western-educated younger generation. An interesting phenomenon is the growing number of middle-aged and elderly Chinese who are converting to the Christian faith.

Several reasons may be offered for the decline of Chinese religion in South Africa: the absence of an active priesthood and temple facilities, and of a systematic body of religious teachings, the successful programme of evangelism by Christian churches, and the development of a materialistic lifestyle. Many South African Chinese Christians face a crisis of cultural continuity. They struggle to reconcile the differences between the ethnic beliefs that appear to contradict their Christian faith, and aspects of their cultural heritage of which they should be proud. The burning of a joss-stick on the anniversary of the death of a father may serve as an example. Does the Christian son commit an idolatrous act or does he merely fulfil his cultural duty as a son?

Traditionalists will welcome the likelihood of a resurgence of ethnic religious practices in the near future. The local Chinese population of 13 000 has been swollen by approximately the same number of overseas Chinese during the 1980s. These recent immigrants come from the Republic of China on Taiwan, the People's Republic of China, and Hong Kong. There are many among them who maintain their traditional beliefs, and it is therefore highly probable that a revitalisation of traditional Chinese beliefs will occur. It remains to be seen whether subsequent generations of the newly arrived immigrants will remain true to the faith of their fathers, or whether they too will gradually convert to the dominant faith of Christianity in South Africa.

SELECT BIBLIOGRAPHY

De Groot, J. J. M., *The Religious Systems of China*, 6 vols. Taipei: Ch'eng-wen, reprint, 1972

Legge, J., *The Notions of the Chinese Concerning God and Spirits*. Taipei: Ch'eng-wen, reprint, 1971

Song, A., 'The Effects of Protestant Christianity on the Chinese Cult of the Ancestors as Practised in the Johannesburg Area.' D.Phil. diss., University of Durban–Westville, 1989

12

Buddhism in South Africa

LOUIS H. VAN LOON

The practice of Buddhism in South Africa differs from that of other religions in that it is, overwhelmingly, an adopted religion. The Christian faith, Hinduism and Islam arrived in this country with settlers from Europe and India who had, by and large, been adherents of these religions in their home countries. As far as can be ascertained, no Buddhists in any significant numbers arrived in South Africa from a traditionally Buddhist nation to form the core of a Buddhist community in this country.[1] And whereas initially some members of the Indian community converted to the religion, it is now virtually extinct amongst them. At present, the strength of the Buddhist following is to be found amongst the white population.

The conversion of some Hindu families to Buddhism started in the early part of the twentieth century. It coincided with severe economic hardships, social disruption and political frustration – the result of an increasingly discriminatory racist policy, enforced by white governments, which aimed to curtail the political rights, freedom of movement and domicile, and educational and trading opportunities of 'non-Europeans'.

The reactions of the Indian community to these problems were many and took forms as varied as confrontation, militant protest, passive resistance, proud self-reliance, and helpless defeatism. Of interest here is the effect these measures had on their religious outlook. For many, conversion to the Christian faith became an attractive option. Pentecostalism in particular aroused the hope that this new religion would help lift Indians out of their inferior position by admitting them to the faith of the ruling class. Others saw in this but a sham answer to their difficulties. Conversion, in fact, left Christian Indians substantially where they were before: underprivileged, politically impotent, racially and socially segregated, and burdened with economic restrictions and curbs on employment. Consequently, many Indians came to feel that it was necessary not to deny their Indian culture, but to make it count. We see a unique expression of this in Mahatma Gandhi's political activities in South Africa, which derived their effectiveness from the ancient Indian religious principles of harmlessness (*ahimsa*) and passive resistance (*Satyagraha*).

Amongst the lower classes of Hindu Indians the additional handicap of caste awareness made it particularly urgent for them to acquire a believable and workable identity. Hindu society in South Africa, more so previously than now, reflected the caste divisions that had been part of Asiatic Indian culture for millennia. In addition to being subjected to political and economic discrimination by the white community, low-caste Indians were also discriminated against within the Indian community itself, and found it especially difficult to make any headway in society. Conversion to Buddhism, as we shall see, was an option that a number of low-caste (mostly Tamil) Hindus took to resolve their many problems.

All this reflected a situation that had arisen in India itself. During the last decade of the nineteenth century, Indian society went through one of its many socio-religious upheavals, this time fuelled by a desire to gain independence from the British Raj. An awakening political awareness, stark economic realities and a new social conscience collided with ancient forms of rulership, spiritual values and tribal customs. Indeed, religion played a considerable role in this. Personalities such as Tagore, Aurobindo and Vivekananda, and groups such as the Theosophists, set out to reinvent the Indian soul. Hindus, Muslims, Sikhs, Jains, Parsees and Christians all contributed their vision of what they believed was best for Mother India.

Buddhism was absent from this political and religious ferment until 1891. Although the Buddha was born in India in the sixth century BCE, disruptive political upheavals, internal decay and, finally, merciless persecution by rival Brahmanical sects and by Muslim invaders from about the seventh century CE onwards, had caused the virtual extinction of Buddhism in the land of its birth. By the fourteenth century, Buddhist monasteries and libraries had been reduced to rubble and ashes, and the monks massacred or forcibly converted to other faiths, or made to flee to neighbouring countries. India had, it seemed, buried its Buddhist past. But remnants remained, not only in the form of ruined temples in the jungles, but also as stories and ideas embedded in Brahmanical and Hindu religious folklore. Later, archaeologists and scholars would uncover them and use them to show that India had once had a very important Buddhist past.

It was in 1891 that a Buddhist monk from Sri Lanka, the Anagarika Dharmapala, visited India on a pilgrimage to ancient Buddhist sites. He was appalled to find the sacred places associated with the Buddha's life and teachings ruined, abused or usurped by other religious sects. As he set about reclaiming these sites for Buddhists worldwide, he aroused Indian peasants and intellectuals alike to take note of their Buddhist past. He claimed, rightly or wrongly, that India's period of glory, prosperity and social justice had coincided with its having been predominantly Buddhist. History, he believed, had shown that India without Buddhism was destined to be undisciplined and subject to superstition and social oppression. To a society searching for its soul, he had added one more challenging element.

Buddhist movements sprung up all across India. One of these was the

South India Buddhist Association, founded in Madras in 1900 by Pandit Iyodhi Dass, a minor scholar of Pali, Sanskrit and Tamil. He conducted research into the background and origins of South Indian Buddhism, the results of which he published in a number of pamphlets and in a Buddhist monthly journal. It was through Iyodhi Dass's son, Rajaram, that his brand of revivalist South Indian Buddhism was introduced to the South African Indian community.

Tens of thousands of Indians had arrived in South Africa in successive waves of immigration from 1860 onwards. They had indentured themselves initially to work in the Natal cane fields, and later as labourers in other menial positions throughout the colony of Natal. Rajaram arrived in 1914. He did not, it seems, play a direct role in the promotion of Buddhism amongst his fellow immigrants. As a young man in his early twenties, working as a waiter in Durban's Royal Hotel and as a part-time actor, he had only a vague idea of his father's Buddhist activities in India. Yet this was enough to arouse the curiosity of some of his friends, who made him promise that upon his return to India – which happened in 1916 – he would send them copies of his father's pamphlets.

These friends were destined to become the nucleus of the South African Indian Buddhist community. In 1917 the first society was formed, the Overport Sakya Buddhist Society, with an initial membership of 25 families, under the leadership of one of Rajaram's friends, N. Munisami, a professional photographer. During the following years, as membership expanded, the name of the society changed, first to the Durban Sakya Buddhist Society and then to the Natal Buddhist Society. Soon a number of affiliated and schismatic groups formed in Malvern and Pietermaritzburg. None of them ever attained a sizeable membership. The 1936 census shows the number of Asiatic Buddhists as 1 771, which amounts to 0.8 per cent of the Indian population.

Hindus seem to have converted to Buddhism for three principal reasons. Firstly, as South Indian Tamils, they were impressed with Pandit Iyodhi Dass's research, which showed that for a period of about ten centuries South India had been predominantly Buddhist and, so it was claimed, relatively free of caste discrimination. Dass maintained that it was only with the demise of Buddhism and the resurgence of Brahmanism that caste injustices were once again imposed upon Indian society. Therefore, by reclaiming Buddhism as their true religious heritage, his followers could consider themselves to be liberated from the stigma associated with Brahmanical Hindu culture, a stigma that continued to determine the social status and circumscribe the economic role of persons of low caste, not only in India, but even in South Africa.[2]

Secondly, Iyodhi Dass had argued that many Hindu religious practices were distortions and appropriations of ancient Buddhist lore. Hindu worship of the Bodhi tree and prayers to Mariammen, for instance, were of Buddhist origin. The early converts to Buddhism therefore felt entitled to claim that much of what went by the name of Hinduism amongst the Natal Indians was but a derivation of an earlier and more authentic heritage, namely Buddhism.

Thirdly, Buddhism appeared to them to be a simple, elegant and intelligent religion, more compatible with a modern Western lifestyle and Christian religious values than Hinduism, which they felt incorporated superstitions and idolatrous beliefs. This attitude was a reflection of yet another development that had its origins in South India at the time: the so-called Self-respect Movement, which aimed to rid Indian society of forms of behaviour and beliefs that were considered irrational, undignified, outmoded and meaningless.

The activities of the Natal Buddhist Society were geared towards promoting an awareness of these issues. Public lectures based on literature received from the South India Buddhist Association were given. Functions were held commemorating the birth and enlightenment of the Buddha. Philanthropic work was carried out amongst the poor and destitute members of the Indian community. However, for a number of reasons, the Buddhist movement never penetrated deeply into South African Indian society. In common with most societies of this kind, the Buddhist movement suffered from personality conflicts, schisms and recrimination amongst its members and leaders. This blemished the image of the society as a movement that was intended to bring solidarity and a sense of direction and purpose to South African Indians. Moreover, membership came from a very poor section of the Indian community, and so no funds were available to promote the causes of the society. As Indian families were forcibly resettled under the Land Tenure and Group Areas Acts, members of the society were scattered over widely separated residential areas, lost touch with fellow members and returned to their previous Hindu practices. In addition, as Indians low on the social scale tended to join the society, it acquired the image of a movement for the poor and the outcast, so that it never attracted a more representative membership of South African Indians. Yet, paradoxically, in the course of time the stigma of caste grew less pronounced, thus depriving the Buddhist movement of one of its most important ideological platforms: to rid Indian society of caste division.

Another problem that afflicted the early Buddhists was that the movement was too secular. Indian religion thrives on gurus, swamis and holy men. These early Buddhist societies were run by sincere and intelligent people, but they were laymen, without orthodox religious authority. They did not have the means available to import monks to lend authority and authenticity to their religious observances, especially those that concerned the consecration of important social events such as marriages, births and deaths. After a promising start, therefore, Buddhist conversion amongst the Hindus soon dwindled. Marriage into Hindu families accelerated the reconversion of Buddhists to Hinduism. When women from nominally Buddhist families married Hindu men, they were expected to follow their husband's religious affiliation. Yet Buddhist men marrying Hindu women were in no position to set adequate standards for their family's devotional practices. As Indian women traditionally conduct domestic religious activities, these Hindu wives of Buddhist men were therefore left to perform the Hindu observances they knew best. There are therefore only a handful of Indian families left today who consider themselves Buddhist. A field survey conducted in 1979 showed that their knowledge and practice of Buddhism were very elementary and suffused with Hindu and Christian concepts and beliefs.[3]

The Natal Buddhist Society continued to exist, rather tenuously, led by one surviving elder, L. Nagamuthu, who had joined the society in 1920 and became its president in 1945. He remained its torch-bearer until his death in 1986. The society has continued to meet once a year for a public celebration, but is now intending to disband as it is not engaged in any other meaningful activities and membership is in continuous decline.

This decline of Buddhism amongst Indians coincided with an increase in interest in the religion amongst the white population. Initially, only a few people were attracted to the philosophy, and practised meditation privately or in very small groups. Amongst them were Molly and Louis van Loon. Their interest in Buddhism was considerably enhanced by their travels to India, Nepal, Thailand, Sri Lanka and Japan where, starting in 1959, they made contact with a number of Buddhist individuals and organisations, amongst them monks, nuns and abbots of monasteries, meditation teachers and scholars, as well as Tibetan lamas and refugees, who made a particularly deep impression on them. They also met the great Tibetan Buddhist scholar, Lama Anagarika Govinda, and his wife, Li Gotami, who visited South Africa at their invitation in 1972. The two visitors gave several public lectures, were interviewed on radio, and opened an exhibition at the Durban Art Gallery of sacred Buddhist art that had been collected by the Van Loons during their visits to the East. It was the earliest publicised visit of internationally renowned Buddhists to South Africa.

In 1969, the Van Loons proceeded to work towards the establishment of a Buddhist movement and meditation centre. They purchased a farm near Ixopo in southern Natal and erected the buildings that now constitute the Buddhist Retreat Centre. The centre was opened in 1980 and has become the major focus for Buddhist activities in the country. It is run by the Buddhist Institute of South Africa, promoting an understanding of Buddhist philosophy, art and culture, and offering public courses in meditation practice.

Louis van Loon also began teaching Buddhism in the Department of Science of Religion at the University of Durban–Westville in 1974 and in the Department of Religious Studies at the University of Cape Town in 1977. Until then, Buddhism had mostly been a somewhat secondary aspect of the religious studies curricula in South African universities. He also began to conduct Buddhist workshops and meditation retreats in Durban, Pretoria, Johannesburg and Cape Town. These public and academic activities brought about some awareness in South Africa of Buddhist philosophy and psychology, chiefly amongst educated whites.

As activities and attendance increased at the Buddhist Retreat Centre, groups of people in the cities of South Africa began to run their own meditation sessions, meeting in their homes and occasionally hiring larger facilities for weekend retreats, particularly when visiting teachers were available to address them. These groups have tended to develop a predilection towards a particular Buddhist tradition or allegiance towards a chosen teacher, sect or method of meditation. As a result there has been a proliferation of distinct Zen, Tibetan or Theravadin groups.

One of the earliest of these groups, the Dojo Marisan Nariji, has been operating in Honeydew, near Johannesburg, since 1979. Its head is a Zen nun, the Ven. Taicho Kyogen, who was ordained in Paris in 1975 by Taisen Desimaru Roshi of the Zen Association Internationale. The group holds regular Soto Zen sessions both at the Dojo and, occasionally, at a retreat in Allandale in the northern Transvaal. Although primarily Zen-orientated, the group has also had visiting teachers in the Theravadin and Tibetan traditions.

A very promising Buddhist community and meditation centre operated for about nine years in Nieu Bethesda, near Graaff-Reinet, in the isolated mountains of the Karoo. It was established by Rob Nairn, who had been interested in Buddhism from an early age and had previously been a magistrate and advocate in Zimbabwe and a lecturer in criminology at the University of Cape Town, before devoting himself fully to running the Nieu Bethesda meditation centre.

Although initially interested in the early or southern tradition of Buddhism (Theravada), he embraced Tibetan Buddhism after he met the Ven. Akong Rinpoché, the head of a well-known Kagyu monastic training and meditation centre in the north of Scotland, Samyé Ling. Nieu Bethesda eventually became a satellite centre of Samyé Ling, called Nieu Bethesda Samyé Ling. The Ven. Akong Rinpoché visited South Africa on a number of occasions, and both he and Rob Nairn ran seminars and meditation retreats in the principal cities of South Africa and at the Buddhist Retreat Centre in Ixopo. As a result, several Tibetan Buddhist groups were formed in Cape Town, Johannesburg, Grahamstown, Port Elizabeth and Durban, all loosely associated with the Nieu Bethesda Centre.

The Nieu Bethesda Centre itself consisted of a cluster of houses which had become available cheaply. In an effort to help the economically depressed people in the area, a non-profit trading store was purchased to serve the local community. A pottery business was started which turned out high-quality products. An attempt was made to teach the local people skills that would make them self-sufficient. Unfortunately, these activities were not successful and it was decided to bring them to an end. When Rob Nairn went on a four-year intensive monastic training retreat at Samyé Ling in Scotland, the lack of a resident teacher brought about the closure of the Centre altogether.

The Dharma Centre in Somerset West in the Cape started life in 1984 as the Heldervue Meditation Centre, three years after its founders, Heila and Rodney Downey, had become acquainted with Buddhist meditation practice at the Buddhist Retreat Centre in Ixopo. Although the Centre welcomes visiting teachers from all branches of Buddhism, its regular practice is rooted in the Zen tradition, initially associated with the Rochester Zen Center in Canada, and more recently with the Kwan Um School of Korean Zen founded by the Ven. Dae Soen Sa Nim.

The Centre invites teachers from the Kwan Um School at least once a year to lead retreats, which are held at the Downeys' large home, now converted into a meditation centre that can accommodate up to 35 practitioners. The Centre conducts formal sitting meditation sessions every Wednesday evening and every other Sunday. Live-in retreats, lasting from two to five days, are held at least four times each year.

Poplar Grove near Colesberg is also a Zen centre associated with the Kwan Um School of Korean Zen. It shares with the Dharma Centre in Somerset West the visiting teachers from that school. The Centre is not an on-going retreat centre in the true sense, but rather a typical Karoo farm and homestead where anyone is welcome to join in the regular daily meditation practice. It is run by Antony Osler, who is an ordained Zen monk, and lives at Poplar Grove with his family. He has been actively involved in various branches of Buddhism since the mid-1970s. He was the first resident teacher at the Buddhist Retreat Centre from its inception in 1980. In 1983 he commenced meditation training under the Japanese Rinzai Zen master Joshu Sasaki Roshi in the USA, but is now attached to the Kwan Um School of Korean Zen. Apart from hosting teachers from the Kwan Um School, Poplar Grove also holds occasional retreats run by Antony Osler himself. He teaches a course in Buddhism once a year at Rhodes University.

This is by no means an exhaustive survey of all the Buddhist groups operating in South Africa. There are groups in almost every city in the country. Some are larger and more active than others and have existed for many years. Others consist of only a few individuals and may fade away after a short while, often to be resuscitated again at a later date.[4]

A vast cultural complex, including a huge Buddhist temple, has been planned for the Taiwanese community in Bronkhorstspruit near Pretoria. Promoted by the abbot of the Fo Kuang Shan organisation, the Ven. Hsing Yun, the project consists of a temple and monastic centre, a cultural–historical museum, a primary and secondary school, a training college for Buddhist monks and a community centre.

Buddhism in South Africa engages exceptionally well with other religions. Although some of the groups adhere strictly to a particular tradition, none are dogmatic or engage in missionary activities. Formal conversion to Buddhism is not their aim. Hence local visitors to the various centres in South Africa come from a great variety of religious, and non-religious, backgrounds, and are not expected to change their particular faith. Generally, emphasis is placed on developing 'mindfulness' (*Sati*). This concerns the establishment of a state of mind that remains calm and clear under all circumstances and is not given to negativity or blind reactivity; or to cravings and attachments, aversions and aggression, obsession and compulsion, confusion and dogmatism. This possibility – of developing a continuous flow of wholesome, positive states of mind, appropriate virtuous behaviour and a deeper understanding of the nature of mental and physical phenomena – is perceived by most people as eminently compatible with other religious beliefs they may hold. Nevertheless, adherents of religious faiths with a strongly exclusive attitude seldom frequent Buddhist centres.

Past census reports do not give a reliable picture of the number of Buddhists in South Africa. The Buddhist groups themselves do not, as a rule, keep a record of those who consider themselves to be confirmed Buddhists. But thousands of people have attended retreats at the Buddhist Retreat Centre since its inception, for instance, many having done so repeatedly. A good percentage would probably claim to be Buddhists if they were asked. People attending retreats tend to be well educated. Most are white, with an occasional interest being shown by Indians and blacks.[5]

There is no single overarching Buddhist authority or organisation in South Africa. Groups following different Buddhist traditions may work together and operate from the same venue but, by and large, each group is autonomous. Teachers are often shared by groups. Most overseas teachers are brought to the country by the Buddhist Institute of South Africa to conduct retreats at the Buddhist Retreat Centre and are then sent to visit groups in the other provinces. They often travel to neighbouring territories as well, such as Lesotho, Botswana, Zambia, Zimbabwe and Mozambique where small groups have established themselves, principally as a result of local people having attended retreats at the Buddhist Retreat Centre. Some of these small groups occasionally invite their own international teachers independently.

How will Buddhism fit into the 'new South Africa'? Historically, Buddhism has shown itself to be extraordinarily resilient during its 2 500 years of existence. It was virtually annihilated in the country of its origin, India, yet has continued to thrive outside its borders. It has withstood determined persecution in China for centuries, surviving even the Red Guards. It is experiencing a resurgence in Chinese-occupied Tibet and now even in Russia, despite 75 years of militant atheism. The growing interest in Buddhism in South Africa over the last troubled decade is perhaps an indication that it, too, has a contribution to make to this country's transition to a more equitable political dispensation.

NOTES

1. Louis H. van Loon, *The Indian Buddhist Community in South Africa: Its Historical Origins and Socio-Religious Attitudes and Practices.* Unpublished paper, 1979, pp. 31ff; and 'The Indian Buddhist Community in South Africa', *Religion in South Africa*, 1, 2 (July 1980), pp. 3–18.

2. That the conversion to Buddhism was of relevance to low and outcaste Hindus was again demonstrated in 1956 when the leader of the Scheduled Castes (the 'Untouchables'), Dr B. R. Ambedkar, embraced the Buddhist religion, together with 500 000 of his followers in a ceremonial mass conversion that eventually grew in momentum until today there are more than 30 million such politicised Ambedkarian Buddhists in India.

3. Van Loon, *Indian Buddhist Community*, pp. 36ff.

4. The Nicheren Soshu sect of Buddhism has been left out of this survey because it has only a glancing connection with the Buddha's teachings and the orthodox practice of them. Based on the teachings of a thirteenth-century reformist Japanese priest, followers of this group chant the title and sections of the Lotus Sutra, a later Buddhist commentarial text, in the belief that that will unfold their 'Buddha nature' and bring about all manner of material benefits. There are about a hundred members of this sect in South Africa, who have no connection with the other Buddhist groups whatsoever.

5. The Buddhist Retreat Centre has, from its inception, been non-discriminatory and multi-racial.

13

Jains and Parsees in South Africa

G. C. OOSTHUIZEN

THE JAIN COMMUNITY

The Jain religion has 2–3 million followers in India. Although there are only about 60 Jains in South Africa, it is necessary to include their religion in this book not only because they are part of the family of faiths found in this country but also because their teaching of non-violence had a profound influence on Mahatma Gandhi. As is well known, he set in motion liberation movements in South Africa and other parts of the world on the basis of that teaching. Gandhi called the founder of Jainism, Baghwan Mahavira, 'the incarnation of non-violence'.

Two new religions arose in India in the sixth century BCE. They were initiated by Gautama Buddha and Mahavira, both reacting against the Brahmans, the Indian priestly class with its ritualistic approach to religion. Answers were needed to the central problem of Indian life at the time, namely how to be released from *karma* and the unending round of rebirths which *karma* implied. Buddhism and Jainism both offered answers to this problem.

Mahavira, originally known by the name Nataputta Vardhamana and most probably of rajah stock, was born towards the end of the sixth century BCE near Vaisali in modern Bihar. His parents, according to tradition, died in accordance with the rite of *sallekhana,* or voluntary self-starvation. Mahavira himself joined an ascetic order. His two basic convictions were that one's soul could only be saved from evil through practising the severest asceticism and that *ahimsa* (non-violence) is basic to the maintenance of purity and integrity.

It may not be quite true that Mahavira was an atheist, but he maintained that every human being is his or her own friend, and questioned the search for a divine friend beyond the self, holding that the gods, if they exist, are subject to the same round of birth and rebirth as humanity. They thus have nothing to do whatsoever with the salvation of human beings. The religion that he founded divided at an early stage into two groups: the Digambaras ('the naked or sky-clad' Jains) and the Svetambaras (the 'white-clad' Jains), who are seen as the more liberal group. (The Jains in South Africa belong to the latter.)

In Jainism, *karma* is seen as a kind of material dust which sticks to the pure *atman* (soul or self) and pollutes it. Jains take vows, the first of which is non-injury (*ahimsa*). Although this idea is also found in the Vedas, the ancient sacred books of Hinduism, it has been highlighted mainly by the Jains. Injuring living beings is believed to have the most harmful karmic effects on the one who inflicts the injury, especially when it is done deliberately. This belief affects the Jains' diet, which has to be strictly vegetarian, and also affects the kind of occupations they may follow. Farming, for example, is out of the question because ploughing the soil is believed to injure the soil and the insect life in it.

Karma, soul, matter and salvation were all given meanings in Jainism that reflected a world-view distinct from that of both Brahmanism and Buddhism. The doctrine of *karma* embodies the Jains' idea that 'the consequences of one's deeds are literally deposited in and on the soul'.[1]

South African Jains fully subscribe to the belief that poisonous and alien material which has penetrated the soul must be thrown off by the soul's activity. Belief in karmic bondage, found in all Indian religions, received an added understanding in Jainism as a negative weight consisting of fine and subtle particles of matter from which the soul must be freed.[2] This aspect of Jainism is also strongly present in the religious approach of South African Jains.

In India and in South Africa, the Jains are on the whole a wealthy community because of the social effects of their religious vows; these have economic as well as religious significance, for they lead to careers in banking, merchandising and property rather than to those occupations which harm living creatures.[3]

The way of salvation

According to Jain belief, three 'jewels' lie on the way of salvation: right knowledge, right faith and right conduct. This implies knowing the Jain creed, believing it and following it. The last is the most important.

Although Jainism does not have a deity, it nevertheless emphasises meditation upon liberated souls, or *Tirthamkaras,* in order to achieve inspiration for those who strive for freedom from *karma* and thus for perfection, or *moksha.* Using a rosary with 108 beads, Jains certainly invoke the *Tirthamkaras* but not as gods. In India, however, many members of the Jain laity pray to Hindu deities.

The end of the Jain year is marked by the most important festival of this religion, Paryushana, during which fasting takes place and special services are held over a period of eight days. The other important festival is the Hindu festival of Diwali (or Deepavali), which is observed in honour of Lakshmi, the Hindu goddess of wealth. For Jains, she symbolises Mahavira's liberation.

Jains thus have an extraordinarily severe and disciplined lifestyle, which culminates in voluntary self-starvation. They are not dependent upon a God or gods, but what they do is achieved through self-effort. They are not selfishly isolationist but are actively involved in the well-being of the public, endowing welfare associations, schools and hospitals.

South African Jains have not only been an exemplary community in religious terms, but have also prospered economically. Between 1901 and 1903 six Jain families entered South Africa, namely those of V. D. Mehta, M. M. Mody, A. N. Goshalia, K. Mehta, P. P. Poonather and P. Sanghve. South Africa's Jains have remained in contact with Jainism in India throughout this century. The small group in South Africa has much more influence than its numbers might indicate. Its members are engaged in business, education, the professions and industry.

Jain lifestyle

Like Jains elsewhere, South Africa's Jain community are vegetarian. They maintain that the structure of the teeth and the intestines in human beings is like that of herbivorous animals rather than carnivores. Because of breaches of the vegetarian diet by some Jains, the year 1991 was declared *Shakahar* Year (Vegetarian Food Year) by the active Jain community in India, and great efforts were made to re-emphasise the vegetarian disposition of the Jain religion. The following year was declared the *Shakahar-Shrawakachar* Year (Vegetarian Food and Jain Conduct Year).[4] Jains in South Africa are not as strict as Indian Jains about the distinction between vegetables that may be eaten (for example, wheat, rice and oil seeds) and those that may not (for example, onions, garlic and potatoes). In common with Jains elsewhere, they avoid intoxicants, tobacco and meat in any form. Jains believe that they have to be faithfully vegetarian, otherwise they and their surroundings will not escape being deformed. Thus, both physically and spiritually, the vegetarian way of life is seen as indispensable.

Jains place great importance on controlling one's acts through the will. For example, a maximum of five items of food will be selected, and only what is necessary to sustain the body is taken. No member of the South African community has ever taken the five great vows of the Jain ascetic or monk. These involve renouncing all killing, dishonesty, taking of anything not given, sexual pleasure, and all attachments, whether small or great, to living or to lifeless things. However, Jains in South Africa adhere to the ten vows for the laity, committing themselves never to knowingly take the life of a sentient creature, to lie, to steal or take what is not given, or to be unchaste; and to refrain from greed, to avoid temptation to sin, to limit the number of things in daily use, to be on one's guard against avoidable evils, to keep special times for meditation, and to observe special periods of self-denial. Of the two further vows, to spend special days as a monk and to give alms in support of ascetics, only the latter is observed.

Weddings are conducted according to the Hindu formula and ritual. As far as death is concerned, only cremation is practised. However, when the body of a loved one is cremated, it is believed that no signs of attachment should be evident. Those present have to move away from the pyre without turning round to look at what is happening. Great attachment is, however, shown to one's loved ones while they are alive. In the Jain community the elderly are never left on their own. They are always treated with great respect and cared for, and are never placed in old age homes. Their children take care of them until they die.

The prayer books

Two prayer books are of special significance for Jains in South Africa. These are the *Samayikh Sutra,* a shortened prayer book, and the *Pratikaram Sutra,* which is the longer form of prayer. The former set of prayers and chants is conducted in contemplation of Mahavira, the founder of the Jain religion, and of the *Tirthamkaras,* or holy prophets. Here the emphasis is on contemplation, described by South African Jains as worship, and although Mahavira is referred to as a 'god' this is for the sake of people who do not understand that religion may not involve a deity. The religious exercise of using the shortened prayer book, the *Samayikh Sutra,* together with the singing of hymns (*mantras*), takes about fifty minutes, and then closes with a prayer.

The *Pratikaram Sutra* is more comprehensive than the *Samayikh Sutra*; reciting the prayers takes over an hour. Forgiveness is asked for any misdeeds committed against anything and anyone in the course of daily life. Even the unconscious trampling on an insect when one is walking is included in these prayers. *Hatya* (harm) to anyone or anything is avoided. No Jains possess firearms, and nowhere does this religion refer to fighting for one's country or one's religion. For Mahavira, *ahimsa* (non-violence) was the supreme *dharma* or religious duty. Jains emphasise that non-violence cannot thrive where there is disparity in social life, and as a result great emphasis is put on correct and honest relationships among human beings, whoever they may be.

These prayers are said at home and can be said at different times by husband or wife or both together, depending on circumstances. Elderly couples usually say the prayers together early in the morning at about six o'clock.

Jain women have been mainly responsible for keeping this religion alive in South Africa. They gather on a weekly basis for prayers and hymn singing. These weekly gatherings take place in turns at their houses once a month during the afternoon.

The Paryushana Parva festival

During the Jain new year, usually around August or September, the festival of Paryushana Parva is celebrated. During the eight days of this festival, prayers are said and hymns sung, and only lentils may be eaten to the exclusion of green vegetables, which, according to Jain belief, are also a form of life and should not be disturbed.

The main emphasis in this festival is on enrichment through renunciation and austerity and on fostering virtues such as knowledge and devotion to Jain principles, as well as on exercising control over one's food and other enjoyments, on study and on hearing the Jain scriptures, on pondering over the self, forgetting enemies and cultivating a genuine spirit of friendship. The noble deeds of Mahavira and their significance for Jains are reflected upon. More particularly, one should shape one's worldly dealings in such a manner that the sorrows of others are seen as one's own; Jains believe one should fully sacrifice all happiness and the amenities of life for the good of society; one should continuously be alert and exercise introspection in order to avoid blemishes because of ignorance and weakness, so that the efforts of the soul do not suffer.

The Samvatsari festival, which takes place on the last day of the Paryushana festival, has special significance for Jains. It involves much introspection in order to establish what small or large blunders may have been committed. It is believed that only through alertness and self-analysis can a human being cultivate sincere relations with others. In this way a person finds liberation from his or her blemishes and establishes the right attitudes towards other people. This festival of introspection thus has benefits for the community. It is believed that the basis of social health is confessing one's faults and seeking the pardon of others. This approach takes place in and between families and in and between communities, and is not restricted to Jains alone but includes others who may have been harmed.

Although they are a very small religious community, the Jains make their presence felt through their business acumen, the strict discipline demanded by their faith, and their positive approach to society, supporting as they do hospitals, schools and charitable organisations. While they do not worship a god or gods, their faith, in honouring its founder and other great spiritual figures, is in the fullest sense a religion, differentiated from a philosophy by its holiness and sense of eternity.

THE PARSEE COMMUNITY

The small South African Parsee community, whose faith goes back to the prophet Zoroaster in ancient Persia over 2 500 years ago, and is thus sometimes called Zoroastrianism, has experienced many difficulties because of racial and religious discrimination. Never more than about 200 strong, South Africa's Parsees have nonetheless retained their religious identity despite these difficulties. They form part of the larger Parsee community world-wide which has 80 000 members in India, 15 000 in the USA, and 5 000 in the United Kingdom. Once a great missionary religion, Zoroastrianism later developed an anti-missionary attitude.

Historical background

Like Hinduism, Zoroastrianism has roots going back to the Vedic Aryans, the Indo-European wanderers who are thought to have separated during the second millennium BCE near the Caspian Sea, with one section moving into India and the other to what is today known as Armenia, Azerbaijan and the northwestern parts of the Iranian plateau. Two separate religions developed among these two groups of Aryans. In India the religion of the Vedas was written down, but the sacred book of the Zoroastrian faith, the Avesta, was preserved for centuries only in oral form and written down as late as the third or fourth centuries BCE. A large part of this ancient literature has been lost forever. The Yasna section of the Avesta is of special significance as it contains the *Gathas,* or Hymns of Zoroaster, written in the Gathic dialect.

The name Zoroaster, by which the founder is known in the West, is derived from the old Iranian name Zarathustra. According to Persian tradition, his birth is placed between 1000 and 500 BCE, with the seventh century as the most probable date – the same period that produced the Buddha, Mahavira, Lao-tzu, Confucius, Jeremiah and other great religious figures.

Several things stand out in the religion of Zoroaster. Firstly, he rejected the numerous gods of his people and taught a unique ethical monotheism in which the deity is known as Ahura Mazda (later known as Ormuzd). By the will of Ahura Mazda, all things came into being. God is good, while Angra Mainyu, later called Ahriman, is the very antithesis of Ahura Mazda. Accordingly, each person's soul is the seat of a struggle between good and evil. However, Ahura Mazda will eventually be victorious. He expresses his will through a Holy Spirit, Spenta Mainyu, and through the various modes of divine action called Amesha Spentas (Immortal Holy Ones). It was taught that a general resurrection will take place at the end of the present world order, with good and evil being subjected to an ordeal of fire and molten metal. Zoroaster retained the sacred fire as a precious symbol of Ahura Mazda. Among his reforms, religious ceremonial was reduced to an essential core. Magic and idolatry were purged, animal sacrifices eliminated and ritual intoxication condemned. Finally, his reform was a practical one, emphasising faithful performance of daily tasks and giving them religious significance.

Various changes later took place, especially between 226 and 251 CE, such as the introduction of powerful *mantras* for use as spells and incantations to counteract evil. Furthermore, the doctrine of the future life was worked out in graphic detail. Zoroastrians emphasise that one's own moral consciousness determines one's destiny.

The influence of Zoroastrian ideas on orthodox Judaism and on the pre-Islamic Arabs, including the young camel-driver from Mecca destined to become the Prophet Muhammad, is held by some to have been considerable. In 651 CE the Sassanid empire, the stronghold of Zoroastrianism, fell to Islam. A century later, many Parsees emigrated and, after a sojourn on the coast near the Persian Gulf, settled on an island off the coast of India and eventually in India itself. Groups of other Zoroastrians joined them, and they were accepted by the tolerant Hindus, who allowed them to practise their faith freely.

Zoroastrianism has retained a presence in Persia (or Iran). Its members there refer to themselves as Zardusthians or Bahdinan ('those of the good religion'). They have remained faithful to their ancient religion, and their priests are trained and initiated in the traditional Zoroastrian way.

The Parsees in India

Most of the Parsees still live in Gujarat and have made Gujarati their home language. The men usually wear Western clothes, though often with closely fitting white trousers, while the women wear saris without veils. The Parsees are a wealthy community in India, and are known for being progressive and for their success in trade and industry. Emigration has spread their faith into various parts of the English-speaking world, especially England, the USA, Canada, Australia, Hong Kong, South Africa, France and Singapore. In South Africa they have numbered two hundred at most. Towards non-Zoroastrians they usually have a reserved attitude, and as a non-Parsee cannot become a Parsee there is no outgoing approach to other religions.

The Parsee priests regulate Zoroastrian ceremonial life. The priesthood is hereditary and is headed by high priests called *dasturs*. Ceremonies in their fire temples are performed by ritual officials known as *mobeds*. These temples do not differ from other buildings, in order to make them less conspicuous. In Iran, however, a separate room in a dwelling often serves this purpose. The ceremony for kindling the temple fire is very elaborate and is done in honour of Ahura Mazda. Such a fire is made by compounding sixteen different fires, and each of these is kindled according to a very involved ritual. When the fire is first kindled, the priest has to cover his face in order not to pollute the sacred flame. Worshippers enter the temple precinct at any time and, after washing the uncovered parts of the body, recite the *kusti* prayer in Avestan, the Aryan language, take off their shoes and enter the inner hall of the fire chamber. There the priest receives the offering of sandalwood and money, while a handful of ashes is passed to the worshippers to rub on their foreheads and eyelids. Then they offer prayers, bow towards the fire, retrieve their shoes and leave.

Where numbers are sufficient, the fire ritual of modern Zoroastrianism is its main feature. This secretly conducted ritual, which non-Parsees are not allowed to attend, is performed by properly ordained and ritually prepared representatives of the hereditary priesthood.

On the Parsee New Year's Day, worshippers rise early, bathe, put on new clothes specially acquired for the occasion, and worship at the fire temple. Then alms are given, and the rest of the day is spent in a festive atmosphere.

The annual ceremonies of the Parsees are based on the religion of the Avesta and include the festival of Mithra, whose seat is the sun and who inculcates truth, friendship and devotion. The festival of Fravadin, the deity who presides over the departed ancestors, is very solemn. On this occasion the *fravashis* (ancestors) revisit the homes of their descendants. Ceremonies are held on the hills to welcome them. The six phases of creation are also commemorated, namely heaven, water, earth, trees, animals and human beings.

Funeral practices include the ceremonial washing of the body; after various rituals, it is draped in a white sheet. In India the bodies of Parsees are disposed of in *dakhmas*, or towers of silence, which are usually situated on hilltops. These traditionally take the form of a stone floor with a circular brick or stone wall around it. In the centre of the floor is a pit with three sections, the shallowest being for men, the next for women, and the deepest for children. Six bearers bring the body to the *dakhma*, followed by mourners in white. After the funeral procession has viewed the body for the last time, six bearers take it into the tower, put it in a separate shallow pit, and then partially uncover the body by cutting the clothes with scissors.

After the mourners have left the tower of silence, vultures strip the body into a skeleton within a short space of time. When the bones have dried after a few days, the corpse bearers enter the tower and put the bones into the central well, where they crumble away. In places where Parsees are not present in large numbers and where there are no vultures, underground stone chambers or lead coffins are used for interment. In South Africa interment in graves is practised.

Parsees in South Africa

Parsees arrived in South Africa from India towards the end of the nineteenth century. They paid their own way and did not arrive as indentured workers. However, they retained their historical affinity with the Indian community, both locally and in the motherland.

Pioneer Parsee families such as the Rustomjee, Dinshar, Randeria, Dorabjee and Dunjibhoy families settled in Natal; the Davaria, Talati, Camay and Wadia families in Johannesburg; and the Macherjee family in Cape Town. Since their arrival they have played a prominent role in the Indian community. At the beginning of this century they received special rights in the Transvaal. Some of them even held government positions; a certain Camay was postmaster of the central Johannesburg post office. They also unofficially enjoyed special privileges. Paul Kruger, the President of the Transvaal, befriended the Talati family and stayed at their hotel when he visited Krugersdorp. Some Parsees in the Transvaal petitioned the British Colonial Secretary in 1906 for the same privileges as those who enjoyed British citizenship.[5]

The Parsees rejected their special privileges when Gandhi started his campaign against racial discrimination, and identified themselves fully with the Indian community. They then suffered the same restrictions under which Indians had to exist. It was a Parsee lawyer, Sorabji S. Adajania, who entered the Transvaal in 1908 and challenged the Immigration Registration Act of 1905, which controlled the entry of Indians into the Transvaal through a special permit system. Ordinance 29 of the Transvaal subjected all Indians to compulsory registration and identification by means of fingerprints. They had to carry passes and produce them on request to a police officer under penalty of a fine or imprisonment. Ordered to leave the Transvaal within seven days, Sorabji Adajania refused and was sentenced to one month's hard labour.[6]

The number of Parsees in South Africa grew to just under two hundred but has now decreased, as a result of apartheid policies, to under one hundred. The Immigrants Regulation Act of 1913 consolidated the existing immigration laws of the pre-Union colonies and excluded all persons whom the Union considered unsuitable on economic grounds or on account of their supposed standard or habits of life. The Act as amended excluded all immigration of Asians to South Africa, except the wives and minor children of those already domiciled in South Africa.[7]

This legal bombardment against the growth of the Indian community through immigration deeply affected the Parsees. The Nationalist government from 1948 onwards continued these destructive policies, promulgating the 1953 Immigration Regulation Amendment Act, which prohibited the entry, after February 1953, of Asiatic women born outside the Union who had married South Africans of Asian descent overseas. The Act also prohibited the minor children of these women from entering the Union without special permission.[8]

This Act was a severe blow to the Parsee community. Parsees are not allowed to marry members of another faith, and a person from another faith will not be accepted as a member of the Zoroastrian religion. One has to be a Zoroastrian by birth. The result was that most young Parsees, because their community was so small, had to go to India to find marriage partners. This problem was brought to the attention of the authorities by Dr R. N. Randeria, a South African Parsee. Dr Randeria's attempts to get permission to bring his fiancée, Dr J. D. Modi, a cancer researcher, Parsee and Indian citizen, into South Africa were unsuccessful. His application was dismissed after several attempts by himself and others, including the High Priest of the Zoroastrian faith in London, Dr H. K. Mirza, who acted on behalf of Parsees in South Africa. The most comprehensive document drawn up in this connection, with the aid of a Dutch Reformed Church member and Dean of the Faculty of Theology at the University of South Africa, Professor J. A. Lombard, entitled 'The dilemma of marriage as it affects the minority Parsee community in the Republic of South Africa', was addressed to the Department of Indian Affairs, but in spite of the fact that the lives of two leading personalities were involved, the apartheid government rejected the plea yet again. It was disturbing to see young Parsees leaving South Africa in order to marry and settling abroad, while others had to remain unmarried rather than marry outside the Parsee community. Dr Randeria applied immediately after he had completed his studies as an ophthalmologist in Edinburgh in 1953 to bring a bride to South Africa but succeeded only after eighteen years when the Minister of Internal Affairs gave 'special permission' for him to bring his wife to South Africa after they were married in Bombay in 1971. Only in 1981 did the government finally decide to allow a few other Indian men to bring their brides into South Africa.

Through the years the Parsees in South Africa have excelled in various professions – as medical practitioners (Dr Freni Manchershaw was the first woman doctor from the Indian community, while another became superintendent of a large hospital in Durban), as attorneys, insurance brokers, estate agents, shipping agents, traders, accountants and university lecturers. Some took a stand in the political sphere such as Sorabji and J. G. Rustomjee, referred to as Parsi Rustomjee, who was closely involved with Gandhi's passive resistance campaign. His son, Sorabji Rustomjee, was the president of the South Africa Indian Congress at the time of the Second Round Table Conference in 1932 to discuss the situation of Indians in South Africa. He was in 'the forefront of all opposition to discriminatory laws of the Government directed at the Indian community'.[9]

Parsees have found themselves in a difficult position in South Africa. They have contributed their expertise and acumen to the country but the implications of their religious affiliation have not been respected by the authorities until quite recently. A lax attitude towards their tradition and religion has developed among some of the Parsee youth. Gathering places for Parsees have disappeared, and community interests have waned. Nevertheless, there are those who uphold the culture, tradition and religion of this faith, keeping a dynamic but small community together.

The practice of the Parsee religion in South Africa

Parsees in South Africa do not have fire temples as in Iran and India. They observe the various ceremonies which are prescribed for them but have adapted them to their circumstances. They are assisted by two members in their community who, in a part-time capacity, conduct the ceremonies and rituals.

All Parsees are required to observe the *naojote* ceremony and the marriage, funeral and *jashan* ceremonies. Some are not entirely faithful, but most Parsees perform the ceremonies expected of them.

The *naojote* ceremony is the ritual of initiation by which a Parsee child is accepted in the faith as a new (*nao*) worshipper (*jote*). Both sexes go through this ritual at about the age of nine at the youngest, though it can be performed for an older child as long as he or she is not much beyond the age of puberty. In earlier years Parsee children were often taken to India for this important ritual. It is never performed on infants, as *naojote* is an initiation into the responsibilities of the religion when the child confesses his or her faith. The child is given a sacred shirt and cord at the ceremony and is shown how to tie the cord over the shirt. Prayers are directed to Ahura Mazda, to whom the child promises obedience. The sacred shirt and cord are symbols of the child's subjection to Ahura Mazda and to the Zoroastrian religion. The shirt (*sudreh*), made of pure cotton, signifies loyalty to the Parsee faith. The cord (*kusti*), made of pure lamb's wool (symbol of innocence and gentleness), is tied and untied five times a day round the waist to the accompaniment of traditional prayers. It reminds the wearer of the three cardinal virtues of the Zoroastrian faith, namely *humata* (good thoughts), *hukhata* (good words) and *huvarshata* (good deeds).

Marriages of Parsees in South Africa have been few because of the restricted choice of partners for young people in such a small community. Marriage is considered to be an act beneficial to the community as a whole. Unfortunately, only two Parsee marriage ceremonies have been performed in South Africa during the past quarter of a century.

The four-day marriage ceremonies of the Parsees are filled with symbolic rituals. The first day is called *Mandawsaro*. It commences with prayers and the planting of a twig from a mango tree, signifying fertility, near the door of the house which the bridal couple will occupy. The second and third days are devoted to *varadh patra*, honouring the dead, who are held in high esteem in the Parsee religion. The fourth day witnesses the marriage itself after sunset, with elaborate ceremonies and a sacred bath as symbol of complete purification.

In the Zoroastrian context, death is evidence of the temporary victory of evil, and it is believed that where it takes place, the forces of evil gather. In order to limit the spread of evil, the body is removed as soon as possible to a place of isolation. Funeral rites are acts performed to counteract the spreading of this evil. After the isolation of the corpse it is washed and dressed in old clothes (so as not to cause waste), and the funeral takes place, if possible, on the day of death.

Reference has already been made to the funeral ceremonies. After the corpse has been put in the tower of silence, various ceremonies are observed at home for three days. It is believed that the soul hovers round the body for three nights protected by the angel Sraosha. During this period friends and family experience a time of anguish at the thought of the soul's misdeeds in life and consolation at the thought of its merits. After the third night the soul is believed to proceed to its judgement. On the last day the amount of money collected in memory of the deceased for charitable purposes (not for a tombstone) is announced.

In South Africa, Parsees have no choice but to resort to the burial of bodies and even to cremation. For centuries Parsees did not practise cremation because fire is considered to be sacred – it is maintained that decomposing bodies contaminate the sacredness of fire. However, the Hindu practice of cremation has had an influence on some Parsees. Family and friends cover the body in a cotton cloth after the final bath as a symbol of purification against ever-present evil. Thereafter, the sacred shirt and cord are put on the corpse. If available, sandalwood is used for the fire in the room as well as for incense. A prayer lamp is put in the room, and the *Ahimavaiti Gatha,* consisting of the first fire hymns composed by Zoroaster, is chanted.

Parsees do not have a special day during the week for religious purposes, but certain days in the month are auspicious for giving special attention to fire, water and the ancestors. On specials occasion a *jashan* (a form of thanksgiving) is performed. When a family decides to hold a *jashan,* a day suitable for the priest to say prayers is chosen, and guests are invited to the home.

There still exists a definite Parsee identity among members of this community in South Africa, despite all the adversity with which they have had to contend. This identity is grounded in the basics of their religion, which secularism has not destroyed, and although some Parsees have contact with the more philosophical type of Hinduism, they retain their Zoroastrian basis intact. There is no religious contact between them and either Christianity or Islam. Parsees live and work within the context of Zoroastrian values. The faith into which a Parsee is born – and in no other way can he or she be a Parsee – runs deeply in the Parsee system. The Parsees, however, have gradually made concessions with regard to marrying non-Parsees. Within their communities, the faith remains intact and free of any syncretistic tendencies. This devout community, which has been in South Africa for a century without any officially trained priests, has remained true to its faith with the help of members who have taken over religious leadership duties.

The negative forces of apartheid have been largely responsible for harming South Africa's Parsee community, which in greater numbers would have been an even more valuable asset in this country. This is therefore yet another sad chapter in the discriminatory history of the country. Some of the harm done could be overcome if efforts were to be made to encourage Parsees to return or come to South Africa. The simplicity of the requirements of the Parsee faith, the high ideals it sets before its adherents and the courage it gives them, matters which have kept this religion alive for an immensely long time and through great adversity, will be of special significance in the new South Africa.

NOTES

1. J. B. Noss, *Man's Religions*. London: Macmillan, 1969, p. 116.

2. K. V. Mardia, *The Scientific Foundations of Jainism*. Delhi: Motilal Banarsidass Publishers, 1990, pp. 10–17.

3. P. Sukhalalji, *Essence of Jainism*. Ahmedabad: Institute of Indology, 1998, pp. 92–107.

4. H. C. Bharill, *Vegetation Food and Jain Conduct*. Jaipur: Pandit J. Smarak Trust, 1992, pp. 1–26.

5. S. Bhana and B. Pachai, *A Documentary History of Indian South Africans*. Cape Town: David Philip, 1984, p. 24.

6. T. Naidoo, *The Parsee Community in South Africa*. Durban: University of Durban–Westville, Institute for Social and Economic Research, 1987, p. 15.

7. F. Meer, *Portrait of Indian South Africans*. Durban: Avan House, 1969, p. 44.

8. *Ibid.*, p. 45.

9. Naidoo, *Parsee Community*, p. 48.

SELECT BIBLIOGRAPHY

Hofmeyr, J. and Oosthuizen, G. C., *Religion in the South African Indian Community*. Durban: University of Durban–Westville, Institute for Social and Economic Research, 1981

Naidoo, T., *The Parsee Community in South Africa*. Durban: University of Durban–Westville, Institute for Social and Economic Research, 1987

Oosthuizen, G. C., *Die Godsdienste van die Wêreld*. Pretoria: NG Boekhandel, 1978

Randeria, D. N., *The Parsee Mind: A Zoroastrian Asset to Culture*. New Delhi: Munshiram Publishers, 1993

Randeria, D. N., 'The Zoroastrian Viewpoint', in G. C. Oosthuizen, H. A. Shapiro and S. A. Strauss (eds.), *Genetics and Society*. Cape Town: Oxford University Press, 1980

Zaehner, R. C., *The Dawn and Twilight of Zoroastrianism*. London: Putnam, 1961

Appendix 1

Important Events in the History of South Africa's Religions

MARTIN PROZESKY

1. Before the arrival of European settlers

About 1,75 million years ago: earliest human ancestors in South Africa

About 100 000 years ago: *Homo sapiens* (anatomically modern humans) present in South Africa

About 30 000 years ago: origins of hunter–gatherer Khoisan culture

About 2000 years ago: arrival of metal-using farmers from the north, ancestors of the Bantu-speaking people

About 2000 years ago: emergence of pastoralist Khoikhoi culture

By 1488: extensive Bantu-speaking settlement in most of the eastern half of South Africa including the highveld; Khoikhoi clans in the western and southern Cape; San in the hinterland and mountains of much of South Africa

2. Foreign exploration, settlement and conquest: from 1488 to 1902

Before Dutch settlement: 1488–1652

1488	Dias lands on southern Cape coast: first known Christian act in SA is his cross-raising at Kwaaihoek on the southeastern coast
1497	Da Gama gives a Christian name to eastern coastal area, *Tierra da Natal* ('Land of the Nativity') sighted on Christmas day
1560	Portuguese Jesuits begin missions in southwestern and southeastern Africa, e.g. Luanda and the Zambezi valley

The period of Dutch colonial control: 1652–1806

1652	Arrival of Dutch party under Jan van Riebeeck
1652–65	Period when sole religious official at Cape was the 'sick-comforter'
1658	Arrival of Mardyckers (first free Muslims) at Cape from Moluccan Islands
1660	A French Catholic bishop, shipwrecked at the Cape, is denied permission to say mass

1665	Johan van Arckel, first Dutch Reformed minister, arrives at Cape; consistory formed
1669	First record of a Jewish presence at the Cape when two young Jews convert to Christianity
1688	Party of Jesuit astronomers visit Cape and minister to Catholics among the Dutch
1688	Edict of Nantes revoked in France; French Huguenots begin to arrive at the Cape
1694	Arrival of exiled Shaykh Yusuf at the Cape
1737	Arrival of first Protestant missionary, the Moravian George Schmidt
1744	Schmidt establishes Genadendal mission station but leaves soon afterwards
1750	Three DRC ministers in Cape: Cape Town, Stellenbosch, Drakenstein
1780	Arrival of Tuang Guru, second spiritual father of Islam at the Cape
1792	Return of Moravian missionaries
1795	London Missionary Society (LMS) founded
1795	First British occupation of the Cape
1799	LMS missionary Johannes van der Kemp arrives
1803	Resumption of Dutch control of the Cape under the Batavian Republic
1804	De Mist's ordinance of religious toleration issued
1804	Fathers Lansink, Nelissen and Prinsen arrive at Cape (first Catholic priests)
1804	Approximate date of building of first mosque in Dorp Street, Cape Town

The period of British colonial control: 1806–1910

1806	Second British occupation begins; General Baird expels the three Catholic priests
1806	Methodist and Congregational soldiers at the Cape build chapels in Cape Town
1813	Presbyterian church forms at the Cape
1814	Barnabas Shaw, Methodist missionary, arrives
1817	Robert Moffat, LMS missionary, arrives
1820	English settlement of Eastern Cape begins
1820	Dr John Philip (LMS) arrives
1820	William Shaw arrives in Eastern Cape as chaplain to party of Methodist settlers
1821	William Shaw begins to build first church in Grahamstown
1821	John Philip establishes mission station across Orange River at Philippolis
1822	Andrew Murray, Snr, commences DRC pastorate at Graaff-Reinet
1822	Father Scully starts to build first Catholic church in Cape Town

1823–30   Expansion of Methodist missions into Eastern Cape and Transkei

1824   Lovedale founded in Eastern Cape by Church of Scotland missionaries, John Bennie and John Scott

1824   First DRC commission on missions at Cape

1825   Robert Moffat founds Kuruman mission station

1828   Publication of Dr John Philip's book *Researches in South Africa*

1832   First Anglican church in Eastern Cape at Bathurst

1835   Daniel Lindley, American missionary, arrives and becomes the first regular minister to the Voortrekkers

1836   First DRC mission to black people

1836   Great Trek commences

1837   Cape DRC deplores Trek

1838   First Roman Catholic Bishop, Patrick Griffith, arrives at Cape

1838   Voortrekker vow at Blood River

1840   First Catholic mission station founded near Malmesbury in the Western Cape

1840   Arrival of David Livingstone (LMS)

1841   Beginning of an established Jewish community in South Africa with the founding of the first congregation in Cape Town

1844   First Jewish marriage solemnised in Cape Town

1845   First recorded Jew born in SA

1847   First recorded scroll of the Torah brought into SA

1848   Robert Gray appointed first Anglican Bishop of Cape Town

1849   First synagogue built in Cape Town

1853   John William Colenso appointed first Anglican Bishop of Natal

1853   Nederduitsch Hervormde Kerk forms in Transvaal

1856   Transvaal Republican constitution declares no equality between black and white in church and state

1857   NGK Synod at the Cape permits separate worship because of the 'weakness of some' (i.e. whites)

1857   Xhosa 'cattle-killing'

1857   DRC theological seminary established at Stellenbosch

1859   Gereformeerde Kerk forms in Transvaal

1860   Indian settlements in Natal commence, marking the beginnings of Hinduism in South Africa and of Islam in Natal

1860   NHK becomes official church of Transvaal Republic

1860   Andrew Murray, Jnr, commences his influential ministry in the Cape

1861   Bishop Colenso publishes his controversial commentary on the Epistle to the Romans

1862   Building of the St John's Street Synagogue or 'Old Synagogue' in Cape Town – the first to be specifically designed as a synagogue

1863   Bishop Colenso tried and convicted of heresy by his church; excommunicated and deposed, he appeals successfully to the Privy Council in England

1863   Abubakr Effendi, a Turk of Kurdish descent, is sent to the Cape by the Ottoman Sultan at the request of the British Crown to serve the Muslims

1865	Privy Council rules in favour of Colenso's reinstatement
1867	Discovery of diamonds near Kimberley
1870	Proposed union of DRC and Anglicans in the Cape
1872	First Black Independent Christian church (in Lesotho)
1879	Anglican diocese established in Transvaal
1879	Anglo-Zulu War
1881	Beginning of large influx of East European Jews into South Africa
1882	Mariannhill Monastery near Durban founded by Roman Catholic Trappists
1882	Muslims at Cape resist state vaccination measures on religious grounds
1883	Death of Bishop Colenso
1884	Nehemiah Tile sets up the independent Tembu National Church
1884	Building of Grey Street mosque in Durban, first mosque in Natal
1886	Cape Muslims resist the authorities during the cemetery riots
1886	Discovery of Witwatersrand goldfields
1887	Building of mosque in central Pretoria
1892	Mangena Mokone founds his Ethiopian Church in Transvaal
1893	M. K. Gandhi arrives in Durban from India
1893	Gandhi ejected from a train at Pietermaritzburg station because of his colour: this marks a turning point in his life
1894	Ahmad Effendi stands for Cape parliament, first 'non-white' person to do so
1895	Establishment of first (African Christian) Zionist congregation, in Johannesburg
1895	Decision made to establish the Roeland Street Synagogue in Cape Town, the first synagogue in the East European tradition (consecrated in 1902)
1896	James Dwane becomes superintendent-general of the Ethiopian Church, from which develops the Order of Ethiopia
1898	South African Zionist Federation formed
1899	Anglo-Boer War begins
1902	Peace of Vereeniging

3. Domination, the liberation struggle and religion: 1902–1990

Foundations of apartheid: 1902–1948

1902	Enactment of the Cape Immigration Restriction Act restricts the entry of Jews and Indians into South Africa
1903	Dr Abdullah Abdurahman, a leading Muslim, makes his entry into civic affairs and politics
1903	Transvaal Jewish Board of Deputies formed
1904	Cape Jewish Board of Deputies formed

1904	South African General Missionary Council formed
1904	Gandhi and others establish the Phoenix Settlement near Durban
1905	Establishment of the Hindu Young Men's Association in Natal
1907	Passive resistance movement launched by Gandhi and others
1908	Formation of Apostolic Faith Mission (AFM)
1910	Union of South Africa formed
1911	Isaiah Shembe starts the Nazareth Baptist Church
1911	Census reveals that more than 25 per cent of the African people are Christian
1911	End of Indian immigration to South Africa
1912	South African Native National Congress (SANNC) formed in Bloemfontein
1912	South African Jewish Board of Deputies established
1912	Formation of South African Hindu Maha Sabha
1914	Gandhi leaves South Africa after 21 years
1914	National Party formed
1914	Formation of Assemblies of God
1915	Judah Leo Landau appointed first Chief Rabbi
1917	Overport Sakya Buddhist Society founded in Durban
1918	Afrikaner Broederbond formed
1920	Full Gospel Church established
1921	Massacre by government troops of 'Israelite' millenarian group at Bulhoek in Eastern Cape
1922	First Apostolic Delegate appointed to South Africa
1922	Founding of Jamiat al-'Ulama (Islamic Association of the Learned) in the Transvaal
1923	SANNC renamed the African National Congress
1923	Bantu Presbyterian Church founded
1923	Cape Malay Association (CMA) founded
1925	Establishment of the Arya Pratinidhi Sabha, national umbrella body of the Hindu Arya Samaj in South Africa
1929	Inauguration of the Cape United Council of Orthodox Hebrew Congregations
1930	Immigration Quota Act severely limits immigration of Jews from Eastern Europe to South Africa
1931	Methodist Church of South Africa formed through union of three branches of Methodism
1932	Baptist Union condemns government policy towards the 'Native Peoples'
1933	Formation of the Federation of Synagogues in Johannesburg
1933	Establishment of reform Judaism in SA
1934	First visit to SA by a representative of the Ramakrishna Mission in India, Swami Adhyanand
1934	First woman ordained to the Christian ministry in South Africa, in the Congregational Church
1936	Christian Council founded

1937	Aliens Act effectively halts Jewish immigration from Germany to South Africa
1937	Emilie Solomon elected chair of the Congregational Union, the first woman to hold a leadership position in a South African church
1941	NG Kerk participation in Christian Council ends
1942	Formation of Moslem Progressive Society
1943	Militant younger members of the ANC form the Congress Youth League
1945	Formation of Muslim Judicial Council
1946	Founding of the Ramakrishna Centre of South Africa in Durban
1947	Southern African Catholic Bishops' Conference formed
1947	Ecumenical Faculty of Divinity established at Rhodes University
1948	National Party government under D. F. Malan, former NGK minister, comes to power
1948	World Council of Churches founded in Amsterdam
1948	State of Israel comes into being
1948	First Jewish day school established in Johannesburg

The high noon of apartheid: 1948–1976

1949	Christian Council convenes a conference at Rosettenville on 'The Christian Citizen in a Multi-racial Society'
1949	First branch of the Divine Life Society starts
1950	The Arabic Study Circle is formed in Durban
1951	Roman Catholic Church sets up a hierarchy of four archbishoprics and numerous bishoprics
1953	Bantu Education Act effectively ends missionary education for black people
1954	Annual Methodist Conference narrowly defeats an attempt to segregate the Methodist Church
1955	Congress of the People at Kliptown adopts the Freedom Charter
1955	Second Assembly of the World Council of Churches at Evanston, Illinois, condemns racism
1955	Founding of Natal Jamiat al-'Ulama
1957	'Church clause' in Native Laws Amendment Act, which would obstruct black people wishing to worship in white group areas
1957	Anglican Archbishop Geoffrey Clayton dies; succeeded by Joost de Blank
1957	Roman Catholic Archbishop Whelan of Bloemfontein declares apartheid is nothing less than a heresy
1957	Formation of the District Six-based Muslim Youth Movement
1958	The Claremont Muslim Association is founded by Imam Abdullah Haron
1959	Pan Africanist Congress (PAC) formed
1960	Sharpeville massacre on 21 March
1960	Government bans the ANC and PAC

1960	Consultation of churches at Cottesloe, Johannesburg, condemns apartheid
1960	Federal Theological Seminary established at Alice, in the Eastern Cape
1960	Alphaeus Zulu becomes Suffragan Bishop of Zululand, the first black Anglican bishop
1961	Cape and Transvaal Synods of NG Kerk withdraw from World Council of Churches
1963	Christian Institute of Southern Africa founded with Beyers Naudé as its first director
1963	Regional Dutch Reformed Churches federate by means of a General Synod
1964	Seth Mokitimi becomes first black President of the Conference of the Methodist Church
1966	Federation of Evangelical Lutheran Churches of Southern Africa formed
1967	Formation of the United Congregational Church of South Africa
1967	Christian Council renamed the South African Council of Churches
1967	Church Unity Commission formed
1967	University Christian Movement (UCM) formed
1968	Publication of *The Message to the People of South Africa* by the SACC and the Christian Institute
1969	Death in detention of Imam Abdullah Haron in Cape Town
1969	First known Sai Baba (Hindu) group formed in Durban
1970	Formation of Muslim Youth Movement of South Africa, in Durban
1971	World Council of Churches launches its Programme to Combat Racism
1972	Roman Catholic hierarchy issues its 'Call to Conscience'
1973	Congress on Mission and Evangelism in Durban, under auspices of SACC and Africa Enterprise
1974	NG Kerk General Synod issues *Human Relations in the Light of the Scriptures,* providing legitimation for government policy on the race question
1975	Evangelical Lutheran Church of Southern Africa formed
1975	Formation of Islamic Council of South Africa
1976	Soweto uprising on 16 June; nationwide unrest begins

Crisis and collapse of apartheid: 1976–1990

1976	Roman Catholic Church decides to integrate its schools
1977	Banning of Christian Institute by government, along with certain other organisations and publications
1977	Launch of *Odyssey* magazine, vehicle for 'new age' ideas
1978	Desmond Tutu becomes General Secretary of the SACC
1978	DRC severs ties with the Reformed Church in the Netherlands over its support for liberation movements
1978	Formation of the Sunni Jamiat al-'Ulama of South Africa

1979	Islamic revolution in Iran
1979	South African Christian Leadership Assembly (SACLA) organised by Africa Enterprise
1980	Formation of Qiblah Mass Movement, which identifies with revolutionary (Iranian) Islam
1980	Opening of Buddhist Retreat Centre near Ixopo
1981	Alliance of Black Reformed Christians in South Africa (ABRECSA) formed
1982	Dr Allan Boesak elected Moderator of the World Alliance of Reformed Churches (WARC) in Ottawa, Canada
1982	NG Sendingkerk issues the *Belhar Confession*, stressing the unity of the church over against apartheid
1983	Tricameral constitution adopted by white parliament, with freedom of religion for all but still favouring Christianity
1983	United Democratic Front launched against apartheid
1983–4	Eloff Commission of Enquiry into SACC
1984	Call of Islam (COI) breaks away from MYMSA on issue of political alliances with United Democratic Front
1985	Jewish Board of Deputies condemns apartheid at its 33rd National Congress
1985	Jews for Justice and Jews for Social Justice formed in Cape Town and Johannesburg, respectively
1985	Launching of National Initiative for Reconciliation in Pietermaritzburg
1985	Publication of *Kairos Document*
1985	Opening of Hare Krishna Temple in Chatsworth, near Durban
1986	NHK resolves to remain white
1986	Desmond Tutu becomes Archbishop of Cape Town
1986	NGK General Synod issues *Kerk en Samelewing*, rejecting theological justifications of apartheid
1986	Formation of the Union of Orthodox Synagogues of South Africa
1986	Formation of short-lived Hindu Alliance of South Africa
1987	SACC National Conference discusses Christianity and violence in SA
1990	National conference of church leaders at Rustenburg issues the *Rustenburg Declaration*, completely rejecting apartheid

Appendix 2

Religious Affiliation in South Africa

Table 1. *Membership of the various religions as a percentage of the total*

Religion	1980 census	1991 census
Christian churches	77,0	66,4
Hinduism	1,8	1,3
Islam	1,1	1,1
Judaism	0,4	0,2
Other faiths	0,1	0,1
No religion	2,1	1,2
Nothing/object	3,1	29,7*
Uncertain	14,4*	

*The people in these two categories are believed to include many members of the African traditional religions.

Table 2. *Membership of the Christian churches as a percentage of the total*

Churches	1980 census	1991 census
African Independent Churches	26,6*	33,5*
Dutch Reformed Churches (NGK)	17,9	15,6
Roman Catholic	12,3	11,4
Methodist	11,4	8,8
Anglican	8,4	5,7
Lutheran	4,6	3,8
Presbyterian	3,2	2,2
Apostolic Faith Mission	1,5	2,0
Congregational	2,5	1,9
Dutch Reformed Church (NHK)	1,5	1,3
Baptist	1,3	1,2
Dutch Reformed (GK)	1,0	0,8
Other Apostolic Churches	2,5	2,8
Other Pentecostal Churches	2,6	2,3
Other Churches	2,7	6,9

* These figures include members of the Zion Christian Church, whose following rose from 2,7 per cent of all Christians in 1980 to 7,4 per cent in 1991.
Source: J. J. Kritzinger: 'The religious scene in present-day South Africa', in J. Killian (ed.), *Religious Freedom in South Africa.* J. Killian, Pretoria: UNISA, 1993, pp. 2–4

Index